RHETORIC AND FORM

RHETORIC AND FORM:
DECONSTRUCTION AT YALE

Edited and with an Introduction by

Robert Con Davis and Ronald Schleifer

UNIVERSITY OF OKLAHOMA PRESS : NORMAN

BY ROBERT CON DAVIS
The Fictional Father: Lacanian Readings of the Text (editor) (Amherst, 1981)
The Grapes of Wrath: *A Collection of Critical Essays* (editor) (Englewood Cliffs, 1982)
Rhetoric and Form: Deconstruction at Yale (coeditor) (Norman, 1985)

BY RONALD SCHLEIFER
The Genres of the Irish Literary Revival (editor) (Dublin and Norman, 1980)
Kierkegaard and Literature: Irony, Repetition, and Criticism (coeditor) (Norman, 1984)
Rhetoric and Form: Deconstruction at Yale (coeditor) (Norman, 1985)

Library of Congress Cataloging in Publication Data
Main entry under title:

Rhetoric and form.

    Bibliography: p. 239
    Includes index.
    1. Deconstruction—Addresses, essays, lectures.
I. Davis, Robert Con, 1948–   . II. Schleifer, Ronald.
PN98.D43R44 1985   801'.95   85–1002
ISBN O–8061–1895–4

To the memory of Paul de Man

Preface

Literary studies in the United States have undergone a radical transformation in the last twenty-five years from the almost total hegemony of New Criticism, with its privileging of the "autonomous" literary work and close readings of particular literary texts, to an explosion of interest in interdisciplinary approaches to literature. This major shift has overwhelmed the academic study of literature and raised the most fundamental questions concerning the nature of literary "work," the generation of meaning in language and literature, and the nature of literary response. In large part this revolution began with the importation of Continental philosophical and literary studies to the once insulated Anglo-American academy. "A radical displacement," Jacques Derrida wrote in "The Ends of Man," "can only come from the outside," and we can understand the fruitful transformation of literary studies in our country as such a displacement.

This transformation, however, has been accomplished not by the mere translation and dissemination of foreign ideas (in fact, if the transformation we are talking about has any "central" import, it is that such notions of free-floating, self-subsisting ideas must be examined with great care and become the objects of a thoroughgoing critique). Rather, in an important way, this displacement is the result of the engagement of American critics and scholars with new and seemingly foreign ways of questioning experience. In the last two decades this engagement has taken place most notably at Yale University. J. Hillis Miller, Geoffrey Hartman, and Paul de Man, along with their sometime colleague at Yale, Derrida himself, have transformed literary studies in the United States by redefining the kinds of fundamental questions that can be asked concerning language, literature, and culture. Their engagement with literature and with so-called theoretical questions has resulted in the reinterpretation of major works in our own literature. By clearly engaging and repossessing those literary texts, they simultaneously give currency to the "foreign" notions. Moreover, the Yale critics have revolutionized not only the study of literature but that of culture in general, and they have spawned a generation of younger scholars whose works elicit the same excitement and exhilaration that can be found in their mentors' writings. In important ways, as Robert Con Davis argues in this volume, the careers of the critics at Yale trace the development of literary criticism in the United States over the last twenty years. Their students—and we are all, even the detractors among us, students of Miller, Hartman, and de Man—have discovered in their work new ways of conceiving of and responding to literature and criticism. In the symposium included in this volume Miller cites Derrida's contention that deconstruction is quintessentially American, and, although we suspect that in his comment Derrida may well be trying to make deconstruction foreign to France (something "from the outside"), his observation is nevertheless an implicit acknowledgment of the work of the critics at Yale.

We are honored, then, to invite a younger generation to examine the work of Miller, Hartman, and de Man in a volume of essays that includes contributions from Miller and Hartman. In Part One, "The Yale Critics," Miller and Hartman individually position themselves within the current reorientation of literary studies that the Yale critics themselves initiated. Miller articulates the basic "grounds" of literary study in light of this Continental transformation, and Hartman returns to Wordsworth to situate his deconstructive reading in the context of his evolving postdeconstructionist project of reconceiving literature. Juliet MacCannell offers a retrospective overview of the career of Paul de Man in this section. Concluding Part One is a symposium in which Miller, Barbara Johnson, and Louis Mackey engage students of deconstruction on its relationship to Marxism.

In Part Two, "Controversies," a younger generation of critics presents readings of the Yale critics from the viewpoints of feminism (Barbara Johnson), Marxism (Barbara Foley), and psychoanalysis (Robert Con Davis). Even as they question the Yale critics, however, we can see the ways in which Miller, Hartman, and de Man have opened literary studies to the most wide-ranging questions of our social, intellectual, and personal lives.

Finally, Part Three, "Theory and Practice," explores and extends the work of Miller, Hartman, and de Man. Robert Markley examines the place of style in the work of Miller and, implicitly, in deconstructive criticism altogether; Herman Rapaport reads literary and musical texts in exciting new ways suggested by the redirection of Hartman's most recent work. Christopher Norris and Ronald Schleifer read de Man in the contexts of the British "common-sense" philosophy of William Empson and the structural linguistics of A. J. Greimas.

This volume grows out of the Oklahoma Conference on Contemporary Genre Theory and the Yale School sponsored by the University of Oklahoma, the Department of English, and *Genre*, held in Norman from May 31 to June 1, 1984. The featured speakers at the conference were Miller, Johnson, and Hartman; the papers they presented are included in this volume. In addition, scholars from all over the United States joined us in Norman to offer papers dealing with contemporary literary theory and deconstruction at Yale. Before his death last winter Paul de Man had agreed, with the graciousness familiar to those who had the opportunity of working with him, to join our conference. The editors of this book join the contributors in dedicating our work to his memory.

The conference was designed to inaugurate a new graduate concentration in literary theory to be offered by the Department of English in the University of Oklahoma. Support for both the conference and the new graduate concentration came from many areas of the University. The editors would like to thank James Burwell, Dean of the College of Arts and Sciences; Kenneth Hoving, Dean of the Graduate College and Vice-Provost for Research Administration; and J. R. Morris, Provost and Senior Vice-President of the University, for their strong support of the conference and their continuing support of *Genre*.

Many others contributed to this project in important ways. George D. Economou, Chair of the Department of English, helped with patience, advice, and departmental aid. He also served as the keynote speaker and a panel participant at the conference. President William Banowsky took time out of his busy schedule to welcome scholars to the University of Oklahoma and to the conference; Jerome Weber, Vice-Provost of the University, provided timely financial aid; Michael Flanigan, David Gross, and Larry Frank, of the English Department, contributed their time, energy, and expertise to the conference. Allene Hone and Sue Perna, of the Oklahoma College of Continuing Education, organized the logistics of the conference with cheerful efficiency. We would also like to acknowledge the generous support of the Oklahoma Foundation for the Humanities and the National Endowment for the Humanities, whose grants allowed scores of Oklahoma educators to come to Norman to participate in the conference. Finally, we would like to thank Gita Rajan, who compiled the bibliography and the index with great care.

The conference and this volume are the culmination of a year's collaboration between the editors. As always, it has been exciting and fulfilling to work together. Both of us would like to acknowledge the patient and cheerful support of our wives, Melanie Collins Davis and Nancy Mergler. In the interval between the conference and the publication of this collection, Nancy gave birth to Benjamin Whitmore Schleifer; for their patience and a host of other reasons she and Cyrus deserve special thanks.

Robert Con Davis
Ronald Schleifer

Norman, Oklahoma

Contents

Deconstruction at Yale

Introduction:
The Ends of Deconstruction

Ronald Schleifer and Robert Con Davis
University of Oklahoma

> Time and the temporal mean what is perishable, what passes away in the
> course of time.
>
> —Martin Heidegger

> R. started out by deconstructing the referential system based on the
> metaphor "man" but has substituted for it a new referential system based on
> the pathos of a temporal predicament in which man's self-definition is forever
> deferred.
>
> —Paul de Man

> Is it not better to suppose that words are inscribed for reinscription rather
> than for definitiveness; that all texts are infinitives; that revision,
> reinterpretation, rewriting are not flaws of finitude but the very kind of being
> (*Sein*) we have in time (*Zeit*)?
>
> —Geoffrey Hartman

> The paradox of *mise en abyme* is the following: without the production of some
> schema, some "icon," there can be no glimpse of the abyss, no vertigo of the
> underlying nothingness. Any such schema, however, both opens the chasm,
> creates it or reveals it, and at the same time fills it up, covers it over by
> naming it, gives the groundless a ground, the bottomless a bottom. Any such
> schema almost instantaneously becomes a trivial mechanism, an artifice. It
> becomes something merely made, confected, therefore all-too-human and
> rational.
>
> —J. Hillis Miller

i

The advent of deconstruction in America—deconstruction at Yale—
has made time and its relationship with language a concern for literary
studies in radically new ways: it has rendered temporality, as Paul de
Man has written, a "predicament" (*AR*, p. 199).[1] For the deconstructive
critics at Yale—Paul de Man, J. Hillis Miller, Geoffrey Hartman—this
predicament is more than the fact that we are continually caught and

destroyed by time in the manner of the man in Poe's story, "A Predicament," who sticks his head through a clocktower window and is trapped
and choked by the clock's hands. For the Yale critics it is, rather, the
"predicament" of inhabiting a language which both represents and erases
time. "Time," Hartman writes in *Saving the Text*, "is not against
language (or vice versa) but coterminous with it: to be in the one is to be
in the other" (*ST*, p. 7).[2] This predicament is different from Poe's
because it links to time's deadliness the possibility of signification, what
de Man paradoxically calls a kind of "freedom." "The discovery of
temporality," de Man explains, "coincides with the acts of transgressive
freedom: time relates to space in the same way the imagination relates to
perception, need to passion, etc. The very conception of a future is linked
with the possibility of a free imagination . . ." (*AR*, pp. 140–41). This
freedom is not the subjective freedom of reader-response—it is not, as
Miller says in the Symposium presented here, "infinite free play [which]
. . . can make the text mean anything"—but the freedom of the
possibility of a future.

Temporality, then, for the Yale critics is a *function* as well as a
determination of language: not only does it affect language in ways that
A. J. Greimas describes as "not pertinent to [linguistic] description,"[3]
ways that are as "accidental" as peering out the wrong clocktower
window; it also creates these very "impertinent" determinations by
"generating" in discourse and in the *possibility* of discourse, as de Man
says, "the metaphor of temporality" (*AR*, p. 162). Of *The Social Contract*
de Man writes, "the noncoincidence of the theoretical statement with its
phenomenal manifestation implies that the mode of existence of the
contract is temporal, or that time is the phenomenal category produced
by the discrepancy" (*AR*, p. 273). Another way of saying this is to note,
in terms of speech-act philosophy, that language creates the discrepancy
between its (illusory) representation of what is—its existence as "constative"—and its presentation of its situation, its "performative" force.
That is, language both promises and states and, doing both, is best
figured, metonymically, as a "subjunctive" discourse.

Several of the essays in this collection illustrate that deconstructive
critics tend to emphasize this dimension of language, to write in a kind of
radical subjunctive—a mood and mode that, inscribed in an ambiguous
temporality, assert and deny authority. This is the mode of Hillis
Miller's description of such critics attempting "to escape from the
labyrinth of words, an attempt guided not only by the Apollonian thread
of logic but by Ariadne's thread as she might be imagined to have rescued

it from the too rational and betraying Theseus. . . ."[4] Miller evokes a logic which is not logic and a rational thread which is not a thread. Such a radical subjunctive asserts and denies authority as it erases and creates the "logical category" of causality and the "phenomenal category" of time. The same mode and voice can be found in Miller's essay in our collection: "what I am calling a critique [simultaneously emphasizes] rhetoric as the study of tropes, on the one hand, in a work of whatever genre, and, on the other hand, the way any work of literature, of whatever genre, tells a story with beginning, middle, end, and underlying *logos* or *Grund*, and at the same time interrupts or deconstructs that story." This is the mode, too, of Barbara Johnson's saying that "if we could be sure of the difference between the determinable and the undeterminable, the undeterminable would be comprehended within the determinable. What is undecidable is precisely whether a thing is decidable or not."[5] "What emerges here," in Hartman's words, "is an anti-allegoresis. . . . Interpretation no longer aims at the reconciliation or unification of warring truths" (*ST*, p. 51).

In eschewing reconciliation the rhetorical aim is to create a radical sense of doubt, a formal signal to the reader that what is being said is circumspect and must be taken in some "other" way, "other" than how it might "normally" be read, "other," that is, in the sense of the "otherness" of linguistic repetition and iterability. Derrida develops this sense of "iterability" in his controversy with John Searle and speech-act theory, and he does so by inscribing temporality—that is, repetition—within the seeming timeless "identity" of meaning. "Iterability," he writes,

> supposes a minimal remainder (as well as a minimum of idealization) in order that the identity of the *selfsame* be repeatable and identifiable *in, through*, and even *in view of* its alteration. For the structure of iteration . . . implies *both* identity *and* difference. Iteration in its "purest" form—and it is always impure—contains *in itself* the discrepancy of a difference that constitutes it as iteration.[6]

The authority of such rhetoric, as Robert Markley suggests, is largely "stylistic rather than ideational," and it is so because style (as opposed to "ideas") inscribes time in discourse. Such discourse, for deconstruction, is a reminder that language is a playing out of a presence/absence, fort/da game theatricalized rhetorically as the presence of an absence—*a play on words* which plays, like Miller's *mise en abyme*, a deadly vertigo, a joke—the manner in which language asserts a meaning that it cannot own or control. When such rhetoric works, as it often does for Miller and Johnson, de Man, Hartman and Derrida, this linguistic gaminess stages the *mise en abyme* of unstoppable linguistic regression, the drama of language falling away to reveal other language, repeatedly, temporally.

Conceived in this way, deconstructive rhetoric, deconstructive "style," is an extremely powerful instrument, arguably boundless in its power, flexible and expandable enough to envelop all varieties of paradox and contradiction, chiasmus and catachresis, metaphor and metonymy, original and replica, error and truth. To do this, deconstrution deftly reverses the hierarchies of any opposition or competing practice, reinscribes the dominant chord into the minor one, and the "opposition" has been appropriated into "discourse"—metaphors turned on their head to show a metonymic underside, speech revealed as writing, originals stripped to reveal hidden folds of repetition, man exposed as archiwoman, difference discovered in identity, time in spatial timelessness, and so on. Seemingly nothing can avoid deconstruction's sway just as nothing can avoid temporalization—or, for that matter, spatialization. All is susceptible to reversal in a relentlessly "binary" world. In this way, like T. S. Eliot's "unified sensibility," deconstruction is an instrument possibly tunable to any melody (or non-melody) and a monster (to follow Eliot's shift of metaphors) with an omnivorous appetite and the capability of devouring all opposition—virtually everything.

But just how powerful is deconstructive rhetoric? That is, how powerful is it in the sense that Noam Chomsky talks about a scientific theory's "power" to answer challenges and neutralize opposition—not merely to analyze, but to account for change in time? Chomsky argues throughout his work that a theory that explains too much—that is, is *too powerful*—lacks the capability of being denied, *denegated* in time, and thus lacks force.[7] He means by this that such "global" theories—closer to Kant's analytic rather than synthetic statements—fail to brook contradiction and to engage rigorously and forcefully the challenges posed by diachronic developments. Such theories approach what Miller calls in his essay in this volume "grounds" which occasion either silent assent or discourse at cross purposes. They fail, that is, to be "temporal" (engaging contemporaries) or mortal (creating the possibility of denial); they fail to risk error. Deconstruction deconstructs such "timeless" theories by re-inscribing them in language that is radically temporalized— theatricalized as "temporal," or, more forcefully, as the inscription of "death" in language—so that, as Hartman says, the thinker "discovers that where he thought he was on solid ground—whether terra firma or presupposions or whatever you name the substratum—he is (also) on language; then, that language is not a ground but a groundless veiling of the hypothesis (itself a grounding term) of the ground" (*ST*, p. 64). Such temporalized discourse is ultimately infirm: "to enter language," Hartman explains earlier, "means to risk being named, or recognized by name, to struggle against false names or identities, to live in the knowledge that *reconnaissance* and *mépris(e)* are intertwined . . ." (*ST*, p. 62).

But can such "deconstructive" strategies really appropriate—"take on" and "take in"—*everything*? Can its discourse and style—its language—play any tune, leaving, in effect, no alternative to deconstruction? If so, there is a problem in that deconstructive praxis may have generated theory that is, as Chomsky would say, too *powerful*—too all-encompassing. That is, deconstructive theory and practice may run the risk, in Chomsky's term, of being "vacuous," being so "global" in application as to be lacking in theoretical rigor and usefulness—as true as it is false and, thus, without any real force. These questions circulate, sub rosa, directly and indirectly, through many of the essays in this collection. In fact, the sharp questioning in the symposium on American deconstruction in its second or third phase of development is essential, we will argue, as we begin to understand deconstruction as an historical and theoretical *practice* capable of error and (as a theoretical possibility) virtually at or already arrived at an end.

It is necessary, even crucial, to think of deconstruction in this way, as capable of taking—or as having already taken—a wrong turn, as failing in a particular text or a particular moment in literary history, even as being fundamentally in error, for at least two further reasons. The first involves what deconstruction attempts to accomplish in its promotion of *écriture* as discourse: a particular understanding of both the enabling context that makes writing possible in the first place (the "always already" dimension of language) and the nature of writing within any specific temporal context. The second involves deconstruction-as-a-practice as such and the possible end or death of that practice. In effect, deconstruction is the exposé of language at play, and we must allow for—be able to conceive—the possibility *in practice*, in time, of eventual poor play, even the final closing of the play's play and the rise of another theatricalization in its place. This would not be deconstruction as it describes itself—as a (temporally) continuous twisting in the open dissemination of language defined "deconstructively"—but *deconstruction* as a praxis that may be analyzed and devoured by an as yet unnamed ("unknown" or "unthought") competing practice, deconstruction as the thing appropriated, "devoured," in an "other" discourse. We have to imagine its theater doors actually slamming and being locked. If not, if we cannot imagine the "failure" or "error" of deconstruction, then we deny any reality to the deconstructive project, any breaching of Western metaphysics that its advent entails, any possible impact or intervention by deconstruction in Western culture. In short, we must know deconstruction as *dead*, as radically temporal (or as praxis-toward-death, *already* dying), over with, or ended, or we do not "know" it at all and have no name to call it by—cannot utter anything in its behalf or mark its traces, the presence of its absence. Deconstruction must have an "end" and be capable of failure—exist in but not equal to time—or be nothing at all.

ii

Such a sense of temporalization is inscribed in Paul de Man's important essay, "The Rhetoric of Temporality," in which, as Christopher Norris argues here, de Man recognizes "the temporal predicament of all understanding." Thus, Norris explains, it is

> in terms of allegory—as de Man interprets it—that thought comes to recognize the temporal predicament of all understanding. There is no present moment of self-possessed meaning where signs would so perfectly match up with experience as to obviate the need for further interpretation. Allegory in de Man exerts something like the power of deconstructive leverage that Derrida brings to bear through his key-term *différance*. That is to say, it introduces the idea of a differential play within language that everywhere prevents (or constantly *defers*) the imaginary coincidence of meaning and intent.

In this reading "temporality" itself is a result—an "effect"—of the differential play that is figured as "language," and it is marked *against* its (transcendental) opposite. Temporality has to be "read" against timelessness precisely to achieve what Juliet MacCannell calls the "non-absolutism," the "rhetoric of (anti-)position" in de Man's work. "If there is a *drive* in Paul de Man's writing," MacCannell argues, "it is the drive to otherness, 'toward a conscious *other*.' "

Here we seem to encounter the paradox of deconstructive praxis we are trying to articulate and that is figured in Miller's epigraph as the *mise en abyme*: the "non-absolutism" of deconstruction becomes vacuous if it *endlessly* accommodates everything. This is the argument Barbara Foley presents in her Marxist-Leninist critique of deconstruction: that in its non-absolute validation of "undecidability" deconstruction offers no criteria for timely, *historical* choices. "Each commitment" in deconstruction, Foley writes, "possesses its own 'pragmatic valence' . . . , and none is guided by an overall (totalizing) strategy or plan adjudicating whether some activities are more necessary than others to the movement toward a general human liberation." In this we can see at least a hint of why so many, as MacCannell and Robert Con Davis do here, emphasize de Man's "authoritative" and seemingly "timeless" style. "When he has the most tragic of insights to convey to us . . . ," MacCannell writes, "he does so in an absolutely unsentimental, neutral tone, even when it is, or especially when it is, a question of life and death." Ronald Schleifer and Christopher Norris argue against this reading of "style" in de Man, and they do so to reinscribe temporality into the seeming timelessness of de Man's "philosophism."

Ostensibly like Foley, Schleifer attempts to position de Man's deconstructive praxis within a discourse "other" than itself, in this case to project deconstruction's "end" (or aim) as praxis within discourse about reference: "referential" discourse from Plato through Hjelmslev and such contemporaries as John Austin, John Searle, Jacques Derrida, A. J. Greimas, and Shoshana Felman. In this "referential" discourse deconstructors—Derrida, de Man, Felman—participate in an ongoing Western meditation on the status of epistemological "reference" and "meaning." Schleifer focuses, in particular, on a de Manian "anxiety of reference," "the impossible oppositions of meaning and reference, knowledge and ignorance"—finally, on a de Manian deconstructive epistemological "pathos of distrust" concerning the very possibility of referentiality. Unlike Foley, however, Schleifer is not interested in reifying deconstruction (or de Man's version of it) as a lapse or "error" within another "correct" (or "totalizing") discourse. Rather, in his view, insights or theory about referentiality evolve from several sides—speech-act theory, synchronic linguistics, and so on—and deconstruction's participation in this "discourse" tends to define and mark, in regard to reference anyway, a particular set of "ends" and "aims."

In the debate between Foley and Schleifer the main question concerns whether reference is a fundamentally differential, linguistic "meaning-effect" (as Schleifer, following Felman, suggests) or a substantial and essential entity, an emanation of the "real politic" (as Foley suggests). The contrast becomes most clear when the "object" of reference is time. Is temporality a "metaphor" produced by "discrepancies" embedded in discourse as de Man asserts—what Derrida calls "in effect a 'monumental, stratified, contradictory' history"[8]—or is it "a conception of historical process that is unequivocally linear, though hardly mechanistic or monocausal" as Foley argues? This contrast polarizes the two views, perhaps more than is accurate. Thus Schleifer appears to read the "end" of de Man's deconstruction on the *timeless* axis of "knowledge vs. ignorance" even as de Man's affective rhetoric re-inscribes temporality within it so that its "philosophic" aporias disguise what de Man calls simply "random power, like the power of death"; while Foley inscribes the discourse of deconstruction on the *temporal* axis of "power vs. powerlessness" and then argues that, by finally remaining simply a philosophical discourse, deconstruction erases that temporality so that the "revolutionary" style of deconstruction remains "only" style, its temporalization simply temporizing—dead-end disguised as project. "Deconstruction," she writes, "seeks to counter [political] hegemony not by 'constituting a third term' or 'abolishing' the opposition, but by exposing its internal contradictions: any other strategy, Derrida argues, would end up 'resurrecting' the very exclusionary mode of thought that it seeks to vanquish." In these essays, as in deconstruction, is the play of two "ends"—dead-end and projected aim, the discrepancy between random and totalizing temporality.

Deconstruction's "ends" and their relation to style are evoked in a similarly immediate fashion by Barbara Johnson. Johnson analyzes the specific practice of the Yale School as that of a "Male School" and mounts a critique of Yale deconstruction's gender bias. Severe with Bloom, Hartman, Miller, and de Man, Johnson is particularly harsh with herself. She asks, following Mary Jacobus, "Is there a woman in this text?" and finds that "no book produced by the Yale School seems to have excluded women as effectively as [Johnson's] *The Critical Difference.*" Johnson's charge of error here is serious and far-reaching, and it is more than an immediate and local complaint against Yale deconstruction (and "Yale" as an institution). "The sexes," she writes in a fine simile, "stand in relation to each other not as two distinct entities but as two foreign languages." Thus, she says, in commenting on the work (and, implicitly, the style) of de Man, "the philosopher's place is always within, not outside, the asymmetrical structures of language and of gender, but that place can never, in the final analysis, be proper." The philosopher has to face the "pathos" of his temporal (and sexual) predicament between the all-too-human and the non-human, between totalization and randomness, the "end" as aim and the end as what Yeats calls "Black out." Such "pathos" itself—for de Man the pathos of (temporally un-avoidable) ignorance—signifies the philosopher's diacritical, asymmetrical "place": in this regard Johnson presents, as Felman does in *The Literary Speech Act*, "pleasure" as the binary opposite to "knowledge," rather than de Man's "ignorance," Hartman's "wilderness" and "salvation," Harold Bloom's "anxiety of influence," and Miller's uncanny "manifest strangeness."[9] In the confrontation of daughters and fathers at Yale, as in that between linguistic and Marxist readings of deconstruction, is marked the asymmetrical intersection of the logic and grammar of theory (with its timeless philosophic rhetoric) and the timely (and generational) repetitiousness of the play of practice.

In this collection Hillis Miller engenders a strong sense of deconstruction as an historical *practice* and seems to open the possibility of deconstructive "failure" when he describes four "grounds" or self-evident bases of contemporary theory. He says that current literary criticism rests on a social, psychological, or linguistic ground. Additionally, there is a fourth ground "exceedingly difficult to name in so many words," an "ontology without ontology," a "negative theology," a "something encountered in our relations to other people"—namely, the "death of the other." In the isolation of these "grounds," Miller effectively localizes and historicizes the "criticism" that rests on each. The "ontology without ontology" (like Flannery O'Connor's "Church of Christ Without Christ") is an ideological product that exists only in relation to adjacent "grounds" and is, of course, itself duly local and historical. This "death of the other" is the temporalization of the other (and of opposition altogether), and, like the metaphor of temporality de Man describes, it is produced by discrepancies.

It is Miller's reading of nihilism following Derrida, however, that comes closest to the issue we are addressing. Nihilism, Miller argues, is not a transcendental "philosophic" category but rather an historical response that arose and can possibly end in time. "Following Nietzsche and Heidegger," Miller writes, "Derrida also argues that so-called nihilism is an historical moment which is 'completely symmetrical to, thus dependent on, the principle of reason' (p. 15). Nihilism arises naturally and inevitably during a period, the era of technology, when the principle of universal accountability holds sway in the organization of society. . . ." Such a reading of this concept is a reading of time, and it indicates what most of our essays suggest, that time itself—*temporality*—is not only an "absolute" opposite to transcendental concepts such as space or timelessness or neutrality and so on, but also plays and participates in them, marking timeless oppositions and temporalizing (and temporizing) them at the same time. "Temporalization," in these terms, is not a new "ground," a simple origin, but rather, as Derrida says of *dissemination*, "marks an irreducible and *generative* multiplicity . . . forbidding an exhaustive and closed formalization of [the text], or at least a saturating taxonomy of its themes, its signified, its meaning" (*Positions*, p. 45).

Thus, while deconstruction *can* be understood as the pure good of theory as opposed to practice (as Norris reads de Man and Empson *against* New Criticism) or (in Foley's case) practice without theory, Barbara Johnson suggests in the Symposium that it can also be understood differently: "insight is produced," she says, "in that space between theoretical generalizations and the documentation of uncertainty." "The sort of interrogation for which I am calling," Miller says,

> is neither a work of "pure theory" nor a work of pure praxis, a series of explictions. It is something between those two or preparatory to them, a clearing of the ground and an attempt to sink foundations. It is "criticism" in the fundamental sense of "critique," discriminating, testing out. . . . If criticism as critique is between theory and practice, it is also neither to be identified with hermeneutics, or the search for intentional meaning, on the one side, nor with poetics, or the theory of how texts have meaning, on the other side. . . .

Placing himself between alternatives, Miller is here situating himself in the middle. This position, as Robert Markley argues, implies a style that is altogether temporal: Miller's "strategies of isolating, expanding upon, and charting the metamorphoses of key words and images," Markley writes, "describe what I would call a rhetoric of *delay*—not the outright rejection of the interpretive act but its open-ended deferral." The activity of Miller's criticism is, as Kierkegaard says, *interesting*—both "in between" and a "concern"; it is, again in Kierkegaard's term, *timely*.

Such activity is timely in the sense that Geoffrey Hartman develops in his essay here: it is a *response* to something outside and beside the point, at once "local" and yet transcendental. It is both because a human response to experience—what Miller calls an all-too-human response—is to "perceive" and emphasize transcendental signification. Thus, in a "local" reading of Wordsworth's Intimation Ode Hartman "deconstructively" attempts to emphasize "the letter in the spirit," that is, to allow words "to evoke their intertextual echoes," which in turn rest on a linguistic "ground" which is thoroughly "timely." Such a linguistic ground supports the *text* "on which . . . intertextual leaping comes to rest." Both Miller and Hartman, far more than is often thought about the highly "theoretical" Yale critics, insist upon such "local" readings (calling, as Miller says, "Back to the text!") and, thus, upon the potential for failed and "mis-" readings, or errors in deconstructive reading if not in deconstruction itself. However, in Hartman's treatment of Wordsworth the "theoretical" ("all-too-human") resistence to the temporalization of deconstruction is a fact, too—not, as in de Man, in a "neutral" style, but in a tendency to thematize "timeliness." Even the structure of Hartman's essay—a detective story with its "discovery" of the "timely utterance" that saved Wordsworth at the end—resists the implication of its "local" emphasis on the letter in the spirit by articulating the possibility of discourse as pure spirit in the *signifying* "disturbance" of temporal continuity.

Here indeed—and Davis emphasizes this in his reading of "error" in Hartman—is an abrupt "end" to deconstruction with a vengeance, an apocalyptic locking up of deconstruction in what Hartman calls his "mildly deconstructive reading" that emphasizes the materiality and temporality of language. Hartman writes that "the construction of an intertextual field is disconcerting as well as enriching because intertextual concordance produces a reality-discord, a overlay or distancing of the referential function of speech, or the word-thing, word-experience relationship." The (particular and local) problem here is that the "intertext" Hartman chooses to "hear," the "referent" he "discovers" in Wordsworth's discourse, is not one among many, but rather God's *fiat*, a "referent" that authorizes transcendental textuality (and referentiality) as well as originating temporality in a world that is seemingly unequivocally linear.

Hartman's project is truly a kind of "saving," what Miller calls an attempt at a "cure" and what Herman Rapaport describes as the "phatic buffer or shelter" that the sound shapes of language—the *materiality* of language—provide for the speaking subject: "a protective covering which is always already part of the speech of an other, a covering which is identified with the voices which others have spoken." Such materiality marks not a linear, but an ambiguous temporality, conceived as a saving of performed consciousness *and* as the marking of the destructive futurity of repetitious time. "What will be of interest," Rapaport writes,

> is not so much a saving of the text as cultural artifact, but a saving of consciousness as the performance and behavior of *chora*, a saving we will find

more troubled as we proceed. For certainly by the time we consider Alban
Berg, the performance or behavior of sound will be a performance of the
composer's dying. What is saved or treasured up is sound, a saving that in
Berg is a symptom of a sickness or abscess in being. . . .

Here, then, are articulated the "ends" of deconstruction and especially
deconstruction at Yale: the inscription of temporality in readings that
are at once "local" and "theoretical," and a temporality which is itself
equivocally conceived. As Derrida writes in "The Ends of Man," "the
transcendental end can appear to itself and unfold before itself only in the
condition of mortality, of relation to finitude as the origin of ideality. . . . It has meaning only in this eschato-teleological situation."
Thus, as he says of man, the end of deconstruction "has always been
prescribed, and this prescription has never served except to modulate the
equivocality of the *end*, in the interplay of *telos* and death."[10]

iii

All of this brings us back to the possibility of "error" at Yale, a
"swerving" in American deconstruction that is both its "end" and its
"aim," a "tremendous capacity" in the Yale critics, as Davis writes," for
being wrong, for advancing a criticism continually different from itself—for being critically in error." "This propensity for error," Davis
goes on, "posited in part as the willingness repeatedly 'to make it new,' is
a de Manian accounting of the tremendous productivity (and importance) of these critics." This view of deconstruction at Yale as
fruitfully error-ridden—apart from Davis's enthusiasm—does not merely depict correctable swervings and a theoretical "cure," even a "curing."
At stake here is error, too, in a nonrecuperable sense, so that deconstruction once "lost," as Derrida says about Poe's purloined letter, "would not
be found; it might always not be found."[11] Here Derrida presents a
"sense" of loss in the nonrecuperability of time (impossibly) conceived
beyond discourse. In fact, as we might extend Derrida's comment,
deconstruction is always not being found, is always erring in the movement toward its own aim/end, its own trajectory as praxis-toward-death.
Conversely, the deconstruction that is *always* findable and non-falsifiable
is a "purveyor of truth," vacuous and chimerical, neither dead, alive, nor
"undead," but simply without force—a theory that *never was*.

We are suggesting that this collection-as-symposium—with its Yale
criticism and its rereadings of Yale deconstruction—attempts to insinuate deconstructive ends within deconstruction, to read deconstruc-

tion as "always already" in error, as "always already" a text. Various of these rereadings necessarily reinscribe deconstruction as a "transcendental" methodology provoking new questions and new readings. But all of them challenge deconstruction and demand its answerability to the concerns of time, to the responsibilities and freedom of the local discourse deconstruction has initiated. "Deconstruction" does not in truth control its own developments and "offspring" and cannot, in any absolute sense, be held accountable for them. It is precisely this lack of control in deconstruction that makes it a local and error-ridden practice. As this collection's essays show, deconstruction is read most productively as a romantic poem, attempting in its dismantling of binarity and atemporal structures to be somehow closer to the nick of time, to enable itself to play in the temporal labyrinth—finally, to approach and be (nearly) adequate to the very (unlocatable) tracings of time itself. This inscription of romantic poetry, in fact, is rather telling, and it appears in deconstruction in many different ways, most prominently in the Yale reliance on rereadings of romantic texts—Hölderlin, Shelley, Rousseau, Wordsworth, Hegel, and so forth. It may well be that the "desire" of deconstruction is defined by that of the greatest romantic poetry, the "great endeavor" whose desire (aim/end), as René Wellek said long ago, is "to overcome the split between subject and object, the self and the world"[12]—the split between *telos* and death. Deconstruction attempts not to overcome but to acknowledge and reinscribe the split already inscribed in discourse, "temporality" and the "ends" of man. Neither the romantic desire to overcome nor the deconstructive acknowledgment of the split in time between *telos* and death can fully succeed, master its own ends, or erase its errors. But as this "reinscription" of romanticism in deconstruction demonstrates, the failure to transcend an end/aim— the absoluteness of death—does not preclude further inscription— further discourse. Deconstruction's "end," as this collection shows, does not and will not preclude further discourse either.

NOTES

1. Paul de Man, *Allegories of Reading* (Yale University Press: New Haven, 1979); abbreviated *AR*.

2. Geoffrey Hartman, *Saving the Text: Literature/Derrida/Philosophy* (Johns Hopkins University Press: Baltimore, 1981); abbreviated *ST*.

3. A. J. Greimas, *Structural Semantics*, trans. Daniele McDowell, Ronald Schleifer, Alan Velie (University of Nebraska Press: Lincoln, 1983), p. 175.

4. J. Hillis Miller, "Stevens' Rock and Criticism as Cure," *GaR*, 30 (1976), 336.

5. Barbara Johnson, "The Frame of Reference: Poe, Lacan, Derrida," *YFS, Literature and Psychoanalysis*, ed. Shoshana Felman, 55/56 (1977), 504.

6. Jacques Derrida, "Limited Inc.," trans. Samuel Weber, *Glyph* 2 (1977), 190.

7. *Denegation* is a term A. J. Greimas develops in *Structual Semantics* to account for a "functional" (as opposed to a "synchronic") understanding of discourse and which he defines (with J. Courtés) in *Semiotics and Language: An Analytical Dictionary*, trans. Larry Crist, Daniel Patte, et. al. (Bloomington: Indiana University Press, 1982) as distinct from "negation": "While negation is paradigmatically the contrary of assertion, the operation of *denial*[denegation]presupposes the existence of a preceding utterance of assertion or of negation. Thus denial implies a syntagmatic perspective 'in which the relation of implication is actualized" (p. 72). Thus, in the opposition "negation vs. denial" Greimas inscribes Chomsky's opposition between "too-powerful" and "forceful" theories.

8. Derrida, *Positions*, trans. Alan Bass (University of Chicago Press: Chicago, 1981), p. 57.

9. For Miller's "strangeness," see *Fiction and Repetition* (Cambridge: Harvard University Press, 1982), p. 18; Hartman, *Criticism in the Wilderness* (Yale University Press: New Haven, 1980); de Man, *Allegories of Reading*, p. 19; and Harold Bloom, *The Anxiety of Influence* (Oxford University Press: New York, 1973). Bloom remains a prominent "Yale critics" who is virtually absent from this collection. (Johnson and Davis, however, do allude to his work.) His absence is our tacit acknowledgment that, while his work is forcefully important in American criticism, it does not share with de Man, Miller and Hartman, the "ends" of deconstruction we are describing here. Derrida's "influence" is less apparent in his work; and the kind of complicated temporality we are attempting to articulate here is more simply in Bloom the "misreading" of predecessors rather than "errors" inherent in time diacritically conceived as "monumental, stratified, contradictory" that Derrida suggests.

10. Derrida, "The Ends of Man," trans. Edouard Morot-Sir, Wesley Piersol, Hubert Dreyfus, Barbara Reid, *Philosophy and Phenomenological Research*, 30 (1969), pp. 44, 55.

11. Derrida, "The Purveyor of Truth," *YFS, Graphesis*, ed. Marie-Rose Logan, 52 (1975), 64.

12. René Wellek, "Romanticism Re-Examined," in *Romanticism Reconsidered*, ed. Northrop Frye (Columbia University Press: New York, 1963), p. 132.

Part One
The Yale Critics

The Search for Grounds in Literary Study

J. Hillis Miller
Yale University

> You ask me in what I think or have thought you going wrong: in this: that
> you would never take your assiette as something determined final and
> unchangeable for you and proceed to work away on the basis of that: but were
> always poking and patching and cobbling at the assiette itself—
> (Matthew Arnold, Letters to Clough)[1]

> . . . perhaps one is a philologist still, that is to say, a teacher of slow
> reading [*ein Lehrer des langsamen Lesens*].
> (Friedrich Nietzsche, "Preface" to Daybreak)[2]

An important passage in George Eliot's *Daniel Deronda* (1876) speaks
of the liability of the heroine, Gwendolen Harleth, to sudden, inexplicable fits of hysterical terror or of "spiritual dread." She has these fits when
faced with open spaces: "Solitude in any wide scene impressed her with
an undefined feeling of immeasurable existence aloof from her, in the
midst of which she was helplessly incapable of asserting herself."[3]

A strange little paragraph by Maurice Blanchot entitled "Une scène
primitive," "A Primitive Scene," and published just a century later, in
1976, describes a "similar" "experience," ascribed this time to a child of
seven or eight standing at the window and looking at a wintry urban or
suburban scene outside:

> Ce qu'il voit, le jardin, les arbres d'hiver, le mur d'une maison; tandis qu'il
> voit, sans doute à la manière d'un enfant, son espace de jeu, il se lasse et
> lentement regarde en haut vers le ciel ordinaire, avec les nuages, la lumière
> grise, le jour terne et sans lointain. Ce qui se passe ensuite: le ciel, le *même* ciel,
> soudain ouvert, noir absolument et vide absolument, révélant (comme par la
> vitre brisée) une telle absence que tout s'y est depuis toujours et à jamais
> perdu, au point que s'y affirme et s'y dissipe le savoir vertigineux que rien est
> ce qu'il y a, et d'abord rien au-delà.

> [What he saw, the garden, the winter trees, the wall of a house; while he
> looked, no doubt in the way a child does, at his play area, he got bored and
> slowly looked higher toward the ordinary sky, with the clouds, the grey

light, the day flat and without distance. What happened then: the sky, the *same* sky, suddenly opened, black absolutely and empty absolutely, revealing (as if the window had been broken) such an absence that everything is since forever and for forever lost, to the point at which there was affirmed and dispersed there the vertiginous knowledge that nothing is what there is there, and especially nothing beyond.][4]

"Rien est ce qu'il y a, et d'abord rien au-delà": nothing is what there is there, and first of all nothing beyond. As in the case of Wallace Stevens' "The Snow Man," where the listener and watcher in the snow, "nothing himself, beholds / Nothing that is not there and the nothing that is,"[5] the devastating experience of a transfiguration of the scene which leaves it nevertheless exactly the same, the *same* sky, is the confrontation of a nothing which somehow is, has being, and which absorbs into itself any beyond or transcendence. In this primitive scene, original and originating, for Blanchot's child, or possibly even for Blanchot as a child, the sky definitely does not open to reveal heavenly light or choirs of angels singing "Glory, glory, glory." It the effect on Gwendolen Harleth in Eliot's novel of confronting open space in solitude is sometimes hysterical outbursts, the effect on Blanchot's child of an opening of the sky which does not open is seemingly endless tears of a "ravaging joy [joie ravagéant]."

I take these details from *Daniel Deronda* and from Blanchot's little scene, quite arbitrarily, or almost quite arbitrarily, as parables for the terror or dread readers may experience when they confront a text which seems irreducibly strange, inexplicable, perhaps even mad, for example Blanchot's *Death Sentence* [*L'arrêt de mort*]. As long as we have not identified the law by which the text can be made reasonable, explicable, it is as if we have come face to face with an immeasurable existence aloof from us, perhaps malign, perhaps benign, in any case something we have not yet mastered and assimilated into what we already know. It is as if the sky had opened, while still remaining the same sky, for are not those words there on the page familiar and ordinary words, words in our own language or mother tongue, words whose meaning we know? And yet they have suddenly opened and become terrifying, inexplicable. On the one hand, our task as readers is to transfer to reading Henry James's injunction to the observer of life, the novice writer: "Try to be one of those on whom nothing is lost." A good reader, that is, especially notices oddnesses, gaps, anacoluthons, non sequiturs, apparently irrelevant details, in short, all the marks of the inexplicable, all the marks of the unaccountable, perhaps of the mad, in a text. On the other hand, the reader's task is to reduce the inexplicable to the explicable, to find its reason, its law, its ground, to make the mad sane. The task of the reader, it will be seen, is not too different from the task of the psychoanalyst.

Current criticism tends to propose one or another of the three following grounds on the basis of which the anomalies of literature may be made lawful, the unaccountable accountable: society, the more or less hidden social or ideological pressures which impose themselves on literature and reveal themselves in oddnesses; individual psychology, the more or less hidden psychic pressures which impose themselves on a work of literature and make it odd, unaccountable; language, the more or less hidden rhetorical pressures, or pressures from some torsion within language itself as such, which impose themselves on the writer and make it impossible for his work to maintain itself as an absolutely lucid and reasonable account.

The stories or *récits* of Maurice Blanchot, as well as his criticism, propose a fourth possibility. Though this possibility is, in the case of Blanchot at least, exceedingly difficult to name in so many words, and though the whole task of the reader of Blanchot could be defined as a (perhaps impossible) attempt to make this definition clear to oneself or to others, it can be said that this fourth possibility for the disturber of narrative sanity and coherence, a disruptive energy neither society nor individual psychology nor language itself, is properly religious, metaphysical, or ontological, though hardly in a traditional or conventional way. To borrow a mode of locution familiar to readers of Blanchot it is an ontology without ontology. Nor is it to be defined simply as a species of negative theology. Blanchot gives to this "something" that enters into the words or between the words the names, among others, of it [*il*]; the thing [*la chose*]; dying [*mourir*]; the neutral [*le neutre*]; the non-presence of the eternal return [*le retour éternel*]; writing [*écrire*]; the thought [*la pensée*]; the truth [*la verité*]; the other of the other [*l'autre de l'autre*]; meaning something encountered in our relations to other people, especially relations involving love, betrayal, and that ultimate betrayal by the other of our love for him or her, the death of the other. To list these names in this way cannot possibly convey very much, except possibly, in their multiplicity and incoherence, a glimpse of the inadequacy of any one of them and of the fact that all of them must in one way or another be figurative rather than literal. What sort of "thing" is it which cannot be pinned down and labelled with one single name, so that all names for it are improper, whether proper or generic? All Blanchot's writing is a patient, continual, long-maintained attempt to answer this question, the question posed by the experience recorded in "A Primitive Scene."

Two further features may be identified of my four proposed modes of rationalizing or accounting for or finding grounds for the irrational or unaccountable in any literary account.

The first feature seems obvious enough, though it is evaded often enough to need emphasizing. This is the exclusivity or imperialism of any one of the four. Each has a mode of explanation or of grounding the anomalous in literature demands to exercise sovereign control over the others, to make the others find their ground in *it*. You cannot have all four at once or even any two of them without ultimately grounding, or rather without having already implicitly grounded, all but one in the single regal ur-explanation. Psychological explanations tend to see linguistic, religious, or social explanations as ultimately finding *their* cause in individual human psychology. Social explanations see human psychology, language, and religion as epiphenomena of underlying and determining social forces, the "real" conditions of class, production, consumption, exchange. Linguistic explanations tend to imply or even openly to assert that society, psychology, and religion are "all language," generated by language in the first place and ultimately to be explained by features of language. Metaphysical explanations see society, psychology, and language as secondary, peripheral. Each of these modes of grounding explanation asserts that it is the true "principle of reason," the true *Satz vom Grund*, the others bogus, an abyss not a ground. Each asserts a jealous will to power over the others.

The second feature of these four modes of explaining oddnesses in literature is the strong resistance each of them seems to generate in those to whom they are proposed. The resistance, for example, to Sigmund Freud's assertion of a universal unconscious sexual etiology for neurosis is notorious, and that resistance has by no means subsided. In Marxist theory, for example that of Louis Althusser in *For Marx*, "ideology" is the name given to the imaginary structures, whereby men and women resist facing directly the real economic and social conditions of their existence. "Ideology, then," says Althusser, "is the expression of the relation between men and their 'world,' that is, the (overdetermined) unity of the real relation and the imaginary relation between them and their real conditions of existence."[6] There is a tremendous resistance to totalizing explanations which say, "It's all language," the resistance encountered, for example, by structuralism, semiotics, and by misunderstandings of so-called "deconstruction" today. Many people, finally, seem able to live on from day to day and year to year, even as readers of literature, without seeing religious or metaphysical questions as having any sort of force or substance. It is not the case that man is everywhere and universally a religious or metaphysical animal. George Eliot, speaking still of Gwendolen, describes eloquently the latter's resistance to two of my sovereign principles of grounding:

> She had no permanent consciousness of other fetters, or of more spiritual restraints, having always disliked whatever was presented to her under the name of religion, in the same way that some people dislike arithmetic and accounts: it had raised no other emotion in her, no alarm, no longing; so that the question whether she believed it had not occurred to her, any more than it had occurred to her to inquire into the conditions of colonial property and banking, on which, as she had had many opportunities of knowing, the family fortune was dependent. (pp. 89–90)

Why this resistance to looking into things, including works of literature, all the way down to the bottom is so strong and so universal I shall not attempt here to explain. Perhaps it is inexplicable. Perhaps it is a general consensus that, as Conrad's Winnie Verloc in *The Secret Agent* puts it, "life doesn't stand much looking into."[7] It might be better not to know.

Is it legitimate to seek in literature a serious concern for such serious topics, to see works of literature as in one way or another interrogations of the ground, taking ground in the sense of a sustaining metaphysical foundation outside language, outside nature, and outside the human mind? The role granted to poetry or to "literature" within our culture and in particular within our colleges and universities today is curiously contradictory. The contradiction is an historical inheritance going back at least to Kant and to eighteenth-century aesthetic theory or "critical philosophy." The tradition comes down from the enlightenment through romantic literary theory and later by way of such figures as Matthew Arnold (crucial to the development of the "humanities" in American higher education) to the New Criticism and the academic humanism of our own day. On the one hand the enjoyment of poetry is supposed to be the "disinterested" aesthetic contemplation of beautiful or sublime organic forms made of words. It is supposed to be "value free," without contamination by use of the poem for any cognitive, practical, ethical, or political purposes. Such appropriations, it is said, are a misuse of poetry. According to this aestheticizing assumption one ought to be able to read Dante and Milton, for example, or Aeschylus and Shelley, without raising either the question of the truth or falsity of their philosophical and religious beliefs, or the question of the practical consequences of acting on those beliefs. Cleanth Brooks, for example, in a recent essay vigorously reaffirming the tenets of the New Criticism, presents *Paradise Lost* as a case in point: "Milton tells us in the opening lines of *Paradise Lost* that his purpose is to 'justify the ways of God to men,' and there is no reason to doubt that this was what he hoped to do. But what we actually have in the poem is a wonderful interconnected story of events in heaven and hell and upon earth, with grand and awesome scenes brilliantly painted and with heroic actions dramatically rendered. In short, generations of readers have found that the grandeur of the poem far exceeds any direct statement of theological views. The point is underscored by the fact that some readers who reject Milton's theology altogether nevertheless regard *Paradise Lost* as a great poem."[8]

On the other hand, literature has been weighted down in our culture with the burden of carrying from generation to generation the whole freight of the values of that culture, what Matthew Arnold called "the best that is known and thought in the world."[9] Cleanth Brooks elsewhere in his essay also reiterates this traditional assumption about literature. Walter Jackson Bate, in a recent polemical essay, sees specialization, including the New Criticism's specialization of close reading, as greatly weakening the humanities generally and departments of English in particular. Bate regrets the good old days (from 1930 to 1950) when departments of English taught everything under the sun but reading as such, in a modern reincarnation of the Renaissance ideal of *litterae humaniores*. The literature components of the humanities in our colleges and universities, and departments of English in particular, have with a good conscience undertaken, after hurrying through a soupçon of rhetoric and poetics, to teach theology, metaphysics, psychology, ethics, politics, social and intellectual history, even the history of science and natural history, in short, "Allerleiwissenschaft," like Carlyle's Professor Diogenes Teufelsdröck.[10]

The implicit reasoning behind this apparently blatant contradiction may not be all that difficult to grasp, though the reasoning will only restate the contradiction. It is just because, and only because, works of literature are stable, self-contained, value-free objects of disinterested aesthetic contemplation that they can be trustworthy vehicles of the immense weight of values they carry from generation to generation uncontaminated by the distortions of gross reality. Just because the values are enshrined in works of literature, uninvested, not collecting interest, not put out to vulgar practical use, they remain pure, not used up, still free to be reappropriated for whatever use we may want to make of them. Has not Kant in the third critique, the *Critique of Judgment*, once and for all set works of art as reliable and indispensible middle member (*Mittelglied*), between cognition (pure reason, theory, the subject of the first critique) and ethics (practical reason, praxis, ethics, the subject of the second critique)? And has not Kant defined beauty, as embodied for example in a poem, as "the symbol of morality [*Symbol der Sittlichkeit*]"?[11] Both Bate and René Wellek, the latter in another outspoken polemical essay with the nice title of "Destroying Literary Studies," invoke Kant, or rather their understanding of Kant, as having settled these matters once and for all, as if there were no more need to worry about them, and as if our understanding of Kant, or rather theirs, could safely be taken for granted: ". . . Why not," asks Bate, "turn to David Hume, the greatest skeptic in the history of thought . . . and then turn to Kant, by whom so much of this is answered?" (p. 52); "One can doubt the very existence of aesthetic experience," says Wellek, "and refuse to recognize the distinctions, clearly formulated in Immanuel Kant's *Critique of Judgment*, between the good, the true, the useful, and the beautiful."[12] So much is at stake here that it is probably a good idea to go back and read Kant for ourselves, no easy task to be sure, in order to be certain that he says what Bate and Wellek say he says.

When Matthew Arnold, the founding father, so to speak, of the American concept of the humanities, praises the virtues of disinterested contemplation, he is being faithful to the Kantian inheritance, no doubt by way of its somewhat vulgarizing distortions in Schiller. It was, and is, by no means necessary to have read Kant to be a Kantian of sorts. Arnold's full formulaic definition of criticism, in "The Function of Criticism at the Present Time" (1864), is "a disinterested endeavour to learn and propagate the best that is known and thought in the world."[13] He speaks elsewhere in the same essay of the "disinterested love of a free play of the mind on all subjects, for its own sake."[14] When Arnold, in a well-known statement in "The Study of Poetry" (1880) which has echoed down the decades as the implicit credo of many American departments of English, says: "The future of poetry is immense, because in poetry, where it is worthy of its high destinies, our race, as time goes on, will find an ever surer and surer stay," he goes on to make it clear that poetry is a "stay" just because it is detached from the question of its truth or falsity as fact. Poetry can therefore replace religion when the fact fails religion. Poetry is cut off from such questions, sequestered in a realm of disinterested fiction. Just for this reason poetry is a "stay," a firm resting place when all else gives way, like a building without a solid foundation. "There is not a creed which is not shaken," says Arnold in his melancholy litany, "not an accredited dogma which is not shown to be questionable, not a received tradition which does not threaten to dissolve. Our religion has materialized itself in the fact, in the supposed fact; it has attached its emotion to the fact, and now the fact is failing it. But for poetry the idea is everything; the rest is a world of illusion, of divine illusion. Poetry attaches its emotion to the idea; the idea *is* the fact."[15] The image here is that of a self-sustaining linguistic fiction or illusion which holds itself up by a kind of intrinsic magic of levitation over the abyss, like an aerial floating bridge over chaos, as long as one does not poke and patch at the assiette. This bridge or platform may therefore hold up also the ideas the poem contains and the readers who sustain themselves by these ideas.

Arnold had this double or even triple notion of the staying power of poetry already in mind when, in 1848 or 1849, many years before writing "The Study of Poetry," he wrote to Arthur Hugh Clough: "Those who cannot read G[ree]k sh[ou]ld read nothing but Milton and parts of Wordsworth: the state should see to it. . . ."[16] Most Freshman and Sophomore courses in American colleges and universities in "Major English Authors" are still conceived in the spirit of Arnold's categorical dictum. The uplifting moral value of reading Milton and parts of Wordsworth, so important that it should be enforced by the highest civil authority, is initially stylistic. Arnold opposes the solemn, elevated, composing "grand" style of Homer, or, failing that, of Milton and parts of Wordsworth, to the "confused multitudinousness" (*ibid.*) of Browning, Keats, and Tennyson, the romantics and Victorians generally, excepting that part of Wordsworth. The occasion of Arnold's letter to Clough is the devastating effect on him of reading Keats's letters: "What a brute you were to tell me to read Keats's Letters. However it is over now: and reflexion resumes her power over agitation" (p. 96). From Keats Arnold turns to the Greeks, to Milton, and to those parts of Wordsworth to subdue his inner agitation as well as to protect himself from the agitation without.

Only secondary to the sustaining effect of the grand style as such are the "ideas" expressed in that style. A writer, says Arnold, "must begin with an Idea of the world in order not to be prevailed over by the world's multitudinousness" (*ibid.*, p. 97). The Idea, so to speak, is the style, or the style is the Idea, since the grand style is nothing but the notion of composure, elevation, coherence, objectivity, that is, just the characteristics of the grand style. This combination of grand elevated style and presupposed, preconceived, or pre-posited grand comprehensive Idea of the world (never mind whether it is empirically verifiable) not only composes and elevates the mind but also fences it off from the confused multitudinousness outside and the danger therefore of confused multitudinousness within. The latter, Arnold, in the "Preface" of 1853, calls "the dialogue of the mind with itself."[17] He associates it especially with the modern spirit, and fears it more than anything else. It is the dissolution of the mind's objectivity, calm, and unity with itself. This composing, lifting up, and fencing out through literature takes place, to borrow from one of the authors Arnold tells us exclusively to read, as God organizes chaos in the work of creation, or as Milton, at the beginning of *Paradise Lost*, prays that his interior chaos, likened to the unformed Abyss, may be illuminated, elevated, impregnated, and grounded by the Holy Spirit or heavenly muse: "Thou from the first / Was present, and with mighty wings outspread / Dove-like satst brooding on the vast Abyss / And madst it pregnant: What in me is dark / Illumine, what is low raise and support" (*Paradise Lost*, I, 19–23).

It is only a step from Kant's image in paragraph 59 of the *Critique of Judgment* of art or poetry as *hypotyposis* [*Hypotypose*], indirect symbols of intuitions for which there is no direct expression,[18] to Hegel's assertion that sublime poetry, like parable, fable, and apologue, is characterized by the non-adequation and dissimilarity between symbol and symbolized, what he calls the *Sichnichtentsprechen beider*, the non-correspondence of the two.[19] It is only another step beyond that to I. A. Richards' assertion, in *Principles of Literary Criticism*, with some help from Jeremy Bentham's theory of fictions, that the function of poetry is to produce an equilibrium among painfully conflicting impulses and thereby to provide fictive solutions to real psychological problems. Another step in this sequence (which is not even a progression, radicalizing or deepening, but a movement in place), takes us to Wallace Stevens' resonant formulation in the *Adagia* of what all these writers in somewhat different ways are saying: "The final belief is to believe in a fiction, which you know to be a fiction, there being nothing else. The exquisite truth is to know that it is a fiction and that you believe in it willingly."[20]

Proof that Matthew Arnold still plays an indispensable role within this sequence as the presumed base for a conservative humanism is a forceful recent article by Eugene Goodheart, "Arnold at the Present Time," with accompanying essays and responses by George Levine, Morris Dickstein, and Stuart M. Tave.[21] As is not surprising, the oppositions among these essays come down to a question of how one reads Arnold. If Goodheart grossly misrepresents "deconstruction" and the sort of "criticism as critique" I advocate (which is not surprising), he is also a bad reader or a non-reader of Arnold. Goodheart takes for granted the traditional misreading of Arnold which has been necessary to make him, as Goodheart puts it, "the inspiration of humanistic study in England and America" (p. 451). Levine, Dickstein, and Tave are, it happens, far better and more searching readers of Arnold. Adjudication of differences here is of course possible only by a response to that call, "Back to the texts!," which must be performed again and again in literary study. Nothing previous critics have said can be taken for granted, however authoritative it may seem. Each reader must do again for himself the laborious task of a scrupulous slow reading, trying to find out what the texts actually say rather than imposing on them what she or he wants them to say or wishes they said. Advances in literary study are not made by the free invention of new conceptual or historical schemes (which always turn out to be old ones anew in any case), but by that grappling with the texts which always has to be done over once more by each new reader. In the case of Arnold the poetry and prose must be read together, not assumed to be discontinuous units or an early negative stage and a late affirmative stage negating the earlier negation. Far from offering a firm "assiette" to the sort of humanism Goodheart advocates, such a careful reading of Arnold will reveal him to be a nihilist writer through and through, nihilist in the precise sense in which Nietzsche or Heidegger defines the term: as a specifically historical designation of the moment within the development of Western metaphysics when the highest values devalue themselves and come to nothing as their transcendent base dissolves:[22] "There is not a creed which is not shaken, not an accredited dogma which is not shown to be questionable, not a received tradition which does not threaten to dissolve." "I am nothing and very probably never shall be anything," said Arnold in one of the letters to Clough.[23]

A house built on sand, in this case a humanistic tradition built on the shaky foundation of a misreading of Matthew Arnold, cannot stand firmly. To put this another way, the affirmations of Goodheart, Bate, Wellek, and others like them participate inevitably in the historical movement of nihilism ("the history of the next two centuries," Nietzsche called it)[24] which they contest. Most of all they do this in the act itself of contestation. "The question arises," says Heidegger in the section on nihilism in his *Nietzsche*, "whether the innermost essence of nihilism and the power of its dominion do not consist precisely in considering the nothing merely as a nullity [*nur für etwas Nichtiges*], considering nihilism as an apotheosis of the merely vacuous [*der blossen*

Leere], as a negation [*eine Verneinung*] that can be set to rights at once by an energetic affirmation."[25]

In a brilliant essay on "The Principle of Reason: The University in the Eyes of its Pupils,"[26] Jacques Derrida identifies the way the modern university and the study of literature within it are based on the domination of the Leibnizian principle of reason, what in German is called "der Satz vom Grund," the notion that everything can and should be accounted for, *Omnis veritatis reddi ratio potest*, that nothing is without reason, *nihil est sine ratione*. Following Nietzsche and Heidegger, Derrida also argues that so-called nihilism is an historical moment which is "completely symmetrical to, thus dependent on, the principle of reason" (p. 15). Nihilism arises naturally and inevitably during a period, the era of technology, when the principle of universal accountability holds sway in the organization of society and of the universities accountable to that society. "For the principle of reason," says Derrida, "may have obscurantist and nihilist effects. They can be seen more or less everywhere, in Europe and America among those who believe they are defending philosophy, literature and the humanities against these new modes of questioning that are also a new relation to language and tradition, a new affirmation, and new ways of taking responsibility. We can easily see on which side obscurantism and nihilism are lurking when on occasion great professors or representatives of prestigious institutions lose all sense of proportion and control; on such occasions they forget their principles that they claim to defend in their work and suddenly begin to heap insults, to say whatever comes into their heads on the subject of texts that they obviously have never opened or that they have encountered through a mediocre journalism that in other circumstances they would pretend to scorn" (p. 15). Obviously much is at stake here, and we must go carefully, looking before and after, testing the ground carefully, taking nothing for granted.

If such a tremendous burden is being placed on literature throughout all the period from Kant to academic humanists of our own day like Bate and Goodheart, it is of crucial importance to be sure that literature is able to bear the weight, or that it is a suitable instrument to perform its function. The question is too grave for its answer to be left untested. To raise the question of the weight-bearing capacities of the medium of poetry is of course not the only thing criticism can do or ought to do, but I claim it is one all-important task of literary study. The question in question here is not of the thematic content of or the assertions made by works of literature but of the weight-bearing characteristics of the

medium of literature, that is, of language. It is a question of what the
language of poetry is and does. Is it indeed solid enough and trustworthy
enough to serve, according to the metaphor Kant proposes at the end of
the introduction to the *Critique of Judgment*, as the fundamentally necessary bridge passing back and forth between pure cognition and moral
action, between *theoria* and *praxis*? "The realm of the natural concept
under the one legislation," says Kant, "and that of the concept of
freedom under the other are entirely removed [*gänzlich abgesondert*] from
all mutual influence [*wechselseitigen Einfluss*] which they might have on
one another (each according to its fundamental laws) by the great gulf
[*die grosse Kluft*] that separates the supersensible from phenomena [*das
Übersinnliche von den Erscheinungen*]. The concept of freedom determines
nothing in respect of the theoretical cognition of nature, and the internal
concept determines nothing in respect of the practical laws of freedom.
So far, then, it is not possible to throw a bridge from the one realm to the
other [*eine Brücke von einem Gebiete zu dem andern hinüber zu schlagen*]"[27]
    Art or the aesthetic experience. is the only candidate for a possible
bridge. The whole of the *Critique of Judgment* is written to test out the
solidity, so to speak, of the planks by which this indispensable bridge
from the realm of knowledge to the realm of moral action might be built,
across the great gulf that separates them. If the "beauty" of the work of
art is the sensible symbol of morality, it is, on the other hand, the
sensible embodiment of the pure idea, what Hegel was to call, in a
famous formulation, and in echo of Kant's word *Erscheinungen*, "the
sensible shining forth of the idea [*das sinnliche 'scheinen' der Idee*]."[28] As
Hegel elsewhere puts it, "art occupies the intermediate ground between
the purely sensory and pure thought [*steht in der 'Mitte' zwischen der
umittelbaren Sinnlichkeit und dem ideellen Gedanken*]" (*Ibid.*, I, 60, my
trans.). Whether Kant or Hegel establish satisfactorily the solidity of
this ground, its adequacy as a bridge, is another question, one that a full
reading of Kant's third *Kritik* and of Hegel's *Ästhetik* would be necessary
to answer. That the answer is affirmative does not go without saying, nor
of course that it is negative either. Others are at work on this task of
re-reading Kant and Hegel.
    The sort of interrogation for which I am calling is neither a work of
"pure theory" nor a work of pure praxis, a series of explications. It is
something between those two or preparatory to them, a clearing of the
ground and an attempt to sink foundations. It is "criticism" in the
fundamental sense of "critique," discriminating testing out, in this case
a testing out of the medium of which the bridge between theory and

practice is made. If criticism as critique is between theory and practice, it is also neither to be identified with hermeneutics, or the search for intentional meaning, on the one side, nor with poetics, or the theory of how texts have meaning, on the other side, though it is closely related to the latter. Critique, however, is a testing of the grounding of language in this or that particular text, not in the abstract or in abstraction from any particular case.

If this sort of investigation of the weight-bearing features of language is often an object of suspicion these days from the point of view of a certain traditional humanism, the humanism of *litterae humaniores*, it is also under attack from the other direction, from the point of view of those who see the central work of literary study as the reinsertion of the work of literature within its social context. The reproaches from the opposite political directions are strangely similar or symmetrical. They often come to the same thing or are couched in the same words. It is as if there were an unconscious alliance of the left and the right to suppress something which is the bad conscience of both a conservative humanism and a "radical" politicizing or sociologizing of the study of literature. A specific problematic is associated with the latter move, which attempts to put literature under the law of economy, under the laws of economic change and social power. I shall examine this problematic in detail elsewhere,[29] but it may be said here that the most resolute attempts to bracket linguistic considerations in the study of literature, to take the language of literature for granted and shift from the study of the relations of word with word to the study of the relations of words with things or with subjectivities, will only lead back in the end to the study of language. Any conceivable encounter with things or with subjectivities in literature or in discourse about literature must already have represented things and subjects in words, numbers, or other signs. Any conceivable representation of the relations of words to things, powers, persons, modes of production and exchange, juridical or political systems (or whatever name the presumably non-linguistic may be given) will turn out to be one or another figure of speech. As such, it will require a rhetorical interpretation, such as that given by Marx in *Capital* and in the *Grundrisse*. Among such figures are that of mimesis, mirroring reflection or representation. This turns out to be a species of metaphor. Another such figure is that of part to whole, work to surrounding and determining milieu, text to context, container to thing contained. This relation is one variety or another of synecdoche or of metonymy. Another figure of the relation of text to social context is that of anamorphosis or of ideology, which is a species of affirmation by denial, abnegation, what Freud called *Verneinung*. Sociologists of literature still all too often do no more than set some social fact side by side with some citation from a literary work and assert that the latter reflects the former, or is accounted for by it, or is determined by it, or is an intrinsic part of it, or is grounded in it. It is just in this place, in the interpretation of this asserted liaison, that the work of rhetorical analysis is indispensable. The necessary dialogue between those practicing poetics or rhetoric and sociologists of literature has scarcely begun. Conservative humanists and "radical" sociologists of literature have this at least in common: both tend to suppress, displace, or replace what I call the linguistic moment in literature.[30] Here too, however, denegation is affirmation. The covering over always leaves traces behind, tracks which may be followed back to those questions about language I am raising.

Kant, once more, in the "Preface" to the *Critique of Judgment* has admirably formulated the necessity of this work of critique: "For if such a system is one day to be completed [*einmal zu Stande kommen soll*] under the general name of metaphysic . . . , the soil for the ediface [*den Boden zu diesem Gebaude*] must be explored by critique [*die Kritik*] as deep down as the foundation [*die erste Grundlage*] of the faculty of principles independent of experience, in order that it may sink in no part [*damit es nicht an irgend einem Teile sinke*], for this would inevitably bring about the downfall [*Einsturz*] of the whole" (Eng. 4; Ger. 74–75). Elsewhere, in the *Critique of Pure Reason*, the same metaphor has already been posited as the foundation of the edifice of pure thought: "But though the following out of these considerations is what gives to philosophy its peculiar dignity, we must meantime occupy ourselves with a less resplendent [*nicht so glänzenden*], but still meritorious task, namely, to level the ground, and to render it sufficiently secure for moral edifices of these majestic dimensions [*den Boden zu jenen majestätischen sittlichen Gebäuden eben und baufest zu machen*]. For this ground has been honeycombed by subterranean workings [*allerlei Maulwurfsgänge*: all sorts of mole tunnels: Smith's translation effaces the figure] which reason, in its confident but fruitless search for hidden treasures has carried out in all directions, and which threaten the security of the superstructures [*und die jenes Bauwerk unsicher machen*]."[31]

Which is critique? Is it groundbreaking to be distinguished from mole-tunnelling and a repair of it, as the second quotation claims, or is critique, as the first quotation affirms, the work of tunnelling itself, the underground search for bedrock which in that process hollows out the soil? Does this contradiction in Kant's formulations not have something to do with the fact that Kant uses a metaphor from art, or to put this another way, throws out a little artwork of his own in the form of an architectural metaphor, in order to define the work of criticism which is supposed to be a testing out of the very instrument of bridging of which the definition makes use? This is an example of a *mise en abyme* in the technical sense of placing within the larger sign system a miniature image of that larger one, a smaller one potentially within that, and so on, in a filling in and covering over of the abyss, gulf, or *Kluft* which is at the same time an opening of the abyss. Such a simultaneous opening and covering over is the regular law of the *mise en abyme*.

Have I not, finally, by an intrinsic and unavoidable necessity, done the same thing as Kant, with my images of bridges, tunnels, bedrock, pathways, and so on, and with my strategy of borrowing citations from Arnold, Kant, and the rest to describe obliquely my own enterprise? This somersaulting, self-constructing, self-undermining form of language, the throwing out of a bridge where no firm bedrock exists, in place of the bedrock, is a fundamental feature of what I call critique. Groundlevelling, it appears, becomes inevitably tunnelling down in search of bedrock, as, to quote Milton again, beneath the lowest deep a lower deep still opens.

I end by drawing several conclusions from what I have said, and by briefly relating what I have said to the question of genre. The first conclusion is a reiteration of my assertion that the stakes are so large in the present quarrels among students of literature that we must go slowly and circumspectly, testing the ground carefully and taking nothing for granted, returning once more to those founding texts of our modern tradition of literary study and reading them anew with patience and care. To put this another way, the teaching of philology, of that "slow reading" or *langsamen Lesen* for which Nietzsche calls, is still a fundamental responsibility of the humanities, at no time more needed than today. Second conclusion: Disagreements among students of literature can often be traced to often more covert disagreements about the presupposed ground of literature—whether that ground is assumed to be society, the self, language, or the "thing." One of these four presuppositions may be taken so for granted by a given critic that he is not even aware that it determines all his procedures and strategies of interpretation. Much will be gained by bringing the fundamental causes of these disagreements into the open. Third conclusion: Though the intellectual activity of ground-testing and of testing out the very idea of the ground or of the principle of reason, through slow reading, has a long and venerable tradition under the names of philology and of critical philosophy, nevertheless such testing has a peculiar role in the university. It is likely to seem subversive, threatening, outside the pale of what is a legitimate activity within the university, if research within the university, including research and teaching in the humanities, is all under the sovereign and unquestioned rule of the principle of reason. Nevertheless, moving forward to the necessary new affirmation and the new taking of responsibility for the humanities and within the humanities depends now, as it always has, on allowing that interrogation to take place.

This new taking of responsibility for language and literature, for the language of literature, which I am calling critique, has, finally, important implications for genre theory or for generic criticism. What I have said would imply not that generic classifications or distinctions and the use of these as a guide to interpretation and evaluation are illegitimate, without grounds, but that they are in a certain sense superficial. They do not go all the way to the ground, and the choice of a ground (or being chosen by one) may be more decisive for literary interpretation than generic distinctions and even determine those generic distinctions and their import. It is only on the grounds of a commitment to language, society, the self, or the "it," one or another of these, that generic distinctions make sense and have force. The choice of a ground determines both the definition of each genre and the implicit or explicit hierarchy among them. It is possible, it makes sense, to say "This is a lyric poem," or "This is a novel," and to proceed on the basis of that to follow certain interpretative procedures and ultimately to say, "This is a good lyric poem," or "This is a bad novel." Nevertheless, it is possible and makes sense to do these things only on the grounds of a prior commitment, perhaps one entirely implicit or even unthought, to founding assumptions about the ultimate ground on which all these genres are erected as so many different dwelling places or cultural forms for the human spirit to live in and use.

Beyond that, it might be added that what I am calling critique, in its double emphasis on rhetoric as the study of tropes, on the one hand, in a work of whatever genre, and, on the other hand, on the way any work of literature, of whatever genre, tells a story with beginning, middle, end, and underlying *logos* or *Grund* and at the same time interrupts or deconstructs that story—this double emphasis tends to break down generic distinctions and to recognize, for example, the fundamental role of tropes in novels, the way any lyric poem tells a story and can be interpreted as a narrative, or the way a work of philosophy may be read in terms of its tropological patterns or in terms of the story it tells. Much important criticism today goes against the grain of traditional generic distinctions, while at the same time perpetuating them in new ways in relation to one or another of my four grounds, just as many important works of recent primary literature do not fit easily into any one generic pigeon-hole.

NOTES

1. *The Letters of Matthew Arnold to Arthur Hugh Clough*, ed. H. F. Lowry (London and New York: Oxford University Press, 1932), p. 130.

2. Friedrich Nietzsche, *Daybreak: Thoughts on the Prejudices of Morality*, trans. R. J. Hollingdale (Cambridge: Cambridge University Press, 1982), p. 5, trans. slightly altered; German: Friedrich Nietzsche, *Morgenröte*, "Vorrede," *Werke in Drei Bänden*, ed. Karl Schlecta, I (Munich: Carl Hanser Verlag, 1966), 1016. Further citations will be from these editions.

3. George Eliot, *Daniel Deronda*, I, *Works*, Cabinet Edition (Edinburgh and London: William Blackwood and Sons, n. d.), Ch. 6, p. 90. Further references will be to this volume of this edition.

4. In *Première Livraison* (1976), my trans.

5. Wallace Stevens, *The Collected Poems* (New York: Alfred A. Knopf, 1954), p. 10.

6. Louis Althusser, *For Marx*, trans. Ben Brewster (New York: Vintage Books, 1970), pp. 233–34.

7. Joseph Conrad. *The Secret Agent* (Garden City, N.Y.: Doubleday, Page, 1925), p. xiii.

8. Cleanth Brooks, "The Primacy of the Author," *The Missouri Review*, 6 (1982), 162.

9. Matthew Arnold, "The Function of Criticism at the Present Time," *Lectures and Essays in Criticism, The Complete Prose Works*, ed. R. H. Super, III (Ann Arbor: The University of Michigan Press, 1962), 270.

10. See Walter Jackson Bate, "The Crisis in English Studies," *Harvard Magazine*, 85, No. 1, (1982), 46–53, esp. pp. 46–47. For a vigorous reply to Bate's essay see Paul de Man, "The Return to Philology," *The Times Literary Supplement*, No. 4,158 (Friday, December 10, 1982), 1355–56.

11 Immanuel Kant, paragraph 59, "Of Beauty as the Symbol of Morality," *Critique of Judgment*, trans. J. H. Bernard (New York: Hafner Publishing Company, 1951), p. 196; German: *Kritik der Urteilskraft, Werkausgabe*, ed. Wilhelm Weischedel, X (Frankfurt am Main: Suhrkamp Verlag, 1979), 294.

12 René Wellek, "Destroying Literary Studies," *The New Criterion* (December 1983), p. 2.

13. Matthew Arnold, "The Function of Criticism at the Present Time," p. 282.

14. *Ibid.*, p. 268.

15. Matthew Arnold, "The Study of Poetry," *English Literature and Irish Politics, The Complete Prose Works*, ed. R. H. Super, IX (Ann Arbor: The University of Michigan Press, 1973), 161.

16. *Letters to Clough*, p. 97.

17. Matthew Arnold, *Poems*, ed. Kenneth Allott (London: Longmans, Green and Co. Ltd., 1965), p. 591.

18. See Kant, *Critique of Judgment*, eds. cit.: Eng., pp. 197–98; Ger., pp. 295–297.

19. G. W. F. von Hegel, *Aesthetics: Lectures on Fine Art*, trans. T. M. Knox, I (New

York: Oxford University Press, 1975), 378; *Vorlesungen über die Ästhetik*, I (Frankfurt am Main: Surhkamp, 1970), 486.

20. Wallace Stevens, *Opus Posthumous* (New York: Alfred A. Knopf, 1957), p. 163.

21. "The Function of Matthew Arnold at the Present Time," *Critical Inquiry*, 9 (1983), 451–516. Goodheart's essay, "Arnold at the Present Time," is on pp. 451–68.

22. See Friedrich Nietzsche, "European Nihilism," *The Will to Power*, trans. Walter Kaufmann and R. J. Hollingdale (New York: Vintage Books, 1968), pp. 5–82. These notes are dispersed in chronological order with the other notes traditionally making up *Der Wille zur Macht* in Nietzsche, "Aus dem Nachlass der Achtzigerjahre," *Werke in Drei Bänden*, III, 415–925. See also Martin Heidegger, "Nihilism," *Nietzsche*, trans. Frank A. Capuzzi, IV (San Francisco: Harper & Row, Publishers, 1982); German: *Nietzsche*, II (Pfullingen: Verlag Günther Neske, 1961), 31–256; 335–98.

23. *Letters to Clough*, p. 135.

24. *The Will to Power*, p. 3.

25. Heidegger, "Nihilism," *Nietzsche*, IV, 21; German: *Nietzsche*, II, 53.

26. Trans. Catherine Porter and Edward P. Morris, *Diacritics*, 13 (1983), 3–20.

27. Kant, *Critique of Judgment*, Eng., p. 32; Ger., p. 106.

28. Hegel, *Ästhetik*, I, 151, my trans.

29. In "Economy," in *Penelope's Web: On the External Relations of Narrative,* forthcoming.

30. A book on nineteenth and twentieth-century poetry with that title is forthcoming from Princeton University Press.

31. Immanuel Kant, *Critique of Pure Reason*, trans. Norman Kemp Smith (New York: St. Martin's Press, 1965), pp. 313–14; German: *Kritik der reinen Vernunft*, A (1781), p. 319; B (1787), pp. 375–76, *Werkausgabe*, ed. cit., III, 325–26. For a discussion of the image of the mole in Kant, Hegel, and Nietzsche see David Farrell Krell, *"Der Maulwurf: Die philosophische Wühlarbeit bei Kant, Hegel und Nietzsche/The Mole: Philosophic Burrowings in Kant, Hegel, and Nietzsche," Boundary 2*, 9 and 10 (Spring/Fall, 1981), 155–79.

"Timely Utterance" Once More

Geoffrey H. Hartman
Yale University

et sonitus me sacer intus agit
—Milton

"It would be not only interesting but also useful to know what the 'timely utterance' was," Lionel Trilling wrote in 1941 concerning Wordsworth's Intimation Ode. He eventually does "hazard a guess."[1] Time has not diminished our fascination with the phrase: the guessing continues, while Trilling's interpretation has become part of the poem's aura and has entered the consciousness of many readers. Just as we find a ring of cosmic junk around planets, so it is with interpretive solutions stabilized by the gravitational field of a well-known poem. Moreover, Trilling's critical style is itself of interest. To "hazard a guess" indicates a modest attitude (he does not speak as a specialist, rather as an educated, reflective reader) but also, perhaps, a subdued sense of venture. For Wordsworth's diction is a riddle as well as a puzzle, and we answer it at the risk of appearing foolish, of exposing our superficial views on language and life.[2]

"Timely utterance," of course, is not the only crux in Wordsworth's Ode, nor the only mystery-phrase singled out by readers. There is the bombast (Coleridge's term) of stanza 8, addressed to the Child as Prophet and Philosopher; there is the delicate vatic vagueness of "fields of sleep"; there is, at the end, "thoughts that do often lie too deep for tears."

These cruxes—and there are others—all share a problem of reference: we do not know what the "timely utterance" was; "fields of sleep" is a periphrasis that should yield a proper name, perhaps of a place as mythic as the Elysian fields ("fields of light," cf. *Aeneid* 6.640); the sublime words that describe the infant seem really to describe some other, more fitting, subject; and who knows what the deep thoughts are about.

Let me clarify, in a preliminary way, this problem of reference. Those deep thoughts: their occasion is clear (the simplest thing, the meanest flower), and their emotional impact also is clear. But where precisely do

37

they lie, where is "too deep for tears"? Is it, to quote a moving sonnet in which Wordsworth mourns the loss of his daughter Catherine, that "spot which no vicissitude can find"?[3] Or is the obverse suggested, that they are *not* thoughts of loss, mortality, or the grave, but arise from a still deeper level, from under or beyond the grave? Or is Wordsworth adjuring himself not to cry, not to give in to a pathos permitted even to Aeneas ("Sunt lacrymae rerum . . . ," *Aeneid* 1.468), as he forbids mourning despite nature's valedictory intimations:

> And O, ye Fountains, Meadows, Hills, and Groves,
> Forebode not any severing of our loves!

I multiply questions because I suspect that a simple solution, or stabilizing specificity, cannot be found. Yet the nonspecific quality of such verses does not harm them. It acts somewhat like formal perspective, in which an abstract reference-point allows the imaginative construction of naturalistic space. For, with the partial exception of stanza 8 on the sublime Child, we remain very much in a familiar world. Wordsworth extends, it is true, the boundary of natural events, yet never crosses it decisively into another region. Plato's doctrine of anamnesis or pre-existence is made to support ordinary feelings, to give them a memorable frame, not to justify fantastic speculation. The Ode's closing sentiment even limits the kind of thoughtful brooding (the "philosophic mind") that is its very concern: there is neither analytic nor visionary excess.

The more we press toward precision of reference, the more a Wordsworthian thought-limit appears. One is tempted to ask: are the thoughts secretly apocalyptic? Or so sentimental that they border on a crazy sort of concreteness, as mind passes from the "meanest" sign to the sublimest natural laws via an elided corpse? (For one could imagine the poet thinking: This flower at my feet may be nourished by the putrefaction of the dead, who are remembered unto life in this way.)[4]

Matthew Arnold's eulogy of the poet is to the point.

> The cloud of mortal destiny,
> Others will front it fearlessly—
> But who, like him, will put it by?

Wordsworth's poetry has the strength to absorb thoughts that potentially unbalance the mind. "Dim sadness—and blind thoughts," he calls them in "Resolution and Independence," "I knew not, nor could name." The "burthen of the mystery" is acknowledged—and lightened. Alas, the "burthen of the mystery" is another of those strange phrases, strong yet vague. I turn now to what occasioned these preliminary reflections: "timely utterance."

i

The context is not as much help as it might be.

> To me alone there came a thought of grief:
> A timely utterance gave that thought relief. . . .

(22-23)

The thought is almost as unspecific as what gives it relief. Perhaps it does not have to be specific, since the stanza's first verses suggest that what mattered was the contrast of thought and season. To me alone, among all beings, there came this untoward thought, like an untimely echo. Hence, after it is dispelled, Wordsworth vows: "No more shall grief of mine the season wrong." Only "seasonable sweets" (Keats) from now on. One possibility for interpretation, therefore, is that he was interested in expressing a relation, or a broken and then restored relation, rather than the precise detail of a single experience. The broken relation between his heart and the "heart of May" is always to be repaired. There may even be a repetition of that relational structure in the very next lines:

> The cataracts blow their trumpets from the steep;
> No more shall grief of mine the season wrong;
> I hear the Echoes through the mountains throng,
> The Winds come to me from the fields of sleep. . . .

(25-28)

Two types of utterance are presented here in asyndetic sequence: one comes from nature (the cataracts) and seems to heighten, like a punctuation from above, the timely utterance (indeed, there is a possibility that it was the timely utterance); and one comes from within the poet ("No more shall grief . . ."), as if to answer or echo nature (relation having been restored) and so to confirm that the disturbing fancy has passed. This echo-structure is made literal by "I hear the Echoes through the mountains throng." Together with "The Winds come to me from the fields of sleep," it suggests an extension of sensibility, some inner horizon opening up, as the poet hears into the distance. What is heard is not just waterfall or winds (whatever their message), but the principle of echo itself. Hence the echoes "throng"; they are suddenly everywhere; as thick as sheep at folding time. The stanza as a whole evokes a *correspond-*

ence of breezes, sounds, feelings, one that has absorbed discordant elements (cf. 1850 *Prelude* 1.85, 96 ff., 340–50). Its culmination is the hallooing of "Shout round me, let me hear they shouts, thou happy Shepherd boy!" (Ode, 35).

In this verse, which concludes the stanza, the movement of empathy is so strong that we almost feel its apostrophe as a self-address, representing the poet as that "Child of Joy" (34). His flock, as in Shelley's "Adonais," is composed of "quick Dreams, / The passion-winged Ministers of thought." And though we are moving toward the opposite of a pastoral elegy, the double or echo aspect of this provisional climax ("Shout . . . shout") may be modifying as well as intensifying. Is not the cry optative rather than indicative in mood, an utterance that *projects* an ideal utterance, so that it is hard to tell the spontaneous from the anticipated joy? The "let me hear" repeats as a variant "Shout round me" and points it inward: it seems to appeal for a sound so strong that the poet cannot but hear. Yet "I hear, I hear, with joy I hear" is delayed to the next stanza, and then immediately counterpointed: "—But there's a Tree, of many, one . . . ." An inward and meeting echo, a reciprocal response, is not assured even now.

ii

Broken column, broken tower, broken . . . response. The theme of lost Hellenic grace or harmony is not relevant except as it is also more than Hellenic and recalls the "echo" formula of a poetry at once pastoral and elegiac:

> All as the sheepe, such was the shepeheards looke,

Spenser writes in "January," the first eclogue of the *Shepheardes Calender*. And

> Thou barrein ground, whome winters wrath hath wasted,
> Art made a myrrhour, to behold my plight. . . .

This correspondence of season with mood, or of nature with human feelings, is the simplest form of the echo-principle in pastoral verse. Echo is something more than a figure of speech:

> Now lay those sorrowfull complaints aside,
> And hauing all your heads with girland crownd,
> Helpe me mine owne loues prayses to resound,
> Ne let the same of any be enuide:

So Orpheus did for his owne bride,
So I vnto my selfe alone will sing,
The woods shall to me answer and my Eccho ring.

Spenser gives himself away in an *Epithalamion* of his own making: his poetry participates in the marriage, it weds the world, the word, to his desire, or more exactly to the *timing* which builds his rhyme, and which can call for silence ("And cease till then our tymely joyes to sing, / The woods no more vs answer, nor our eccho ring") as well as for reponsive sound. In this sense, poetry is itself the "timely utterance"—not Spenser's *Epithalamion* as such, nor "Resolution and Independence" (or a part of it, as Trilling and Barzun suggest[5]), or any other identifiable set of verses.

Yet what is meant by *poetry* cannot be formalized, as I have seemed to suggest, in terms of generic features. I might like to claim that "timely utterance" opens every poetic form to the incursion of pastoral;[6] and Wordsworth himself gives some purchase on such a view:

—The Poets, in their elegies and songs
Lamenting the departed, call the groves,
They call upon the hills and streams to mourn,
And senseless rocks; nor idly; for they speak,
In these their invocations, with a voice
Obedient to the strong creative power
Of human passion.
(*The Excursion* 1.475-81)

Yet what matters is neither the pastoral setting nor the overt, figurative expression of sympathy ("Sympathies there are," Wordsworth continues, "More tranquil, yet perhaps of kindred birth, / That steal upon the meditative mind, and grow with thought." What matters is the sense of a *bond* between and nature, of a *responsiveness* that overcomes the difference of human speech and creaturely muteness, or articulate and inarticulate utterance.

. . . Far and wide the clouds were touched,
And in their silent faces could be read
Unutterable love.
. . . in the mountains did he *feel* his faith.
All things, responsive to the writing, there
Breathed immortality, revolving life,
And greatness still revolving; infinite. . . .
(*The Excursion* 1.203-05; 206–29)

The capacity for "timely utterance" in this timeless, mute, or unutterable situation maintains the bond, and justifies the poetry. "The strong creative power / Of human passion" is equivalent to poetry in this respect. "Passion" often has, for Wordsworth, the sense of passionate speech that identifies with "mute, insensate things." "My heart leaps up"—an "extempore" lyric whose final lines come to serve as an epigraph to the Intimations Ode, and which has been nominated by some scholars as the "timely utterance"—is about this bond. The lyric is remarkable as an utterance, as a speech act that falls somewhere between vow and passionate wish:

> My heart leaps up when I behold
>   A rainbow in the sky:
> So was it when my life began;
> So is it now I am a man;
> So be it when I shall grow old,
>   Or let me die!

That "Or let me die!" is a true "fit of passion," one of those Wordsworthian moments where feeling seems to overflow and be in excess of its occasion. It is, one might say, *untimely*.

Yet we intuit its emotional truth, and it becomes timely again once we recall another utterance, that of the creator when he makes the rainbow a sign of *His* bond:

> I have set My bow in the cloud, and it shall be a token of a covenant between Me and the earth. And it shall come to pass, when I bring clouds over the earth, and the bow is seen in the cloud, that I will remember My covenant, which is between Me and you and every living creature of all flesh; and the waters shall no more become a flood to destroy all flesh.
>
> (Genesis 9:13-16)

If Wordsworth's vow recalls that primal vow, it is a response that says: This is *my* bond, *my* way of binding each day to each and continuing in time. Cut the link of nature to human feelings and the bond is broken. Once dead to nature, I might as well die. Poetry is a marriage-covenant with nature, a "spousal verse" even more demanding of "dew" response than Spenser's *Epithalamion*.

iii

To utter things in a timely way is the ideal situation, of course; and Wordsworth usually represents the ideal in its wishful or miscarried form. So the hyperbolic "Or let me die!" is followed by a second hyperbole that expresses more patently a disturbed sense of temporal continuity. "The Child is father of the Man" reverses the way we think about fathers and children; yet it quickly naturalizes itself as a sort of proverb. We assimilate its unexpectedness, as with "Or let me die!"; and since the words themselves are simple enough (however complex the thought), we do not have to, indeed we cannot, keep unfolding them. The very opening of *The Prelude*, similarly, is a "passion" that makes us aware, as it generates itself, of an ideal of harmony or correspondence that proves fallible. As an utterance it comes closer to "tempest" than "tempus." The "correspondent breeze" turns into "A tempest, a redundant energy / Vexing its own creation" (*Prelude* 1.37-8). There is a disproportion or discord between the "gentle breeze" of the poem's first verse and this tempestuous, self-forcing power. The *untimely* is never far away (cf. 1.94–105).

But our own solution may have been untimely, that is, premature. Even should "timely utterance" be an inspired periphrasis for "poetry," and exclude the promoting of a particular poem or passage, we continue to think of poetry as a *manifold* of utterances that is *one* only if the idea of vocation is adduced: if poetry is also "poesy." Poetic utterances are not only characterized by being timely (either vis-a-vis others or oneself); they are unified by being timely. That should be their essential quality, or the predicate pointing to a predicament. A reader alerted by the Vergilian motto of the Ode ("paulo majora canamus") would recognize the question of poetic growth and maturation: of the *career* of the poet. Is there a future for Wordsworth as poet, or for poetry itself? Has the time for poetry, as "timely utterance," passed?

Moreover, the Ode's vacillating strain, its blend of humble and prophetic tones, recalls Milton's stylized hesitation in *Lycidas:* poetry is conceived by Milton as a precarious venture that may be prematurely launched, untimely tried by "forc'd fingers rude." It is Milton who linked poetry's timeliness explicitly to a vocation that was imperious, prophetic, hazardous. If not now, when?

The "Now" that begins stanza 3 of Wordsworth's Ode may therefore be more than a pivoting or idling word. Its place in time, as well as its syntactical position, is not easily fixed. It is like the anchor of hope. Its prepositional and propositional components fuse into an absolute construction. The word stands outside the events it qualifies: like a symbol in mathematics it could refer to every phrase that follows. The sequence of tenses in stanza 3 shifts, moreover, from present to past to present, as everything tends toward that "Now." Coming to it, after two reflective and chiefly elegiac stanzas, it is as if a person were to draw a deep breath, then to exhale it, signaling a new start. The present, or this very utterance, cancels what has been. "Now" is, in its virtuality, the temporal word *par excellence*.

To make so ordinary a word extraordinary may be self-defeating in terms of the diction of poetry. Yet poetic language, it could be argued, is ordinary language in its always residual or always future promise. What a difference between this "now" and its two prefigurative echoes in lines 6 and 9 of the first stanza! That common word may also remarkably index "A Presence which is not to be put by" (Ode, 120). It intimates the possibility—not the fact—of a decisive turning point, something about to be, or about to be . . . uttered. Within the flow of language it is an open-vowelled *nunc stans*, a fleeting epiphanic sound. And the transition from "thought of grief" to "relief," which it introduces, and then, in the next stanza, to "blessing," comes through drinking in a surround of sounds: the utterance itself, the cataracts, echoes, winds, and the first clear vocative of the poem, "Shout round me. . . ." It is as if Wordsworth had been released into voice as well as blessing, into a voice that is a blessing.

> Ye blessed Creatures, I have heard the call
>   Ye to each other make. . . .   (36–7)

It is a moment similar to the removal of the curse from the Ancient Mariner in Coleridge's poem. There is the same feeling of relief, the creatures (*res creatae*) are acknowledged and blessed. Coleridge, however, separates blessing and utterance, as if timely utterance were not, or not yet, possible.

> O happy living things! no tongue
> Their beauty might declare:
> A spring of love gushed from my heart,
> And I blessed them unaware.

Yet in Wordsworth too a hesitation of the tongue is felt, or some impediment to the coincidence of voice and blessing. It emerges when we ask whether the action of stanza 4 takes place in real or wishful time. "Ye blessed Creatures, I have heard the call / Ye to each other make; I see / The heavens laugh with you . . ." need not be a descriptive statement about what is happening then and there. It could be an anticipatory and envisioning response to "Shout round me, let me hear thy shouts. . . ."

A wish-fulfillment, then, a proleptic extension of the poet's own vocative, his pausal "Now." The "I have heard" may refer to the past ("There was a time") or it may come so close to the moment of speaking that it is a confirmatory "Roger." Wordsworth does not actually say that *he* is laughing with the creatures; but as he looks round once more, repeating the "turning" described in the opening stanzas, he sees and hears the things he said he could no more.

The reader, of course, no less wishful than the poet, would like to assume that the thought of grief has passed and that the birds and beasts did in fact sing and bound, and that only the discordant heart of the poet had to be tuned. But the "Now" remains slightly apart, hyper-referential, or just plain *hyper*. It is a wishing-word. The music of Wordsworth's Ode is so elaborate that it untunes the timely-happy connection between heaven and nature, as between heart and nature, a connection the poet is always re-establishing. His poem is the most complex Music Ode in English, conveying and absorbing the difference between voice and blessing, words and wishes, being and being-in-time.

iv

All things, responsive to the writing
—Wordsworth

I have offered a mildly deconstructive reading: one that discloses in words "a 'spirit' peculiar to their nature as words" (Kenneth Burke). Such a reading refuses to substitute ideas for words, especially since in the empiricist tradition after Locke ideas are taken to be a faint replica of images, which are themselves directly referable to sense-experience. One way of bringing out the spirit peculiar to words, and so, paradoxically, making them material—emphasizing the letter in the spirit—is to evoke their intertextual echoes. Ideas may be simple, but words always are complex. Yet the construction of an intertextual field is disconcerting as well as enriching because intertextual concordance produces a reality-discord, an overlay or distancing of the referential function of speech, of the word-thing, word-experience relation. Even though the *fact* of correspondence between language and experience is not in question (there is a complex answerability of the one to the other), the *theory* of correspondence remains a problem. I want to conclude my remarks by suggesting that intertextual awareness follows from the character of words, and that it does not divorce us from dearly-beloved experience, or Wordsworth's "the world, which is the world of all of us."

"There was a time" (line 1) immediately introduces the motif of time in a colloquial and inconspicuous way. Yet as the poem proceeds, the expression begins to border on myth. It becomes reminiscent of the *illo tempore*, the "in those days," of mythical thought. Wordsworth locates that mythical epoch at the barely scrutable edge of everyone's memory of childhood. During this numinous time, a "celestial light" invests natural objects, although later we learn also about darker moments, "Blank misgivings of a Creature/Moving about in worlds not realized" (Ode, 144–45). The darkness and the light are intervolved, as in a Grasmere storm. But the metaphor of light predominates, and the poet's loss is described in terms of it.

The third stanza deepens as well as qualifies that sense of loss. The "to me alone" of line 22 points to an event closer to augury than subjective feeling; it singles the poet out. He haruspicates himself. His inability to respond fully to nature, what does it mean? Was the vanished natural light perhaps an inner and now failing light, not *given* from outside but rather *bestowed* from within by imagination?

That gleam, moreover, whatever its source, seems preternatural. It suggests that the bond between nature and imagination is precarious from the outset, with imagination seeking to wed itself to nature, in order to become poetry rather than prophesy. That is certainly how it seemed to Blake when he read the Ode. He was deeply moved by it, but denounced the "natural man" in Wordsworth always rising up, as he put it, against the imaginative man.

Those acquainted with Wordsworth know that a simple turn of thought can trigger a radical turning about of his mind, and release a near-apocalyptic sense of isolation. Blake is right in the sense that even when the final mood-swing or *"envoi"* of the Ode ends ominously,

And O, ye Fountains, Meadows, Hills, and Groves,
Forebode not any severing of our loves!   (187–88),

Wordsworth pretends that the portent comes from nature rather than from himself. He will not acknowledge that the bond with nature— more psychic than epistemic—is broken. "I could wish my days to be / Bound each to each by natural piety."

"I *could* wish"? How strangely tentative that sounds! The wish hesitates, I suspect, because its very success, its potential fulfillment, might go against nature by confirming the omnipotence of wishful thought. A similar scruple may hover over stanza 3 and the "timely utterance" that allows the Ode to turn upward instead of spiraling downward or breaking off. The very discretion of the phrase protects it from being construed as a wish, or any sort of direct—imperative—speech-act.

"Timely utterance," then, does not pose only a problem of reference. The indirect phrasing involves signifier as well as signified: the poet's attitude toward a higher mode of speech, whether wishful or prophetic. Wordsworth's expression is guarded: he does not actually wish; rather, he "could wish" that the bond with nature should continue, and that the mutability suggested by "There was a time" should not bode an end to time itself, a discontinuity between *illo tempore* and his present or future state. The "timely utterance" meets that anxiety about time; and as "utterance" it suggests that someone else has made a wish for the poet and so relieved him of the responsibility. It is as if a thought had been taken out of his heart and uttered. The structure is similar to that of the famous dedication scene in *The Prelude*, which makes him aware of his calling as poet. "I made no vows, but vows/Were then made for me; bond unknown to me / Was given . . ." (5.534–6).[7] In the Ode too we do not know who utters what. Even if the utterance took place within the poet, it was not his but some other voice. A "discours de l'Autre" (Jacques Lacan) takes away the burden of wishful or visionary speech. There exists, in fact, one such Discourse of the Other that is *timely* and *bonding* and even joins the theme of speaking to that of giving light:

> And God said, Let there be light: and there was light. And God saw the light, that it was good: and God divided the light from the darkness. And God called the light Day, and the darkness he called Night. And there was evening and there was morning, one day.

These are "timely" words indeed: they create time, they establish it beyond all misgiving. What is founded, moreover, bonds a responsive nature (or what is to be nature) to an utterance, and God to his own work, for he acknowledges by direct acts of naming and blessing what has been called into being.

I am tempted, at last, to make an assertion and identify the "timely utterance." "Let there be light: and there was light" utters itself in the poet's mind as a proof-text, that is, not only as a deeply subjective wish for the return of the light whose loss was lamented in the first two stanzas, but also as that wish in the form of God's first words, His "Let there be."

I have taken one phrase as my starting point, and made many angels dance on it. These revels would be in vain if Wordsworth's Ode were not involved in the question of voice as well as light: in what connection there still might be between poetry and prophecy. "A Voice to Light gave Being," Wordsworth writes in a later Great Ode, alluding to fiat or logos. Yet there is a fear lest poetic voice, in its very power, may call on darkness, and become decreative rather than creative and so a "counter-spirit" or parody of the "divine I AM." Then the prophetic or poetic voice would serve, however involuntarily, the cause of cursing, not of blessing, and wish for an end, a dissolution of word and world. The utterance that surprised Wordsworth is, from one perspective, an arche-typal instance of wish-fulfillment or omnipotence of thoughts. Yet from another perspective it is an exemplary instance of poetry as a creative speech-act that leads to natural piety rather than to apocalyptic solipsism or transcendence.

Wordsworth's most felicitous poetry merges wishing, responding, and blessing: merges, in fact, a first timely utterance, the fiat, and a second timely utterance, the convenant. If, in stanza 3 of his Ode, the sounding cataracts and the "timely utterance" are echo-aspects of each other, it is because what was founded must be founded a second time, on the flood; just as the light that was has to be lit again, now. The Covenant is a second creation confirming the first; while the rainbow as a timely sign recalls an utterance that could make the poet's heart leap up. The Intimations Ode is the third of this series. It is the poet's response, his covenant-sign, his own "timely utterance," incorporating mutely—as silent light—the divine *davar*, that is, the text on which my own intertextual leaping comes to rest.

NOTES

1. "The Immortality Ode," reprinted in *The Liberal Imagination* (New York: Viking, 1950).

2. That we are reluctant to develop the resonances of a critic's prose, even a critic as deliberate as Trilling, does not mean they are not felt. Ironically, Trilling's answer, when it does come (in the fourth section of his essay) is one that leads to a displacement from one phrase or word-complex to another, and so enlightens without disburdening the poem. It does not give a final relief to thought.

3. "Surprised by joy—impatient as the Wind" (1815).

4. Compare, in the second stanza of "A slumber did my spirit seal," the verse: "Wheeled round in earth's diurnal course." An image of *gravitational* elides or displaces that of the *grave*; and the tacit verbal pun is reenforced by the fact that "di*urn*al" is followed by "course," a word that sounds like the archaic-poetic pronunciation of "corpse." (I owe this insight to Jay Farness.) Could one show, in Wordsworth, a convergence of nature's eliding (subliming) of the corpse, and poetry's eliding (sublim-ing) of the referent?

5. See Trilling, *The Liberal Imagination*, p. 139.

6. I agree with Paul de Man ("The Dead-End of Formalist Criticism," *Blindness and*

Insight, 2d ed., 1983) in his understanding of pastoral as much more than convention or genre. "There is no doubt that the pastoral theme is, in fact, the only poetic theme, that it is poetry itself." De Man's insight comes by way of a critique of Empson and the doctrine of "reconciliation," a critique that limits the rigorous and principled criticism initiated by Richards.

7. The placement of "unknown" causes an ambiguity. It could refer to the bond or to its character vis-a-vis the receiver. "An unknown bond was given—to me, who was unaware (unknowing) of it at the time." The "unknown" points to what is knowable yet difficult to locate as conscious knowledge at a single spot in time. Its place in the verse-line is self-displacing.

Portrait: de Man

Juliet Flower MacCannell
University of California, Irvine

> Repetition first appears in a form that is not clear, that is not self-evident, like a reproduction, or a making present, *in act.* . . . The resistance of the subject [the "resistance" of the "subject"] . . . becomes at the next moment repetition in act. . . .
>
> —Jacques Lacan

> "A man who dies at the age of thirty-five," said Moritz Heimann once, "is at every point in his life a man who dies at the age of thirty-five." Nothing is more dubious than this sentence—but for the sole reason that the tense is wrong. A man—so says the truth that was meant here—who dies at thirty-five will appear to *remembrance* at every point in his life as a man who dies at the age of thirty-five. In other words, the statement that makes no sense for real life becomes indisputable for remembered life.
>
> —Walter Benjamin

To judge by the first critical attempts to assess the overall importance, impact and, to put it crudely, but in terms appropriate to his thought, the "meaning" and "significance" of his writing, Paul de Man's work has been difficult to take. Though dozens have been guided by his great teaching in their own writing and research, those who have been among the first to offer judgments on the "totality" of his *oeuvre* have tended to be negative, to display remarkable resistances to his insights, and to desire—perhaps to advance their own careers—a kind of Oedipal struggle with the great "authority" figure. "Readings" of Paul de Man (and I think of the term not only literarily but barometrically in these cases) have found their methodological niche at every level of specificity: they range from Stanley Corngold's dispute over the use of "error" for "mistake" (a word or a concept? a signifier or a whole philosophy? what is at stake in mistake?)[1] to questions of his "consistency" or "inconsistency" throughout his career (as in Suzanne Gearhart's pinning him down for never being anything but self-reflexive, a privileger of literature and metaphor as she responds to Rodolphe Gasché's reading of his career as undergoing a deconstructive "reversal"),[2] to the questioning of his

51

attitude toward not only rhetoric but also politics and religion in Frank Lentricchia's recent book—a text which really amounts to a defense of the autochtony of an "American" criticism.[3]   Few have looked for the comprehensive judgment they seek in the sheer *range*—a remarkable range—[4] of his writing on literature, and have instead tried to delimit his scope by means of the devices of terminological (verbal) consistency and/or the classical rhetorical questioning of the ethos of the rhetorician (what is his "stance," "position" or "attitude"?). Yet this seems to be a symptom rather of resistance than of reading, a comprehensiveness without comprehension. "Reading" Paul de Man, as it turns out, will always cause the reader to have to confront the very concepts of *terminological consistency* and *position* as crucial elements in his construction and deconstruction of literary form. Small wonder, then, that his writing occasions resistance. Such resistance comes as no surprise, and is perhaps even—once one reads the work in this light—necessary for the self-preservation and perpetuation of criticism.

i. How to Read Paul de Man

Paul de Man's work cannot be *read* using the basic techniques pioneered by phenomenology (significant excerpting, the dialectical movement of a *cogito*, etc.). It is true that for a time his own work appeared to be identified with the phenomenological movement in literary studies. In the wake of what he once called "L'Impasse de la critique formaliste,"[5] he seemed to espouse phenomenological methods and techniques which offered a provisional counter to the techniques developed by formalist critics. The particular formalism of the New Criticism, whose semiotic forebears were Peirce, Saussure, and the Russian Formalists, via Jakobson and Wellek, had, through its resistance to questions of consciousness outside of form, and in its controversial stance on the status of history,[6] apparently exhausted the play of formal properties conceivable within a text. Close reading had become a sterile technique in the absence of concerns for context and consciousness; more alarmingly, in de Man's critique, it had misread its own context, its own epistemological basis in metaphor. Phenomenology, on the other hand, seemed to hold out the hope of describing what de Man once called the fluidity and invisibility of consciousness, independent of material, earth-bound and ultimately objectified or reified determinations, i.e., a consciousness defined entirely linguistically, by means of a language not rooted in a nostalgia for the natural object.[7]

Whereas the New Criticism, following Coleridgian organicism, founded its conception of metaphor in the prestige of the natural in its objective and spatial form, phenomenology, in its existential, temporal variant, looked not toward but away from the natural, not toward origins (the totality of what already is), but toward the source, as "beginning." To follow phenomenology was to recoup the central sacrifice of formalism: consciousness, the intentional as opposed to the natural object.[8]

A narrative of Paul de Man's career would then see this phenomenological stance ceding to the deconstructive critique made of it by Jacques Derrida in the mid 1960s; a change of heart, and adherence to a new fad or movement of thought, a painful crisis as he moved from one allegiance to another, perhaps without ever really getting "with it." Such, indeed is Suzanne Gearhart's interpretation of the career of Paul de Man.

Such a story would be and is, a false one.

Paul de Man's "deconstructive" technique is operative already in the earliest essays, the technique, as Gasché has outlined it, of reversal followed by a reinscription within tradition. But one cannot only or always read it only in a single essay. If there is any basis to Gearhart's charge that Paul de Man's is limited to being a writing of self-reflexivity, it can only be in the most literal of senses: his writing is self-referential in that each of his texts reads an earlier, prior text of his own. In other words, the theoretical "narcissism" about which his critics complain is not "theoretical"—it is real, and it is his particular practice, but it does not define the limits of his theoretical position. (I, for one, cannot blame him for preferring to read himself as much as others; fellow critics like Sartre and Barthes have done much the same thing. I think his own writing, as a movement of consciousness, interested him most.)

To illustrate why a sequential narrative as well as a phenomenological reading of his texts is a distortion in the interests of creating readable figures, I take now the example of the way in which he worried and worked both phenomenology and the neo-romanticism of Formalism so that each displaces the other, and so that he becomes a proponent of neither.

In the early essay on the impasse of formalism, it is a question of one thing: the mistaking of origin for beginning (Fr.: "*source*"). De Man raises the issue of the ontological status of the text in formalist criticism as it then existed specifically as a question of the *constitution* of the text, as distinct from its genetic origins, or its organic basis—a question he is able to ask at least partly because of the advent of phenomenology. Even before this essay he had published a reading of Montaigne as having raised, to Sartre's dismay perhaps, the question of the transcendental subject and the constitutive agency of the transcendental self in the literary text.[9] Phenomenology was perhaps the first wedge to drive between the unconscious assumption, in formalism, of an organic, quasi-natural "Origin of the Work of Art." Instead of having an "origin"—a theologic concept—literary forming would have an entirely temporal definition, linguistic in its essence. As Husserl once wrote, the whole of human forming is rooted in language as a series of logical propositions.[10] One could follow the critique of formalism with smugness: after all, temporality dissolves its "pseudo-objective" bases, reveals not a natural, but an unnatural history, i.e., a genealogy, rather than a genesis.

But Paul de Man was neither smug nor finished, neither happily becoming an existential phenomenologist, nor severing ties with formalism. For, although, in the years that followed, de Man seemed to adopt a Heideggerian vocabulary and continued to pursue, in "New Criticism and Nouvelle Critique" (and even in the "Rhetoric of Temporality," 1969[11]) the temporality that the new criticisms had left out of their theory of literary form we can be very clear on one point: that de Man's interest in the pursuit had a *methodological* basis, not a *theoretical* one; he was neither an adherent of a philosophy (in the case of Heidegger or Husserl) nor a sectarian of a semi-religious movement of the spirit away from the dryness of form. Instead, here, as in later texts, his method is the tracking of major oversights, omissions, blindnesses, especially as these are of a technical nature, *rather than* of a speculative or ideational nature. In phenomenology's drive toward totalization one might assume that there would be a correct fit between theory and de Man's particular method; indeed many have both explicitly and tacitly assumed this to be the case up to a point in his career.[12] But this was never, strictly speaking, so. For every text in which there is a methodological benefit gained from adopting a phenomenological rather than a formalist technique, the technique's benefit is at least partially offset by recognition of the costs—to literature and history—involved if one were to adopt anything more than the techniques: that is, if one were to adopt the theory whole-cloth. Whether it is Montaigne outthinking Husserl ("Montaigne et la transcendence") or Hölderlin outperforming Heidegger ("Les Exégèses de Hölderlin par Martin Heidegger"), or Proust outwriting Sartre ("Sartre's Confessions") at no point does de Man even hint at a religiously faithful adoption of a theory.[13] And those literary critics that are the most philosophical or systematic in their approach are subject to even more severe criticism: a mere literary "theme" like that of Faust ("La critique thématique devant le thème de Faust") can outdo all the exertions of a Lovejoy in the search for coherence, breadth, and comprehensiveness in the "history of ideas."[14]

Things become really interesting when, in fact, this method—which is as close as de Man ever comes to "consistency" and even there this must be qualified—very quickly comes to be applied *to* phenomenology. And when de Man makes his critique of that orientation, justice is swift and harsh. In the 1960s still we have readings of Binswanger, Poulet, and especially Husserl in "Criticism and Crisis"—as well as the long and (often silent in print) dialogue with the phenomenological psychology criticism of Jean Starobinski on Rousseau[15]—each article or text concerned, again, methodologically, with examining critically the theoretical claims to totality. As Poulet attempts to redress the particular imbalance of formalism's failure to account for temporality and the question of the constitutive as opposed to the organic nature of the subject in the genesis of texts, his dialectical theory of the cogito poses even more difficult problems for this temporality and this subject. In the part of that essay on "The Work of Georges Poulet" in *Blindness and Insight* where he begins to speak of Poulet's method, de Man writes:

> In the more general essays on method that Poulet has recently been writing the notion of identification plays a very prominent part. Reading becomes an act of self-immolation in which the initiative passes entirely into the hands of the author. The critic, in Poulet's words, becomes the "prey" of the author's thought and allows himself to be entirely governed by it. . . . In criticism, the *moment de passage* changes from a temporal act into an intersubjective act or, to be more precise, into the total replacement of one subject by another. We are in fact dealing with a substitutive relationship, in which the place of a self is usurped by another self. Proclaiming himself a passage way (*lieu de passage*) for another person's thought, the critic evades the temporal problem of an anterior past. (*BI*, pp. 95–96)[16]

And although the essay ends on an entirely positive note, he has indeed undone all that seemed to have given Poulet his appeal: temporality and the presence of the subject:

> The quest for the source, which we have found constantly operative in his thought can never be separated from the concern for the self that is the carrier of this quest. Yet this self does not possess the power to engender its own

duration. This power belongs to what Poulet calls "the moment," but "the moment" designates, in fact, the point in time at which the self accepts language as its sole mode of existence. Language, however, is not a source; it is the articulation of the self and language that acquires a degree of prospective power. . . . If one confers upon language the power to originate, one runs the risk of hiding the self. This Poulet fears most of all, as when he asserts: "I want at all costs to save the subjectivity of literature." But if the subject is, in its turn, given the status of origin, one makes it coincide with Being in a self-consuming identity in which language is destroyed. Poulet rejects this alternative just as categorically as he rejects the other. . . . The concern for language can be felt in the tone of anguish that inhabits the whole of his work . . .; the subject that speaks in the criticism of Georges Poulet is a vulnerable and fragile subject whose voice can never become established as a presence. (*BI*, pp. 100–01)

Where is Georges Poulet after this?

The critique of the phenomenological pretention toward totality comes, finally, by drawing our attention to its major exclusions, exclusions we always knew were there, but which ultimately had to be not only stated as such by de Man, but stated in such a way as to bring into question, finally, the entire *technical* basis of a phenomenological reading of form as temporality and subjectivity. These exclusions are, of course, the socio-political domain and the techniques of psychoanalysis. In "Criticism and Crisis" Husserl goes down in a blaze of ignomiy as de Man shows how his "centering" and "presence" in the interest of totality can be read in the light of the *Anschluss* just as surely as Heidegger's claims for poetry's ability to carry the authentic voice of Being must be read in the light of the poet whom Heidegger claimed could best represent this claim, Hölderlin. And finally the entire rhetorical pyrotechnics that are in the hands of recent psychoanalysis are used by de Man to counter the claims of phenomenology (although not entirely; he seemed to support the strange misappropriation of one for the other in Kristeva). [17]

But to return to why Paul de Man's work itself cannot be read phenomenologically: To have demonstrated that he himself exploded phenomenological methods as viable for reading literature would not perforce mean that he himself could not be read using these techniques if it were only a matter of a difference in approach at a different level of analysis. But I do not think such is the case. For in point of fact phenomenological readings are—as I said in jest above, but now I am taking this more seriously; it does have a certain tradition [18]—

barometric: one reads at a certain "moment" (Poulet's, which is not really a time, but an act of acceptance), in a certain "state" (here and now, but not Austria or France), under certain conditions (in the presence of the object, but not, it seems of the *thing*), etc., but one cannot discover, in phenomenology and its correlates, a *method*, a *technology* that is adequate to the linguistic *form* in which all its intuitions must be given.

It is precisely de Man's *linguistic forms* that are overlooked in all the criticisms of his work that have, as of this date, appeared. And it due to this fact that I find I must classify all equally under the heading of the phenomenological as opposed, in the particular way I have started to oppose them here, to the formalist method of reading.

For formalism, as deeply as in error as it may have been philosophically (its "organicism," etc.) was, in the case of the New Criticism, and Reuben Brower at least, and remained, until the advent of the semiological method (which is, in fact, part of the same general enterprise), the only method that dealt with the technical aspects of linguistic and literary form. Whether it was Reuben Brower insisting, through the voice of the Coleridge's Reverend James Bowyer in *In Defense of Reading*[19] that we know how to parse the sentences if we want to be able to read them (" '. . . In the truly great poets he would say, there is a reason assignable not only for every word, but for the position of every word. . . .' "), or René Wellek maniacally tracking the history of a single term, or Ogden and Richards appropriating Malinowski's version of Peirce's version of the sign for the minimal literary unit of analysis, or whether again it is Riffaterre's demystification of one figure of speech by another in Baudelaire's poems, or Greimas's assumption that his square has no ontological status and therefore no rhetorical distortion to it,[20] etc., there is an intense formalist concern for the technical and the methodical. It is in this technology that Paul de Man found, in those essays he published between 1973 and 1983, the most intriguing subjects for his critical writing. And while his approach to formalism in these essays remains as severely, as rigorously critical as it had been for the first critiques of formalism and of phenomenology, it is hardly a question of reiteration of insights of the past. His texts on these texts have an open structure, in the sense that they close no doors—as if de Man had not yet discovered the particular adversary with which to read them deconstructively. (This enterprise was, of course, complicated by the fact that Derridean deconstruction began with an adversarial position on structural semiotics.) There is indeed some delight in being able himself to outformalize the formalists, as in his reading of Riffaterre, or when he overcomes Greimas's square by moving to a chiasmus in the essay on Pascal.[21] (Mathematics indeed looms here in these essays often as the main adversary.)

But I return now to the question of de Man's own literary and linguistic forms, his literary genre, his chosen vehicles of expression: the critical review essay, the light review (*NYRB*), the collection of essays in book form, and those essays with general "philosophical" themes (intentionality, temporality, etc.), and readings of literary texts (*Julie*, "Pygmalion," "Essay on Epitaphs," etc.) (This is the direction in which he was headed; but also simultaneously headed into the broader arena of ideology.) Through the generic diversity, through the topical diversity, one cannot fail to be struck—if one must search for consistency—by the consistency of position that appears throughout. Not political position, in terms of choosing "sides" on an issue, not a moral position, of judging one mode or another "wrong"; nor yet an uncomplicatedly "rhetorical" position, i.e., that is the position of the sophist whose only final commitment is to being aporetical and non-commital in the most frustrating sense of the term.

What we have in a reading of position in de Man is a key formal element that will draw many levels of discourse in his writing, many philosophical, rhetorical, theoretical, critical and methodological *aperçus* under its hegemony. Few can fail to have noted the absolutism of his tone, yet the "authority" for that absolutism lies nowhere in any of the realms for which one has looked and continues to look for it— philosophy, theory, method, in the "privilege" he appears to assign now to "literature," now to "language," now to "metaphor," to figures,[22] etc., each of which is methodically overturned in the course of his writing, if not within one text, then in the next one. It lies solely in its abuse: in the service of non-absolutism.[23] This rhetoric of (anti-)position has a technical basis that I hope to give some account of here.

In what follows I will track the "position" of form in Paul de Man's essays, especially in respect to what he imagines as form's "exotopy": its *other(s)*. Can we account for exactly where *form* seems to fit into his literary understanding—especially his sense of literary history—and for his assessment of his own attempts, among others, to think beyond form? I can show how for de Man form is always a compromise, always an error, but a crucial and perpetual one; it is the only distinctive feature of literature, and it is also the sign of its greatest failure. In its many guises—as figure (shape, rhetorical, geometrical, etc.), as face, and as number—it is the topic most central to his work, and most "identifiable" under his signature. But it is precisely that "signature" that I must question, by posing a question that is implicit in his texts: the very question of position not solely in a theoretical, but in a political sense as well.

ii. The Errors of Form: Being and Nothingness

In the early essay on the "Structure intentionnelle de l'image romantique" (1960), de Man makes explicit why the concept of metaphor as duality (in a later vocabulary, a binary opposition) is both the basis of the language of romanticism and its downfall, why it has been mythified as Narcissus and why it has yielded the prestige of the symbol (the organic object bearing a basic privilege within its structure). But in organizing his particular discourse here, and in subsequent texts that deal with metaphor, de Man has already introduced a structural relation that will become the basis of his later rereading of form, formalism, and especially of semiology.

De Man presents, in this essay, his version of the means of production of romantic language, as well as its intentional structure, by utilizing a fruitful combination of a formalist method and a phenomenological one. Analyzing closely a few lines from Hölderlin on the "origin" and "beginning" of poetic language, de Man shows that the desire for identification with natural objects common to romantic texts is in fact an admission by literary language that it cannot be natural. Language (as Saussure had in fact already told us) has no *origin*, but it can only have a *beginning*. Yet it would like to have the ontological stability of having an origin (divine Being in one vocabulary/simply Being in another). The objective appearance of nature seems to offer an image of such Being, but this is in fact a confusion of *entities* with only one of their manifestations: objects. Paul de Man lays bare the device around which poetic language has structured itself since the end of the Enlightenment: metaphor is defined, poetically, as the nostalgia for Being (seen in the guise of objective Nature) and as such is in a never-ending conflict with the way language ex-ists, i.e., is without *origin*, has no being:

Nous pouvons concevoir l'origine en termes de différence: la source jaillit du besoin d'être ailleurs ou autre chose que ce qui est maintenant ici. Le mot "*ent*-stehen", avec son préfixe disjonctif marquant la distance, introduit aussitôt une notion de différence. Par contre, l'objet naturel ne semble avoir

ni commencement ni fin. . . . Il est clair que, dans le passage cité de
Hölderlin, les mots ne naissent *pas* comme des fleurs. La parole poétique
cherche son origine dans une entité autre qu'elle-même; elle naît d'un
non-être, dans une tentative d'être la première parole à venir au monde
comme naissent des objets naturels. En tant que telle elle demeure profondé-
ment distincte des objets naturels. La proposition de Hölderlin "maintenant
doivent naître des mots comme naissent des fleurs" constitue une parfaite
définition de ce qu'on peut appeler "l'image naturelle," l'image qui indique
le désir d'une épiphanie mais qui nécessairement échoue dans sa tentative
d'être épiphanie parce qu'elle demeure pure origine. Il est de l'essence du
langage d'être capable de ce jaillissement originel mais de ne jamais pouvoir
accomplir cette absolue identité avec soi qui existe dans l'objet naturel. Le
langage poétique ne peut que naître; il est toujours constitutif, c'est-à-dire
qu'on peut *poser* même ce qui *n'est* pas—mais de ce fait même, il demeure
incapable de fonder ce qu'il pose, sinon en tant que l'intention de la conscience. (pp. 72–74)

More concisely stated, the first term of the comparison, *words*, (in which
words can be born *as* things) has no existence anterior to the *metaphoric*
proposition. Words are born by means of it; even though the content—
to want to be born like flowers (which is to say, not born at all, but to be a
natural emanation of Being, like a revelatory epiphany) is a wish that this
were not so. Fulfillment of such a wish (or intention) is absolutely
impossible in the metaphoric mode:

La parole est toujours une libre présence posée par la conscience et au moyen
de laquelle la permanence des êtres naturels peut être mise en question,
rouvrant à l'infini la 'spirale vertigineuse' de la dialectique. (p. 74)

Ironically, the very impossibility of metaphor has resulted in its pre-
ponderance as a figure in literary themes and myths that continually
restage this dilemma:

Dans une infinité de formes différentes, la poésie du dix-neuvième siècle
repète l'experience et représente dramatiquement l'aventure de cet échec; il y
aurait une étude d'ensemble à faire sur les versions romantiques et post-
romantiques de mythes tels que ceux de Narcisse, de Prométhée, de la guerre
des Titans, d'Adonis, de Prosperpine, etc, où, dans chaque cas, la dualité de
la situation mythique reflète la dualité intrinsèque du langage métaphoriqe
lui-même. (p. 74)

De Man proposes an alternative to this specular language, eventually
what he will (following Derrida) refer to as "the language of tropes, the
solar language of cognition that makes the unknown accessible to the

mind and to the senses" ("Autobiography as De-facement," p. 929). If the ontological primacy of the object comes into question, then the perpetual *sacrifice*, within metaphor, of *consciousness* to the object can be questioned in its turn, and the primacy of the imagination, the questioning of the "ontological status of the image" (p. 74) can take place. Such a questioning occurs, de Man feels, in the passages from Wordsworth, Rousseau, and Hölderlin that he analyses in the "Intentional Structure" essay. In these passages the constitutive and expressive, rather than the mimetic and literal, are stressed.

What precisely is the image of this image no longer conceived in terms of objects? What, that is, is the *other* of metaphoric form here—which is only a compromise between "Being and Nothing" that is finally neither? De Man gives a hint, in these texts, of another kind of epiphany, not iconic in the technical sense he has dissected above, but in which consciousness itself is imaged forth, independent of "things," becoming, in a way, an entity: but it is an invisible image, one not based on visual or sense perception, the senses being in this essay for de Man still too clearly tied to the overvaluation of the natural object-as-pseudo-entity. It is, quite simply put, *air*. Invisible, consciousness has for him

> la fluidité totale d'un être qui se trouve entièrement au-delà des choses, que se trouve, comme le "Dieu" dont parle Hölderlin au-dessus de la lumière . . . Les poètes deviennent comme ces nuages que décrit Wordsworth, "Cerulian ether's pure inhabitants" (1. 481); non pas l'azur, ni même la constellation Mallarménne vue de la terre par l'homme en train de sombrer, mais l'objet céleste lui-même, l'habitant du ciel. . . . (pp. 81–2)

And as fruit of the sky, not of the earth, the poetic word born of this consciousness is neither an incarnation (à la Christianity) nor is it metaphoric: it is an ascenscion of consciousness itself

> vers une conscience autre ou cette dualité [de la métaphore] est apaisée. . . . Elle désigne la possibilité de la conscience imageante et pensante de suffire à elle-même, indépendamment de tout rapport avec un objet extérieure et sans être animé par une intention qui vise un tel objet. (p. 82)

Has anyone ever noticed how radical this assertion of a consciousness independent not only of *objects* but of *intentions* is? For although it would be very easy to suppose that this version of consciousness is that of one Husserlian revolution, "la découverture, la révélation d'une nouvelle conception des rapports entre la conscience et les objets" (p. 81), the line is a kind of counter to Bachelard's particular phenomenology of space

that continues to see "nature" as simply terrestrial. Certainly the
"bracketing" of the world and the phenomenological reduction of consciousness to its contents is precisely a reduction to its *intentional objects*;
de Man's emphatic exclusion of these two terms should signal us as to the
radical nature of his revision here, and to how completely *other* than a
phenomenological version of consciousness it implies, even in its Sartrean variant.

What a passage such as this seems to indicate is that if there is a *drive* in
Paul de Man's writing it is the drive to otherness, "toward a consciousness *other*." In this particular case, it is a movement beyond the formal
compromise of a metaphor rooted in the ontological primacy of the
sensually apprehended object, toward an immaterial and non-sensual,
thoroughly de-objectified "consciousness," but such will not always be
the case in his other writings. The particularity of this instance is not
generalizable. In later texts, one will find a movement not of "falling
upwards" so much as that of "ascending downwards," toward the *body*,
which becomes the "other" of the no-thingness of the spirit so designated
in this text (see his essay on Wordsworth, "Autobiography as De-
facement" and "Shelley Disfigured"). De Man was always as much a
Sartrean as a Heideggerian.

Far from the emphasis on consciousness betraying, as Gearhart argues,
a systematic disdain for nature and the natural in all of de Man's work, it
is much fairer (by making the distinction de Man does, that of not
confusing the difference between the *objectivity* of Nature and Being) to
suppose that it is especially the question of the *subject* that it raises, the
question of the subject as a lack of/in Being.

(The antagonism, if one will, is between subject and object; but the
real opposition is between subject and other. The self, metaphoric, is the
conflictual compromise between the two, the compromise that de Man
dissects so coolly and critically. Spirit is, in this early text, hidden
behind the metaphor of the self; in later texts, it will not be *spirit* alone
but *body* that is so hidden: each are equally versions of the *subject*
(including consciousness) that is *other* than that distorted in and by the
compromise of form.)

This is to say that with deconstruction de Man did not undergo what
his students sometimes wanted to see him as undergoing—a conversion.
He was a militant atheist, and one wonders if the form were ever available
to him, although it made a patently readable "story" in 1968 when a
fellow student told it to me. But then de Man had taught me not to
believe in readability. Forms—metaphors, narratives, indeed any *signs*,

always contain, as Peirce has taught us, their own *readings* (Interpretants). De Man repeated this insight, as did Barthes in *Myth Today*, in a negative mode, that is to say, by showing how *resisting* this reading is the most critical activity possible—and also the most foolish.[24]

As that modern philosophy of the subject that begins (in Lacan's wake?) with the Other—or sees the Other as the beginning—deconstruction provided in fact the perfect technical and theoretical procedure for de Man: iterability. Repetition is always, as Derrida writes in "Signature, Evenement, Contexte," the work of the other (*iter* = other). Deconstruction supplied Paul de Man with at least a partial satisfaction of his drive toward "une conscience autre." Even Nietzsche had been unable to satisfy this, although he marks out for de Man some of the terrain by attacking the "most fundamental 'value' of all: the principle of noncontradiction, ground of the identity principle."[25] If de Man could have been said to have any "value of values" it lay exclusively in a principle of contradiction, non-ground of the lack of identity.

But it also was a partial response to that other major problem of formalism, which as de Man never failed to reiterate, was precisely its ignorance of context, its failure to read even its own fictional history as context for its labors. What de Man's application of *iterability* to literature becomes is not de-contexualization, but—if I may be permitted the permutation of a Freudian concept—over-contextualization. It is the fact that the decontextualized citation can and must be "cited," "called up"—given a citation—in a particular other text that is the matter for the Allegory of reading. Far from it being, as critics of intertextuality (Rosiland Coward and John Ellis, for example) would have it, the very essence of the capitalist tradition to free texts from their empirical producers, it is the opposite—an accusation that if an other is indeed the author of what had been thought was one's own "text," it also communalizes what one had thought of as one's personal possession, one's "own" text. The "decontextualization" so often implied by deconstructive critical practice seems to me to differ vastly from de Man's practice and Derrida's praxis as well.

The Rule of Metaphor: But this is *not* to say that such an understanding of the limitations of figure and form in de Man results in any disdain for the power of the binary structure as de Man conceived it to be able to hide the subject. Indeed, no one—apart from Rousseau and Lacan perhaps (even Derrida seems to me, simply by dint of his formal play, to have a certain latitude that de Man felt he lacked)—ever felt more strongly how powerful the Rule of Metaphor is, and sought more assiduously to detail its strictures. And the "middle years" of de Man's critical writing are devoted to the exposition of this rule. If, in the irony that presides over all readings of the deconstructive mode, the perception of his work comes more from these middle years than from the earlier passionate research into questions of the other of form, that he comes to be identified as part of the new Yale Formalists, it is due not only to his faithfulness to the Formal Method, but also to the fact that we fail to read the intellectual and passional basis of his inquiry into form, his version of its binary structure as false compromise, not merely of undecidability and aporia. This matters all the more in that the compromise itself is something we might call "life."

iii. Matters of Life and Death: Getting in Shape

There recurs in many of the earlier texts, a kind of condemnation of the senses, especially insofar as the senses were the perceptual basis for amputating Being and displaying it as "natural." Theoretically this denigration of the senses was apropos, but was it not also a kind of wish? Did he want it to be a kind of sure-fire guarantee of not being trapped in the aesthetic version of form? Aesthetics, shaping, forming—so many terms for the perpetual error of metaphor he uncovers in the 1960 essay on the intentional structure of the romantic image. Even in his late essay on pedagogy, "Resistance to Theory" (1982), he begins by finally freeing himself from the aesthetic position. We had already heard so many remarks about eudaemonism (in the 1975 essay on Nietzsche) about getting beyond sensualist aesthetics which we always found to be confused with ethics, a eudaemonism Kant had precisely sought to put an end to by means of his understanding of aesthetics as formal distance. (Ironically, of course, it is the extreme of aestheticism, which as "a-moralism," seems to be taking hold of younger practicing de-constructionists; even though there is much anti-Kantianism in deconstruction.) In a Heideggerian vein de Man reads such distance on sensual form in a complex manner, in which, while the eudaemonism of sensually conceived form is condemned, the particular value of form as mediation is maintained.

Signs: Metaphors, like all signs, are binaries ("Shelley Disfigured," p. 60) and, hence, specular in structure. De Man writes in "Autobiography as De-facement":

The specular moment that is part of all understanding reveals the tropological structure that underlies all cognitions, including knowledge of the self . . . autobiography, then . . . demonstrates in a striking way the impossibility of closure and of totalization (that is, the impossibility of coming into being) of all textual systems made up of tropological substitutions. (p. 922)

He goes on to speak of the subject of autobiography as "folded back on itself in mirror-like self-understanding" (p. 923). Metaphors operate like the sun in Derrida's "White Mythology," which must go out of and beyond itself to "be" itself (and which is their "source," prior even to language). But metaphors cannot "be," they can only provide the "light" by which reflection—specular self-knowledge—occurs: "The solar language of cognition makes the unknown accessible to the senses" (p. 929). As such, metaphors (figures) exist as the desire for epiphany, for the revelation of Being—a revelation to which they themselves are an obstacle. Perhaps the most fortunate obstacle.

Form is, as de Man once wrote in the article on Heidegger ("Les Exégèses"), that which shelters Dasein, protects it from the direct experience of Being. It is precisely this "direct unmediated experience" that de Man feared and was nonetheless fascinated by. In the Wordsworth essay he writes of aesthetics as the "distance that shelters the author of autobiography from his experience" (p. 919); in the essay on the image of Rousseau in Hölderlin he writes of the extinction of sensation and the experience of Death as linked. But the experience of death is modulated in Hölderlin's vision of Rousseau as embodying "la sagesse et la patience de demeurer fidèle aux limitations que [le] savoir impose, de par ses propres lois, à l'esprit humain"[26]; and he comes to look at rhetoric (in the face of Nietzsche and of the turmoil of the Vietnam War) as "a *text* in that it allows for two incompatible, mutually self-destructive points of view and therefore puts an insurmountable obstacle in the way of any reading or understanding." ("Action and Identity in Nietzsche," p. 29). A remark such as the last one—seen by his critics as nihilistic in the extreme—is in fact the opposite: it is understanding and reading (as described above) that would put us too close to Nothing; it is rhetoric, with its formal compromise, its *mediations* in every conceivable sense of the term, that affords us diversion (in both the Pascalian and the Freudian senses) from Nothing at all. Recall that one of de Man's favorite quotations is from Rousseau's Julie, "tel est le néant des choses humaines que, hors l'Etre existant par lui-même, il n'y a rien de beau que ce qui n'est pas." There is always within de Man this particular tension—the drive toward that which exists beyond the aesthetic (which for him always constitutes a nagging remnant of the eudaemonic, moral and sensualist ethic), that is, from form as sense, to form as mediation and shelter, *and* then its *other*: nothing at all.[27]

Now to translate the terminology we have been using here into the vocabulary he came increasingly to utilize in his later articles, the vocabulary of semiotics, "metaphor" is *iconic*, that is, it is an act of faith that something which is basically unable to be apprehended by the senses can be represented sensually. That is the analogical bridge that all iconic signs must build according to Peirce, and also, according to de Man, all metaphors (see "The Epistemology of Metaphor").[28] Not just Words-worth's texts, but all texts are "constructed of a sequence of mediations between incompatibles" ("Autobiography as De-facement," p. 925).

But what is absolutely unheard of in de Man's own literary and linguistic form—his neutrality of intonation—comes to be understand-able, not, as Lentricchia and Angus Fletcher and even Richard Klein would have it, because he accepted the asceticism of his venture—repeating Kant's pietistic tendencies. At least not entirely (see below). For Bakhtin has taught us that intonation is the "first" metaphor (co-extensive with gesture), and if that is the case, then Paul de Man's work on metaphor in that aspect is surely complex. For when he has the most tragic of insights to convey to us about the structure of metaphoric form—that it is, although a false compromise, the only form that shelters us from Nothingness and Death—he does so in an absolutely unsentimental, neutral tone, even when it is, or especially when it is, a question of life and death. This is crucial for determining exactly where the emotive, expressive and ultimately positional bases of metaphor lie. Neutrality of tone on this life-and-death issue is crucial to a proper evaluation of the "Intentionelle" article. It is one of the few of his early articles that is not constructed around a series of critical queries and assertions in which a certain intonation can usually be heard—a rising voice, an ironic derision, a condemnatory (rarely a laudatory) tone. But in this text, where he makes explicit why the concept of metaphor as a duality is a false compromise and a necessary fiction, a structure that will organize his particular discourse here and in all his subsequent texts that deal with metaphor, de Man has already introduced a structural relation that will become the basis of his later rereading of form, formalism, and especially of semiology. He shows the equal necessity of an impossibility of the metaphoric attitude, and he does so in a neutral form and forum, refusing to take a moral or emotional attitude (they are ultimately the same thing) toward rhetoric. Given the evidence of those who failed to be able either to achieve or maintain such neutrality, including Hölderlin (at times) and Mallarmé, Claudel and Valéry, such a non-evaluative position is remarkable. If denial of the senses was what gave him the strength others lacked, who could deny him that condition of possibility for his courage? For the end result is, of course, that the only form we know which is "prior" to the geometric, spatially and visually conceived form is—Husserl said it—"language as a series of logical propositions." Thus, Paul de Man comes to concentrate not only on the very figures that can possibly be of interest under these conditions—linguistic figures known as tropes—but also to involve himself deeply in the deconstruction of the logic of propositions: as his way of continuing to press *form* for its *other*.

"Death interests me," Paul de Man remarked as we walked last March in New Haven, he pointing out, as he said this, things that might interest me: stories by Henry James; the building that housed Yale's ultra-secret undergraduate society; the fact that the logic of the organization of certain Yale departments seemed to be structured only around one principle—anti-Sovietism. He was also simultaneously experiencing the physical pain of his illness. He did not mind, he said, leaving life. As I tried to express, awkwardly, that there were many of us who would mind his leaving *us*, I also knew how selfish that was, and I wanted to say that we loved him enough to let him rest from his pain. But even here he showed a kind of intellectual appetite for the ultimate experience of otherness that death, in his thinking, was. (I also know that he is the one who showed how Rousseau demystified Julie's Socratic death with her admission of the passional, rather than the rational basis of her existence. He was not, finally, happy to leave the metaphoric illusion(s) of life, if only because he would find in death the end of the possibilities of moving toward otherness.)

iv. Getting Out of Shape/ Coming to One's Senses

Despite the devotion to forms as figure not as sensually conceived, but as media, shelters and life-protecting compromises, —in short *as language* alone—Paul de Man's writing does see form undergo yet another reversal and reinscription in the body of his texts, and in two different ways. For he comes once again to be interested in designating what the escape from form would be like. The essay on Nietzsche ("Action and Identity in Nietzsche," p. 19) is transitional in that Nietzsche radicalized the falsifications of "identity" as *form*: they are rooted in the mistaking of "the sensation of things" for the "knowledge of entities," just as de Man had disclosed of the romantics in his early "Structure intentionelle de l'image romantique" (1960). But, in this particular text on Nietzsche, the reversal also comes to be the case such that *metaphor*—the binary form that is the first step toward overcoming sensation, but which fails to reach *spirit*, fails in the other direction as well: it is supported by *metonymy*, conceived by de Man here as a "link with sensation" (p. 19).[29] In short, it fails to reach the senses. But de Man refuses to stop with such a reversion to sense vs. "sense," and regards Nietzsche's "spatial" reversal here from the point of view of its *other*, time:

> The deconstruction of the metaphor of knowledge into the metonymy of sensation is a surface manifestation of a more inclusive deconstruction that reveals a metaleptic reversal of the categories of anteriority and posteriority, of before and after. (p. 21)

He does this, again, not in the service of fidelity to the category of temporality, but as his strategy of deconstructive criticism. Before the end of the essay, impossibilities have become imperatives ("I cannot = therefore you must"), *acts* become words, "the pure act's paradigm" is "denomination and the deconstruction of its genealogy is best carried out by etymology" (p. 25), etc. But the stage has been set for de Man's own return to the senses as an important critical topos, both theoretically and methodologically. As in the early essay on the romantic image this interest grows as his writing centers once again on the epoch that never ceased to draw his attention—Romanticism: he writes his book on it, he writes once more on Wordsworth and Kleist and Shelley. But this time the reading of the "other" of form, the "subject" of form, is not as Spirit, but as body—not the living, feeling body, but the senseless one, the dead body.

If the most deeply erroneous aspect of the form of language mistaken for a sense perception is voice (see "Autobiography as De-facement," p. 924), in the deconstructive revolution that particular formal difficulty was laid to rest, if only theoretically, and the particular battle with the misapprehensions of the senses seemed unnecessary to continue to fight. But different concerns had evidently come into play with the concentration on the linguistic figure as a compromise and a diversion from death: certainly semiology, especially the Lacanian version of it, but also the literary deconstructionists themselves, with the renewed emphasis on spacing, could not be ignored. With Lacan comes the body, as the Discourse of the Other; with deconstruction comes yet again the question space/or/time; space/and/time—or perhaps space-time (chronotope). And the possibility for reiterating the Other of form again arises, as it had arisen with the earlier phenomenology-formalism conbination.[30]

Writing, for example, is form without compromise such as he might have wished to discover earlier in "Structure intentionelle" (1960). Ideology, deconstructed, could also become the Other of politics as a compromised form.[31] In the Wordsworth essay, he speaks of moving "without compromise, from death *or* life to life *and* death"; in putting it this way he is conceiving of a *structure*—difference—that could deconstruct the pretentions of form to being comprehensive, of "doing both at once" when it is in fact always subordinating one of its conflictual elements to the other. But at the same time he is deconstructing difference by giving it a *form*—a form that permits both elements to cross each other. I offer the following diagram, although I am, of course, aware of the form's limitations:

(1) either/or (or in Barthes' terms, "neither/nor"): always a false opposition that is inherently unstable, hierarchical and/or represses one side of the opposition;

(2) both/and: a pseudo-compromise in which the radical nature of each member is blunted, quiescent;

(3) both and (and both): the chiasmus, difference without opposition.

It is not at all surprising, seen in this way, that he confided to me that his favorite reading had become Pascal, the writer of the chiasmus, of the very hidden God, of the denial of the senses. . . .

v. Positing/position

Gasché has done an excellent job of outlining precisely why the question of positing is important to all philosophies of the subject. And he shows how in the course of de Man's work, *Setzung* becomes *Übersetzung*—translation, or a being moved off of or carried away from the original position. Just as love of self translates into love of others in Rousseau, so, too, Paul de Man's long struggle with the subject in his writing translates into that which also moves beyond its borderlines—or more precisely how it has no borderlines. It is because his middle years were spent working through all the possible varieties of form which attempt to limit the subject that a critic like Gearhart can see in his work a mania for the self-reflexivity that form always implies. But this is a distortion; for not only does it confuse subject and self, which de Man never did, it fails to see how this intensity is a working through of the question of the subject in the literary texts, one by one, in which various pseudo-answers to the question of the subject are offered.

Subject is hidden behind the metaphor of the self; that much of a discrimination in terminology is indeed crucial to de Man. But the question still then remains: if *positing* is, as Gasché shows for early romanticism, absolutely necessary for the determination of a subject, then de Man's *übersetzung*, his over-positioning (or de-positioning), seems to throw the subject in question. After all, is not the subject defined by its attitudes? The one thing subjects can have that objects cannot are attitudes. Is he either constructing a subject not defined attitudinally, positionally, is he betraying the subject to "objectivity"? (I think not; if his writing is anything, it is not "objective" in the crude sense; and yet, in his exclusion of the value judgment that is the hierarchical basis of any form, is not his "objectivity" the most important aspect of his subjectivity?) The question remaining of *why* he attempted his heroic subjectivity without interests, attitudes, opinions, value judgments, and in which he knew he would fail, it seems unanswerable, and unimportant. In the face of his imminent death, there was once again the passion: as we sat in a New Haven café, as we had sat in so many other cafés in Paris, Zürich, New York, he asked me, "What are you working on next?" and I said I had begun to take a real interest in James—*The Portrait, The Princess*. His clear delight broke out—"I *love* Henry James!"

What about "position" in its other than technically philosophical sense that Gasché has so carefully tracked? The question is as crucial to a reading *of* de Man as it was to the reading he himself did of other critics, that is, not only not to accept a purely philosophical definition of any of its own terms, but also—more importantly—to discover how a "philosophical" definition given in a text can be read in and through the form of the text in which it is given. Such a term is position, or positing in Paul de Man—the form of the subject, the subject of form.[32]

NOTES

1. I refer to Stanley Cornold's "Error in Paul de Man" in *The Yale Critics* (eds. J. Arc, W. Godzich, and W. Martin [Minneapolis: Univ. of Minnesota Press, 1983], pp. 90–108), which like any of the recent "readings" of de Man attempts to use Heidegger to get at him. This is an example of the common mistake that de Man was ever a "Heideggerian."

2. Rodolphe Gasché, " 'Setzung' and 'Ubersetzung': Notes on Paul de Man" (*Diacritics*, 11,4[1981], 36–57), had done an admirable job of explicating the role of "positing" in de Man's writing. Gasché links positing, as necessary to any philosophy of self, to de Man's concern with Speech Act Theory, which Gasché uncovers as the teleotype of all philosophies of self-reflexivity. Gasché's is an exposition in the best sense, and I have no quarrel with it conceptually. It simply leaves out the *literary* concern, which always contains a formal element, that was, along with position, also an undeniable part of de Man's enterprise. Interestingly, Suzanne Gearhart in a text which (unfortunately) appeared shortly after de Man's death, criticizes Gasché's article not for this particular lapsus, but because in de-emphasizing the literary she feels Gasché is protecting de Man against the charges he levels elsewhere against the literary abuse of deconstruction. For her Paul de Man is in error simply because, she writes, he "privileged" literature, metaphor, the self. My essay may be considered a response to those charges (and they appear in the form of accusation) in her text. She writes:

> From Gasché's argument here, one could conclude, against de Man, that the literary text and (literary language) never confront an "outside" that would be totally alien to them, but that this is so precisely because they never can be said to confront themselves. The text and (literary) language are at once themselves and other, so radically other that they cannot always be confidently identified as text or literary language. "Philosophy *Before* Literature" (*Diacritics*, 13, 4 [1983], 80).

I hope my essay clarifies certain notions Gearhart purveys here, which although they imitate the gestures of de Man, do not deal adequately with the content of his writing: literature is precisely *not* itself and another at once; it is precisely *not* radically other enough. And certainly literature and language do, *pace* Gasché, confront themselves—this is a structural necessity (see the specular images of "Autobiography as Defacement,"). *MLN*, 94 [1979], 919–30.

3. Frank Lentricchia in *Criticism and Social Change* (Chicago: Univ. of Chicago Press, 1983) has made some amazing statements about de Man's desires that I hope the remainder of this essay belies.

4. Since he was a comparatist who worked equally with literary and philosophical texts, few specialists ever really see the entire spectrum of his writing. It is simply unprecedented within the generic and formal limits he set himself: that is, his is a European (rather than an American) literary style, in which genuinely encyclopedic scholarly knowledge is not called upon for its own sake in the writing of an essay. Essays tend to be written only under conditions where a certain sense of intellectual, moral, or other crisis is involved.

5. *Critique*, 12 (1956), 483–500.

6. The question of history has always dogged Formalism in all its variants, ranging from Trotsky's problems with the Russian Formalists (mirrored by Stalin's attack on Marr's linguistics), to Jakobson's desire, finally, to reduce literary history to "a series of paradigms arrayed along a syntagmatic axis." Derrida once wrote of the difference between a structural figure and a historical totality, and of how they contaminate each other (*De La Grammatologie*). Certainly there is no simple answer to historicity, except to say that some writers—like Benjamin, like de Man—have been able to discern the modern, post-Marxist tendency to mythify history. Gearhart's critique is really aimed at the formalists, not at the profound critique of formalism in de Man's work. I hope my essay will show how her indiscriminate attack fails to distinguish de Man. She writes:

> What de Man offers is a choice between regarding the "extra-linguistic" as the text in masquerade, or as a phenomenal world that can only be perceived of in the substance of naturalism. In either case the perimeter of literature is defended and respected. . . .

But in spite of all de Man's attempts to close off literature and treat it as a discrete object, his work persistently reassures us that literature, literary language, and the text are there all along deconstituting themselves in a process that only confirms their priority and their privilege. According to the logic of such a theory of literature, all forms of history or even of historicity are derived from language. (Gearhart, p. 80)

I cannot see in any of de Man's texts a defense of literary borders: such a *politique* is foreign to this citizen of so many countries, both literary and real. The imprecision in Gearhart's thought is denoted by her switch in vocabulary when she attacks literary form through de Man: "his work . . . reassures us that literature, literary language are there all along *deconstituting* themselves in a process that only confirms their priority and privilege." If there is anything literature wanted to do, it would be to deconstitute itself—and this, is precisely what it can never do. The structure of literary form as the exclusion of the other has nothing whatever to do with social history as Gearhart would like it to operate.

7. "Structure intentionelle de l'image romantique" (*Revue Internationale de philosophie*, 14 [1960]).

8. *Blindness and Insight* (New York: Oxford Univ. Press, 1971), p. 26. Further page citations to this work will be noted in the text.

9. "Montaigne et la transcendence" (*Critique*, 79[Dec. 1953], 1011–22).

10. Bakhtin probably does the best job of showing how the either/or of the forms of space and time (i.e., either structural or historical) in our aesthetics since Kant must be overcome in order for there to be Reading. De Man's essay on the chronotope ("Sign and Symbol in Hegel's *Aesthetics*," *Critical Inquiry*, 8, 4 [1982], 761–75) shows the structure of both and/and both (not both/and) as he sees time *and* space operating chiasmatically as a cross-roads in textuality. In one of his last published essays de Man speaks highly of Bakhtin; and one feels certain that had Bakhtin's version of "temporality" rather than Lukács' become the West's understanding of Marxism and history we would be faced now with a very different set of attitudes toward history.

11. De Man's concern with countering the spatial organicism of the New Critics led him into their authors of choice—Coleridge primarily—and to what is perhaps the most comprehensive of all his writing (in the sense that the reversal and reinscription is contained within the same text): "The Rhetoric of Temporality: Irony and Allegory," (*Interpretation: Theory and Practice*, C. Singleton, ed. [Johns Hopkins Press, 1969], pp. 173–209). All students of literary history would be well-advised to read this essay, as would all critics of Paul de Man. Just as irony seems to be the ultimate "other" of the self (which by now *is* literature for de Man), so, too, "allegory" can become the "other" of irony (as in Stendhal).

12. See Gasché (" 'Setzung' and 'Ubersetzung' ") on the reversal. What is most interesting about those defenders of "historicity" against literary deconstruction is that it seems to me they are victims of a reversal without reinscription: to put it clearly, whereas the older literary scholar could exist in a world of "pure form" uncontaminated by "history" in all that this implied of the too-real, then the equal exasperation of the younger critics with History uncontaminated by "literary forms" is a simple reversal. The real revolution of deconstruction (as of the structuralism before it) was to show how each contaminates the other; there is no purity on either side.

13. "Les Exégèses de Hölderlin par Martin Heidegger" (*Critique*, 11[1955], 800–19). "Sartre's Confessions" (*New York Review of Books*, 5 Nov. 1964, 10–13).

14. "La Critique thématique devant le thème de Faust" (*Critique*, 13[1957], 387–404).

15. Jean Starobinski's work on Rousseau is the target of much of Derrida's critique of the "époque" of Rousseau as well. I have chosen to keep the entire discourse of de Man on Rousseau out of this essay, not only because I have commented on it elsewhere ex-

tensively, but also because it is fitting that the author (Rousseau) who is the allegorical other of so much of de Man's writing should be excluded, if only temporarily, here.

16. One can see here de Man's countering of space with time, even in this quotation, i.e., in the juxtaposition of "moment" and "lieu."

17. A genre I have not dealt with here but at which de Man was becoming more adept was that of the book-jacket blurb, several of which have caused excessive commentary. I refer here to the blurb on Kristeva's *Powers of Horror*, about which I have written (forthcoming in *Semiotica*).

18. The line is from Rousseau's *Reveries*: ". . . j'appliquerais le baromètre à mon ame. . . ."

19. "Symbolic Landscape in Wordsworth and Yeats" (*In Defense of Reading*, eds. R. A. Brower and R. Poirier [New York: Dutton, 1962], 7).

20. A great many of the essays between 1973 and 1982 are devoted to leading semiologists: "Hypogram and Inscription: Michael Riffaterve's Poetics of Reading" (*Diacritics*, 11, 4[1981], 17–35), the essay on "The Resistance to Literary Theory" (*Yale French Studies*, 63[1982], 3–20), which treats Greimas, and of course the justly renowned "Semiology and Rhetoric" (in *Allegories of Reading* [New Haven: Yale Univ. Press, 1979], pp. 3–19). What each of these essays does is to disrupt the formal symmetry implied in "specularity" and to show how, simply because a particular figure unites them, conceptual couples are not necessarily "happily married": grammar and rhetoric do not coexist peacefully, any more than the binary division of the world into pro- and anti-communists can; the paired oppositions of Greimas must be read against the catastrophe also of the chiasmus—as not as straightforward as the great semiotician would like them to be, etc. Riffaterre, it seems, repeats the older fault of seeing perception and thought as specular-symmetrical couples.

21. See "Hypogram and Inscription: Michael Riffaterre's Poetics of Reading" (see note 17) and "Pascal's Allegory of Persuasion" (*Allegory and Representation*, ed. Stephen J. Greenblatt [Baltimore and London: Johns Hopkins Univ. Press, 1981], pp. 1–25).

22. See Gearhart (note 5, above). If there is any privilege in "literary" language it is in respect to ordinary language ("Criticism and Crisis" in *Blindness and Insight*)—or so it seems. For after all, one can, by valuing the "aesthetic" think that saying "Pass the salt" is privileged because it appears in a novel; but from the point of view of the real eater, literary salt would not be so evaluated, and de Man's test certainly does not leave us with a decision on either side. If de Man passes to a close scrutiny of *figures* and figurative language in the later texts this is one aspect of form: not only visible shape, but also figure as face (prosopopeia; "Autobiography as De-facement"), figure as number ("Hypogram and Inscription"), figure as, simply, that which can be disfigured ("Autobiography as De-facement" and "Shelley Disfigured" in *Deconstruction and Criticism* [New York: Seabury, 1979], pp. 39–74).

23. Paul de Man's uncle, Hendrik de Man, was a socialist and a theorist of socialism and leader of the labour party in Belgium before and, briefly, under the Nazis. He was, despite his socialist political persuasion, something of an absolutist, desirous of being a leader, and author of a *Plan van den Arbeid* which was to have depression-era Belgium simply allow socialism to take over the existing capitalist structure and turn it over to socialism without modifying its property and other relations. He staked a great deal on the belief that the Marxist version of historical development would "naturally" prevail over the evident decadence of capitalism demonstrated by Nazism (Erik Hansen, "Hendrik de Man and the Theoretical Foundations of Economic Planning," *European Studies Review*, 9[1978], 235–57). I think Paul de Man was scrupulous to a fault to avoid repeating the mistakes of his notorious relative. When one considers that the *Yale French Studies* essay on theory ("Resistance to Theory") was to have been a "plan" or projection for literary theory—and that its own "resistance to theory" proved unpalatable for the

MLA by whom it was commissioned—one sees how little of the "leader"—or Mafia don—there was in Paul de Man.

24. See de Man's article on semiology in *Allegories of Reading*, but also Peirce's essay on the different types of signs—icon, index and symbol. Dean MacCannell "Sights and Spectacles," forthcoming in *Iconicity: festschrift for Thomas A. Sebeok*, eds., Roland Posner, Paul Bouissac, and Michael Herzfeld) has shown how each sign, according to Peirce, bears a distinctive type of relation to its object: in the icon the relationship of object to representamen is based on faith (e.g., "Love is like a red, red rose" depends on our assimilating the invisible "love" to the sensible "rose"); the index is based on assertion (you *must* see the connection); and the symbol on a collective agreement, historic, among men.

25. "Action and Identity in Nietzsche" (*Yale French Studies*, "Graphesis" [Summer 1975], 16).

26. "L'image de Rousseau dans lapoêsiede Hölderlin" (*Deutsche Beiträge* V, 157–83. 45[1965], 1141–55).

27. In the early "Les Exégèses de Hölderlin par Martin Heidegger" (*Critique*, 11[1955], 800–19) de Man describes fiction specifically as a medium. The Nietzsche essay is very clear on the source of anti-eudaemonism as it is based on "questioning the epistemological authority of perception and of eudemonic patterns of experience" ("Action and Identity in Nietzsche," p. 20). The beginning of the "Resistance to Theory" article is quite open about the overcoming of aesthetics. Which is not to deny to Paul de Man a continuing involvement with aesthetics, for this essay is succeeded, almost immediately, by his writing about Hegel's aesthetics ("Hegel on the Sublime" in *Displacement*, ed. Mark Krupnik [Bloomington: Indiana Univ. Press, 1983]). See note 31 below.

28. "The Epistemology of Metaphor" (*Critical Inquiry*, 5 [1978], 26 ff). Now if icons are literally impossible, so, too, are indices, that is, those signs that coerce the relationship between the representamen and its object: the referential moment. De Man identifies the iconic (aesthetic) and its deconstruction with romantic literary practice; the indexical and its deconstruction (rhetoric) with the theory of Speech Acts (the latter of which he "deconstructs" again in the Nietzsche essay). This leaves the symbol yet to be treated, as indeed it is in an article that appeared in 1983, "Sign and Symbol in Hegel's Aesthetics." The symbol, the conventional pact, the agreement among men and historical associations, politics (the ideological—the Symbolic Order?), was next in line.

29. See my essay on Bakhtin, "The Temporality of Textuality: Bakhtin and Derrida," in *The State of Literary Theory Today* (London: Middlesex Polytechnic/International Assoc. for Philos. and Lit., 1982–83). The essay "Semiology and Rhetoric" in *Allegories of Reading* first, published in 1973, prefigures this same dialectic of metaphor and metonymy, the dialectic that Jakobson named and which has become the commonplace of structuralist and post-structuralist poetics. It is entirely possible to conceive of metonymy in another way, that is, as the silent, non-languaged link between two subjects without the mediation of the Other, as in Bakhtin's "Discourse in Life, Discourse in Art," in Stendhal's writing, etc. (see Bakhtin in *Freudianism: A Marxist Critique* [New York: Academic Press, 1976]).

30. See "Dialogue and Dialogism" (*Poetics Today*, 4, 1 [1983], 99–107) where de Man takes exception to what he sees as Bakhtin's and his critics' overvaluation of dialogism at the expense of his brilliant insights on exotopy and the chronotope.

31. The working title of a text planned for publication in 1984–85 was "Aesthetics, Rhetoric and Ideology" (on Kant, Hegel, Kierkegaard, and Marx).

32. Interestingly, he mentions Diderot in the "Intentional Structure" essay as being the real other of the romantics, for in some respects it is Diderot who will come closest in his theory of language to de Man: the origin of language, Diderot tells us, is in the pre-position.

Marxism and Deconstruction:
Symposium at the Conference on Contemporary Genre Theory and the Yale School
1 June 1984

Panelists: Barbara Johnson, Louis Mackey, J. Hillis Miller

Introduction

The Symposium at the Conference on Contemporary Genre Theory and the Yale School took place on June 1, 1984 at the Center for Continuing Education on the University of Oklahoma campus in Norman. Panelists Barbara Johnson, Louis Mackey and J. Hillis Miller fielded questions for two hours from about one hundred students and scholars who had gathered to hear their remarks. Scheduled for the last day of the Conference, the Symposium gave the students an opportunity to raise questions and engage the panelists in a dialogue while allowing the panelists to respond to other papers given at the conference and to clarify or expand on their own presentations. The dynamics of this session, the clash of viewpoints and the theoretical, philosophical and political differences which emerged from this discussion made the Symposium one of the most stimulating events of the Conference.

The Symposium had not been designed by the conference organizers to address as exclusively as it did the question of the relationship between Marxism and deconstruction. The discussion in the Symposium arose out of what was generally felt to be the unfortunate omission of Marxist viewpoints from the conference schedule. Specifically, the impetus arose from a presentation by David Gross during the session on Drama and Contemporary Theory on "Brecht and Modern Theory." Gross used Brecht's poem "A Worker Reads History" as an illustration of the critical/skeptical attitude toward the act of reading (history)—an example of Brecht's strategy of "estrangement" and Marx's "relentless criticism of everything existing," which seems in significant ways like a deconstructive reading. Gross concluded his presentation with a challenge that deconstruction address economic, social and political institutions much more explicitly.

During the Symposium Barbara Johnson focused on the ways in which both deconstruction and Marxism decenter the subject in a critique of the bourgeois notion of identity and selfhood. Responding to Johnson, Louis Mackey commented on the possibility of rapproachement between these two theories. (Mackey presented a deconstructive reading of St. Anselm's *Proslogium* at the conference.) The result was an exploratory foray into the differences between a critique and a political action, both of which center around the subversion of authority.

What emerged was a discussion of the relationship between linguistic and social/historical modes of analysis in current literary theory. As forms of literary criticism, structuralism and post-structuralism have brought about a revolution in critical theory. Focusing on the conditions of signification, structuralist theories examine the sign and ways in which the sign produces meaning. Deconstruction subverts the structuralist enterprise, taking the analysis deeper into language, philosophically and historically analyzing the basic assumptions of Western culture and how these assumptions affect the way we use language. The result is a literary criticism which has extraliterary implications. As Barbara Johnson noted during the Symposium, deconstruction is "an attack on the way in which discourse functions in patterns of domination." This attack is also relentlessly self-critical in its examination of the hierarchies which perpetuate repression in Western culture—an examination that deconstruction shares with Marxism. Traditional Marxist concern for the structures of economic and political life has expanded in the hands of literary Marxists to include a broad range of cultural and critical activities in which structuralism and post-structuralism have had a significant impact. Like deconstruction, Marxism is also concerned with the ways in which discourse functions in patterns of political effacement and domination.

In practice, however, linguistic theories have tended to ignore history while social/historical approaches have often systematically ignored language. Can Marxism and deconstruction rescue each other from the blindnesses of each approach? Is there a way of combining Marxism and deconstruction that remains loyal to both? Do Marxism and deconstruction share structural similarities as modes of analysis? Will any combining of the two necessarily privilege one over the other? This symposium represents an inquiry into just this area where these two critical theories both overlap and fail to meet.

In the discussion which follows, each of the panelists fuse theory and practice in unique ways. The transcription does, on the whole, retain the original wordings of the questions and the responses from the panelists. We have made changes only when necessary to impose grammatical and syntactical clarity on the flow of spoken discourse.

John Springer
Elizabeth McLemore
University of Oklahoma

Symposium

Robert Con Davis: I would like to start off by asking the three panelists to comment on one of the major papers that was given here. Maybe there is something you would like to touch on before people ask questions.

Barbara Johnson: I'll start by saying something about the issue of the relations between Marxism and deconstruction, which I was surprised to hear brought up only once among the papers I attended. I think it's very important for people working in deconstruction to be asked questions by Marxists. The reason that deconstruction produces social criticism as its left is very complex. Deconstruction, especially in the work of Derrida, has within it the creation of a feeling of imperative; that is, as a critical/analytical attack on the way discourse functions in patterns of domination, deconstruction produces as its necessary shadow or by-product or forerunner, a feeling of increasing imperative, a feeling that if deconstruction can take you this far in the critique of power structures in discourse, then why not go further? Why not actually translate what deconstruction has done on texts into the realm of historical and political action? I think it is the merit of deconstruction to produce that as an inevitable question, and that the intersection between the de-constructive activity and the imperative to go further is where both good Marxist work and good deconstructive work can be done. This is not an easy passage, certainly, for either Marxists or deconstructors to make, and it may be that there is no meeting point, but the continuous worrying of the encounter is immensely productive.

J. Hillis Miller: Since what I have to say is more or less the same thing, perhaps I might speak very briefly next and say I agree with what you've said, and that my remarks were meant to provoke that dialogue. Like all rhetoricians or deconstructors, one of my anxieties is that there could be a kind of sociological or explicitly Marxist criticism which would by-pass the implicit challenges to it that deconstruction has posed, and to think of those problems as in some way solved, perhaps by French Marxists who've done linguistic work themselves.

But I did want to say one or two things that aren't quite what Barbara said. One was that the introduction of the notion of an ethical im-perative, as opposed to a social or political one, into the ingredients of that dialogue seems to me helpful and not evasive. It might be seen as such by those who say you're just trying to get away from talking about politics or political action or society: another example of the way deconstructors are conservative or apolitical or ignore that kind of responsibility. But there is a slight difference between asking about the political relations or social/historical relations and ethical ones. The latter line of inquiry has some advantages in that it asks concrete questions about, for example, whether it makes any sense at all to talk about an ethical responsibility between the student and teacher of literature as a kind of person-to-person or person-to-text relation. That is, after all, mostly what we do. Most teachers of literature are not voting much of the time or writing political manifestoes or being politically active in the overt sense. Mostly we're teaching literature, we're in the classroom, reading people's papers, trying to decide which things ought to be published, applying for grants, etc. For the student and teacher of literature there is a region beyond that of simply worrying about language which talks about the ethical issues involved, ones that may involve conflict. For example, suppose I'm teaching a course which is part of a program in a department which is, in turn, part of an institution where there are all sorts of constraints that surround that whole activity which sets up the curriculum and the syllabus. Then let's say we're studying *Paradise Lost*. Suppose I came to the conclusion that it was not good for this particular group of people to study that work. What would my ethical responsibilities be? We really have a triple responsibility. It would be a responsibility to *Paradise Lost* simply as a kind of ethical imperative, that is, the ethical responsibility of the reader to the text to tell people what you really find there, which may not be what the class or the other critics thought you were going to find.

There would also be a responsibility to the student. It might be that a work would be good for some students and not for others. Two or three times in my long career of teaching I have actually encountered a situation of that sort. I remember a student in a course on the modern novel where we read things like *Heart of Darkness* and *Mrs. Dalloway*. I reached a point in the middle of the course where I wasn't quite sure that reading these novels was a good thing for her. They were troubling her very deeply. For most of the other students you'd think that reading *Heart of Darkness* was a good thing; maybe they'd learn about the evils of imperialism in Africa or about the metaphysical darkness or something. But for this one student I felt I was, in some way, in an ethical situation that was very hard to face.

And there is also an obligation to the institution that has hired us. So I see this as a real region which is connected with those political and social ones but which is not quite the same. It may be a way to think about those issues that would help make them more concrete. The shift from politics to ethics might be useful.

Louis Mackey: I think Barbara Johnson is right in that there has to be lots of dialogue and encounter between Marxism and deconstruction and Freudianism, for that matter. However, I'm wondering about the possibility of any kind of rapprochment between them for this rather simple-minded reason: The Marxist and the Freudian and the deconstructive reader all practice a form of what Ricoeur called "the hermeneutics of suspicion"; that is, you don't just take the text at its word, but you say, "What in the world is going on here that isn't obvious?" The difference between these approaches always seemed to me something like this: that the Marxist and the Freudian, in a sense, already know what's really going on in the text, they have a preconception of what's going on, whereas at least the ideal deconstructive reader is open to whatever might pop up. The Marxist knows that no matter what's going on on the surface there's something down deep about the relations of production, economic matters, things of that sort. The Freudian knows that there is some libidinal thing down there that he's going to find when he gets down and scrapes the barnacles off the underside of discourse. I take it that the deconstructive reader is not supposed to start off with preconceptions about what he is going to find.

BJ: Don't you think that the ideal Freudian or Marxist reader would also want to discover things that they weren't expecting to find?

LM: Would they still be Freudians and Marxists then?

BJ: Did Freud know he was a Freudian? [Johnson first slipped and asked, "Did Freud know he was a Marxist?"—eds.] Marx wasn't a Marxist all along. He was a searching analyst who had been, perhaps, codified too much. But to imitate Marx in his way of leaving open the question and not already knowing the answers would be just as Marxist as to apply a preconceived set of beliefs.

LM: If it is true what you say of Marx and Freud, that they didn't have such preconceptions but were open and waiting to see what happened and what they'd find, and if to be a Marxist or a Freudian means to follow them in that, that is fine. But that isn't what usually is meant by the word. To be a Marxist usually means to be one who follows the teachings of Marx in some sense.

BJ: It depends. People have accused deconstructors of already knowing what they want to find.

LM: That's right, and some of them do.

BJ: Yes, some of them do. So all three of these things are alike in that there is a version that may be seen as dogmatic or already closed and there is a version that leaves things open as best it can. Insight is produced in that space between theoretical generalizations and the documentation of uncertainty. In each of these theoretical fields the insight has met with resistance. That is, revisionism is a real danger in all of these things, and yet revisionism has dogmatism as its counterpart. How can you tell where one leaves off and the other begins?

LM: But isn't there this difference? Marx and Freud may not have known what they were going to find when they set out looking, but when they found it they were both pretty convinced they'd found the truth and propounded what they'd found as such. But doesn't the whole deconstructive enterprise start out with the supposition that whatever we find, we're not going to find a truth that can be handed on to disciples? Doesn't Derrida, in a sense, discourage disciples?

Question: It seems to me that even the methodology of deconstruction contains ideological biases.

BJ: I don't think deconstruction is a methodology in the sense that, at its best, it is constantly testing some previous set of operations in a new arena and hoping to find new strategies. From one book to the next Derrida does completely different things. People who imitate any one of those gestures—and it's the same with some followers of Marx and Freud—people who repeat a gesture that for Derrida was new are making it into a methodology, and it has its usefulness in that sense. But at its best deconstruction is a questioning of its own method all the time.

Q: Which constitutes a method?

BJ: Well, it becomes a method in the sense that it crystallizes in some form in the process of an argument or analysis. There is always an effect of method, as when Barthes speaks of an effect of reality, a reality-effect or method-effect produced by any careful analysis, but to say that it's repeatable in that form and applicable is to oversimplify the promise of the analysis.

Q: I've noticed a great deal of repetition of certain terms by deconstructors. There seems to be quite a jargon associated with deconstruction.

JHM: But not with Derrida. That's an important point. Terms like *différance* have sometimes been seized upon as essential to the deconstructive method. But in Derrida's work, each of those key terms (and there is now a growing list of them: the hymen, the supplement, the pharmakos and so on) arises out of a particular work, and though some claims are made in the course of the analysis for some kind of possible universalizing of terminology, the term is later replaced by another term and yet another term and yet another term. In that sense there is no one term in Derrida's work which is universalized, that's not provisional. But it may be that people have seized on one as being somehow fundamental.

In the case of de Man, whom we take as our archetypal deconstructor, the terms that he uses are traditional rhetorical terms which are, at least implicitly, neutral. That doesn't mean that there is not a certain ideology involved in deciding to use rhetorical terms, but they're not necessarily associated with one particular philosophy. A term like aporia or metonymy, metaphor and so on, is open in the sense that it may be used in different ways, and certainly the use de Man makes of such terms is very different than the use Roman Jakobson makes of them. So there are two methodological ways to free one's self from that danger which Barbara was talking about. And the real danger for deconstruction is that it would become a method, a kind of recipe where you'd sit down and say "I'm now going to deconstruct the 'Prelude.' "

One of the dangers is the freezing of a special jargon. The other would be the appropriation of a more general one. George Poulet's theory was (and it's not unlike Derrida's on this point) that you should draw the terminology with which you analyze a given author from that author or you should use terms that are of such general conceptual import that you can't say they belong to one or another philosophy. Now that's easy to say but it may not be that easy to do, and every critic has his own biases.

I wanted to say a word, if I may, about Freud and Marx. One of the things that deconstruction has done is to reread those authors, perhaps less actively Marx, but certainly Freud. If you look at a line of passages from Freud it is true that he is a dogmatist occasionally, saying "Now we know . . . ," "We know that . . . ," "This means . . . ," those are the kinds of formulations he uses. But on the other hand, there is that wonderful kind of locution which goes all the way from the *Studies in Hysteria* down to a very late paper, a beautiful one for narrative analysis, called "Constructions in Analysis." In the *Studies in Hysteria* he says that what you do is to draw the material out through one of those "clefts" I referred to this morning, and reconstruct it on the outside, thereby creating a picture of the hysterical trauma inside. And he says, "Whether this is really what happens or whether you're constructing something that you've made up, I will not now answer." That's exactly what he says in "Constructions in Analysis," in a slightly different way. He points out that sometimes in analysis you don't get back to the confirmation of the construction you've made until the patient says, "Yes, I remember now." That should happen because what you have done is to take the material and construct a story out of it and the patient should say, "Yes, I remember. I had forgotten that and now I remember it," and then the patient is cured. But what is very strange is that sometimes you don't get the memory but it works anyway. And Freud asks, "What does this mean," and he says once more, "I will not now answer," because obviously it puts in question the whole enterprise.

LM: Well, if that's what it means to read in a Freudian or a Marxist way, then I see no reason why deconstructive, Marxist, and Freudian readings can't go on in cooperation. . . . But in fact I doubt that it *does* mean this. There is, I think, an in-principle difference between deconstruction on the one hand and Marxism and Freudianism on the other; viz., the Marxist and the Freudian are searching for, even if they do not claim possession of, a truth the very nature and possibility of which the deconstructivist is making problematic. This does not imply that Marxists and Freudians cannot be open-minded or that a deconstructivist may not be a dogmatist. And there may be similarities in their ways of reading texts. But their *programs* are different, and the program of deconstruction is precisely to *solicit* the kind of programs Marxists and Freudians are committed to.

Q. Professor Miller spoke of a link between deconstruction and a possible Marxist critique, but the phrase that Barbara Johnson used was the link between deconstruction and political action. Now it seems to me that what is alive with a Marxist critique is the possibility of a realization within what we call the "real world" of some sort of controlled effect. Isn't there a significant difference, then, between talking about a critique and political action, and is there a link between deconstruction and the possibility of political action? Or do we have to keep our politics and our deconstruction separate?

Q: But a critique is a political action. Marxists would say that you can't make a critique which isn't also a political action.

Q: I understand the way in which a critique is also a political action. What I'm asking is, isn't there a horizon of expectation which, linked to that critique, will bring some sort of effective change in the world?

JHM: Not being a Marxist I'm not able to speak from a Marxist point of view, but I think you're right. From a deconstructive point of view it sometimes seems that the Marxists are impatient, that is, they want to make that jump from critique and analysis to political action more rapidly than it can be made and that's, I think, where the dialogue might begin.

For example, a small change in the curriculum of the university that involved the development of a new program which was to be imitated at other schools and involved some change in the way we teach (which is, after all, what we do), might be a much more effective method of political action in the long run. A lot of my colleagues at Yale have been very active with the clerical union. They feel that as Marxists they should be out there making speeches, signing things and acting with the workers, and that that's a political action which is consistent with the Marxism that also appears in their literary criticism. I'm not sure that is the right kind of political action. Changing one course just a little bit, changing the minds of the students at Yale or here at Oklahoma may be the really important mode of political action that we have open to us. It's a question of patience and impatience, and I'm not sure which side is right. I can see the critics on the other side saying, "OK, but by patience you mean wait until the year 2100. That's what they said about racism in the south—'give us time to work this out'—and we never would have." So I see the problem.

BJ: It depends on how you think change takes place. For example, Freud said that sometimes he saw exactly what the patient's problem was, but it was not accepted by the patient, the symptoms didn't disappear, nothing would happen and it would be a confrontation which would not produce change. Whereas the patient who was brought along step by step to recognize small changes, small omissions or symptomatic consistencies, eventually moved him or herself to a point where the same thing in another form was recognized. It could be that this is a kind of model for change, even in the political sense, that could end up being just as effective as a confrontational model of change or intervention.

Q: It appears to me that one of the effects of our reticence to talk about direct engagement in political action is to make the political metaphors that are so evident in deconstructive criticism seem inflated. I happened to jot down a phrase that Barbara Johnson used during one of her talks. It was, "deconstruction subverts the possibility of any authoritative interpretation." I wondered why one would use language that was so politically colored. It reminded me of the charge of "terrorist language" that has been occasionally leveled at the Yale School. I wonder what the alternatives would be to such a politically based, revolutionary metaphor. Instead of "subverting the possibility of authoritative interpretation," something like "constitutively open to interpretation," seems to me a near synonym without the political overtones; overtones which, on occasion, seem to me a kind of paper terrorism, an intellectual, academic terrorism that sometimes informs deconstructive writing.

BJ: I think that that kind of expression is one of the things that produces the Marxist critique of deconstruction—that deconstruction uses a rhetoric of political intervention or of revolutionary action and yet what does it do? It reads texts. In fact, these phrases function as hyperboles that produce their own sense of imperative. Now that may be a rhetorical effect, but it is a real one in the sense that it is picked up by a reader and by the reader's expectations. This kind of hyperbolic structure is provoking two different kinds of reaction. One is the literary establishment's perception that something trivial or dangerous or terroristic is going on in deconstruction, and the other is the political activists who find that deconstruction is all rhetoric and no action. This really does seem to be a function of deconstructive rhetoric, but I think that it's useful for deconstruction to produce those two reactions. What deconstruction wants to do by reading as it does is to keep moving, to keep trying to catch up with itself in that direction. Because if discourse has the kind of formative power that deconstruction seems to indicate that it does, then there is something very fundamental about questioning structures of discourse and how they operate. It is not as much of an exaggeration as it seems to say that something about authority structures could be subverted by an analysis of this type, if an analysis is enough to operate a subversion.

Q: This is in response to, a gloss really, on the last question—deconstructive rhetoric and the accusation of terrorism. If you study the accusation carefully you notice that what is really at issue is a classical lexicon or vocabulary dealing with a classically defined area of discourse (in this case ethics and politics) that goes right back to Aristotle. This ethic and its terminology, the idiom of the ethic, is constantly being dodged by someone like Derrida.

I was recently at a conference in Paris where some traditional French philosophers leveled the following accusation at Derrida: they said, "Why won't you talk about ethics? There is a heavy ethical charge in your writing, why won't you discuss ethics as such?" His answer was very interesting. Basically he said, "I do not wish for my discourse, for which I am responsible" (which is an ethical imperative) "to be appropriated by the classical discourse."

Now he has set himself a very difficult problem: he wishes to discuss ethics and ethical problems but has to "coin" terms and phrase the problems in ways that are not already eaten out and co-opted by the traditional formulae of the discourse. He says we must maintain an ethic whose highest priority is what he calls "respect for the Other"; the other person, the other institution, your colleague in the department or a student, the text certainly. This does not only obtain to the traditional domain of ethics but speaks of a rapport, a latent relation with the singularity of the Other. This necessitates what he calls a "strategy," (and that is a military term) which demands that we be always vigilant vis-a-vis traditional ethics. It requires a "calculus," a calculation of our relationship to these terms. This calculation involves a decision, for example, to defer the use of certain terms and then to use other terms that set you off court from traditional ethics.

Derrida was also accused of never using the term "dialogue." Now dialogue is a very interesting term for its political value, it has non-terrorist resonances and it certainly goes right back to Plato, and yet you find almost never in Derrida's texts any reference to a dialogue. What he does is to "negotiate." Negotiate is his term, his neologism if you will, the term he uses instead of dialogue. And he would never use "dialogue" because it's a term that you can't use without having to appropriate everybody back to Plato. "Negotiate" is a word taken directly from politics and it has several virtues, one of which is that it displaces the question into a fresher and more idiomatic language. Second, it actually forces the stakes out in the open. What the deconstructor does, if he's being scrupulous, is to open up and disclose the real violence at stake in apparently benign academic exchanges. By the way, this conversation occurred in a totally respectable academic context, and I've never been in a more violent, more "terroristic" atmosphere in my life. So terrorism is not too deep a word to use sometimes in this context.

Q: Do you have any particular thoughts on why deconstruction in America has caught on at first primarily among the Victorians and people working in Romantic poetry?

JHM: Has it? I don't know. Probably purely historical accident. But your phrase "deconstruction in America" has reminded me of something. It was suggested to Derrida that the lectures that he gave at Irvine just a few weeks ago be on "Deconstruction in America," but instead he decided to do them on Paul de Man. There's a section at the beginning where he explains why he didn't, and in which he says something that's related to your question. That is, as a Frenchman, he thinks of deconstruction as especially American, and he argues that it is even seen in Europe as being American, even though neither de Man nor himself is American, and his speculation on why that might be involves a political sense. It has something to do with the role of colleges and universities and the academy in general in the United States, that has made America a place where deconstruction has a kind of widespread force in academic life. Deconstruction has taken root here and been an important force. I had never really thought about that, but there may be something to it. In effect he's saying that it's a tautology to say deconstruction in America— deconstruction *is* America. He associates it, somehow, whether he's right or wrong, with something in American culture, some unthought out connection between this particular kind of questioning and our culture generally. He goes on to say that deconstruction is not simply a mode of literary criticism, it has institutional, political, technological, etc. aspects. That's his word, "aspects." It is another one of those terms like "negotiation" where he is very carefully skirting the argument that it has power in these areas. That is part of his thinking out of the question of the relation of deconstruction to the principle of reason. He would see the American university as an institution in the political life of America, as being the high point of that principle of reason. The computer revolution is taking place *here* and deconstruction has a very special relation to that, both being dependent on it and somehow criticizing or undermining or subverting it, to use Barbara's term.

LM: In connection with that, it always seemed to me that American literature would be a wonderful field for deconstructive reading. One thinks of Hawthorne and Melville and all that one could do with them. I know some of the people who are working on deconstructive readings of Pynchon and they're just about to come out. You're going to start seeing deconstructive readings of a lot of American authors. Deconstruction *is* America, it just takes a while to catch on.

Q: Professor Mackey, isn't it always necessary now, regardless of your so-called ideological position, to be a kind of relativist? Implicit in your earlier remarks was the idea that to be a Marxist or a Freudian excluded the possibility of being a relativist, and yet I would think that you would have to be. This morning when Professor Miller mentioned those four grounds of criticism, I'm never really quite sure whether you choose the ground or the ground chooses you. It's not necessarily an intellectual choice, it's a temperamental choice. At the same time, though, you also realize that it is only a partial truth. What I found implicit in your observation was the notion that finally you become trapped by your commitment.

LM: Well, I don't like the word relativist, but I think I like what you mean by it. And I certainly agree with what Hillis Miller said apropos of Marx and Freud. But I do think that things like the introduction to Jameson's last book, where you get the proclamation that Marxism is not another method of interpretation but the untranscendable horizon of all interpretation, sound like absolutist claims. Unless you revise your understanding of Marxism in such a way that you neutralize the absolutism in that claim. . . .

BJ: That might be another hyperbole.

LM: Well it certainly is a hyperbole, but hyperbole can be a way of cloaking absolutist assertions.

Q: I think we should be careful about assuming that Marxism and deconstruction have inherent affinities or intrinsic inclinations. On the one hand, we can take Barbara Johnson as representative of those practitioners who use Marxism and deconstruction simultaneously to interpret texts or structures. At the same time, however, deconstruction has been used and appropriated, not strictly as an instrument of its strategies, by people who have clear rightist inclinations and who, like Stanley Fish (who says outright, publicly, "I voted for Barry Goldwater and I stand for the establishment,"), will use it for their own purposes. In a recent article which appeared in *Critical Inquiry*, he uses this strategy to make it almost impossible to enable change or to produce change in social situations and institutions. His argument is very clever, ingenious really, but it demonstrates that there is no necessary relation between deconstruction and Marxism or leftist ways of thinking.

JHM: I think you've put your finger on something important. Let's take Derrida and Marxism, for example. If I understand Marxist criticism, it would culminate in an explanation which would have something to do with society and it would be satisfied with that. I see in Derrida a commitment to another kind of ultimate explanation which is not purely linguistic (and in that sense there is a difference between Derrida and de Man), that is present in Derrida's continuous interest in Heidegger, who is fundamental for him. There is a genuine ontological dimension in Derrida which might make it possible to say, if I could get him up against the wall on my four principles, that his choice would not be, as you might think, for language as the ultimate grounding explanation but in fact some version of the fourth one. In Derrida language does not come out clean, and that takes some explaining. We've had language for a long time and there are still a lot of problems. As George Eliot puts it, "You can't say what you mean without saying it some other way." I think if we had been able to clear language up we would have done so. Derrida's explanation for this strikes me as extra-linguistic. Of the seminars that he has given over the years since he's been doing that, it is the Heidegger ones that seem most fundamental. That strikes me as a real difference between Derrida and, as I understand it, Marxism.

The Marxist might explain *Daniel Deronda* by saying it's a novel about the displaced middle class in the late Victorian period. Their money came from things like slavery and sugar plantations and the novel says this, and that's what the novel means. Whereas Derrida might choose other parts of the novel and give an explanation which was also possible. He might say that the real explanation is a religious one, and George Eliot is telling us that Gwendolyn's real problem was in some way metaphysical or ontological. That strikes me as a genuine difference. I've talked to people about this before and they always say, "Can't you combine these?" I would be glad to be persuaded that you could because, I'm not going to say that you can't; but at this point it appears to me that ultimately you have to choose one, and that they are not reconcilable except in a hierarchical way.

Q: You seem to be casting Derrida in the role of a Zen master.

Q: I don't think that it is Professor Miller that casts Derrida as the Zen master, I think he casts himself with the sort of mystical, ultimately playful utterance that can't be pinned down. If history means anything it is that it was Derrida and Lacan and other Frenchmen who started deconstruction, working on the backs of Lévi-Strauss and ultimately back to Saussure. America's only claim to any of this would be Peirce who was a cry in the wilderness and not even understood in his own country. But you can't jump from Peirce to deconstruction. This is a French movement. The only possible argument you might make is that it is a movement that had to compete with other strong European movements. There was Sartre, Heidegger, Althusser, but in America there was almost a total vacuum caused by the death of the New Criticism, so that when deconstruction came, it came with a rush.

I hope that if academics can do anything it can make some meaningful distinctions, and I'm a little troubled by this linking of Marxism and deconstruction. When something like deconstruction comes in that is so impressive, people who also have Marxist tendencies will want to combine them. But ultimately—and I think Marx would agree—don't the dialectical process and economic oppression exist regardless of subjective looking-in? The "prison-house of language" has nothing to do with it, whereas deconstructors argue that everything is subjective and that meanings contain their opposites. It seems to me that this mindset leads to inaction. That doesn't mean that the person who deconstructs can't also head the local AFT union or the Progressive Labor Party. It seems to me that real Marxists looking at deconstruction, which is constantly finding binary oppositions everywhere, wouldn't be too patient with it, or shouldn't be.

Q: First of all, I think there are two implicit assumptions that you make that are somewhat erroneous. One is that the whole strategy of binary opposition is precisely what deconstruction wants to overcome, not foreground, the point being that binary opposition is a fiction in the text that structure has created and which deconstruction attempts to deconstruct. So the point is that there isn't symmetry in opposition, that it's not just finding binary oppositions, and that's the difference between deconstruction and structuralism.

The other point is about deconstruction as a French movement. It is true that it certainly has a French genealogy, but it does have Peirce behind it. Derrida explicitly substitutes Peirce's sign for Saussure's sign.

Moreover, it's interesting that one of the things that Derrida is doing is talking very much about there being no such thing as a single language, there are only languages. Crossing the borders between languages is one of the most important strategies which he undertakes and utilizes. If you notice there isn't a single text he's ever written that is in a single language.

Q: Yes, but wasn't it Professor Miller who wrote the article in *Deconstruction and Criticism* about guest and host being essentially the same? So binary opposition is very important in deconstructive analysis.

JHM: I think the point of my analysis was to show that it is not a binary opposition, that the guest turns into the host and the membrane is crossed over on both sides. You start out thinking in terms of the guest/host opposition as a binary opposition, but it doesn't work. I don't claim that that particular opposition has any large valence or applicability.

On the question of deconstruction as a French movement, there's a marvelous movement in the Moynahan interview with de Man which the *Yale Review* is going to publish, where, after a lot of talk about irony, Moynahan says, "Irony is especially French, isn't it?" and de Man replies, "Yes, that's the sort of thing you can say when you want to put something down." You can always say that it's the frivolous French.

I wanted to pick up on one other thing that you said because it links with some things that haven't come up yet, and that is your passing remark that deconstruction is all subjective. I think that is a mistake, partly because it's linked to another fundamental error that a lot of people make about deconstruction, which has something to do with the misunderstanding of Fish and reader-response criticism. It says that the text is a place of infinite free play, and that means that you can make the text mean anything you want. Nothing could be further from the truth about the actual examples we have of deconstruction as a mode of interpretation. Whatever complications Fish has added to his theory, in the end he will say that the text gives nothing whatsoever, it is absolutely empty to the interpretation. Therefore it is free, even though the freedom may be constrained either by an individual who is free to make the text mean what he wants or, in late Fish, interpretive communities that have agreed upon a reading, who say *Paradise Lost* means so and so. That, I don't think, is what deconstruction is about. It says, rather, that the text itself has this kind of homogeneity which a good reading will be coerced into responding to. It gives the priority to the text, not to subjectivity. Now that's not quite the same thing as saying that this is a critique of the idea of subjectivity or selfhood. It has to do with the act of reading and what I meant earlier by the ethics of reading, where the obligation is to the text and what the text does to you. There is a passage from Paul de Man's preface to Carol Jacobs' book, *The Dissimulating Harmonies* (Baltimore: Johns Hopkins, 1978), which, in effect, says that what takes place in any act of reading is what has to happen because of the words, not what one wishes to happen or expects will happen. When you read, in a way it's a no-lose situation; something's going to happen to you, the text is going to make a necessary occurrence take place even in the worst reading. That has nothing to do with subjectivity. It has to do with the language and your response to it. So the notion that it is a free-for-all is not what is at question here. There is a notion of free play, but that is a linguistic notion. I think this is a very important point.

Q: It occurs to me that if Marx or Freud enter into deconstructivist considerations, they enter in the form of a text. One of the first things you are going to have to do is establish that text of Freud's or Marx's after you have established your primary text. Criticism always adds to the primary text so that you have to rehabilitate the texts that you use as intertexts. But from what Professor Miller said this morning, any time you deal with, say, a Freudian critic who quotes Freud at you, what you ought to do is go pick up Freud. So what happens is you displace the criticism with another primary text. Is that right?

JHM: Yes. It might be helpful at this point to invoke the opposition between canonical and noncanonical readings of these grounding texts. It is a presupposition of de Man's criticism, and I think Derrida would agree, that the traditional, as he says, "canonical," readings of most of the major works are wrong; they are misreadings. De Man has an idea that occurs again and again in his work, it's one of the things that fascinates him. He says that if you are reading Rousseau and at a certain point you decide you had better go and see what the great experts on Rousseau have to say, you will discover that the critics make Rousseau say the exact opposite of what he really says. That's a de Manian hypothesis, of which he gives many examples. This is a very interesting phenomenon if it's at all true. Therefore, the canonical reading would be something else, something that happens because it has to happen in certain readers. What I was saying is that you can't rely on a canonical reading of Freud, Marx, anybody, on the basis of which you could then perform a Freudian or a Marxist reading of something else.

Q: Well it seems to me that two things happen. First the reading happens and then the writing about the reading happens. Hartman says that what you've got to do is read as though you were not going to write out of it and then, I suppose, go back and read it again as though you are going to write out of it. So what happens is that you bury that text if you deal with it as an independent reader who has to do the best he can with the thing. But it's almost impossible to write about a text without finding out what the canonical reading is and using it as a constructive motive through the material. It gives you a strong hand or some other kind of force to spring off of in the text.

JHM: But that's a very bold hypothesis and its radical nature should be recognized. What de Man is saying is, here's a professor, very distinguished, who has spent his whole life studying Arnold. He's one of the recognized experts on Arnold. I read him and then I read Arnold, and I find that there is no correspondence between the two. And he finds this as a kind of regular law. When people would ask Professor de Man on what basis he knew he was right and all the others were wrong he would just smile an enigmatic smile.

There is a famous example where the reading in question is the opposition between de Man's reading of Rousseau and Derrida's reading of Rousseau. There is some after-history to that essay in *Blindness and Insight* involving a little bit of change on both sides. In that essay, de Man is saying that Derrida has misread Rousseau, that he has really got Rousseau wrong, but he ascribes to himself as a sort of improvement on Rousseau and the deconstruction of Rousseau, the discovery that Rousseau had already done it for himself. Rousseau, as someone has observed, is almost the only author that de Man will give that kind of absolute allegiance to, and that's very interesting.

Q: I noticed a tendency this morning that when you find a rhetorical inconsistency in critical texts you usually assume that it is unwitting, but if you find a rhetorical inconsistency in a creative text you usually assume that the writer intended us to. Doesn't this privilege certain kinds of rhetorical inconsistencies?

BJ: That might be a definition of the difference between literature and criticism.

Q: But I just finished reading Hartman's *Criticism as Literature*, in which he says the critic has the same opportunities as the writer.

JHM: Hartman appears to say that criticism is really as good as creation, and there are a lot of violent attacks on that. It is obviously another one of those things that annoys a lot of people about deconstruction or about the kind of criticism that Hartman does. The way I would put it (though I'm not sure that it makes it any better) is to say that the critic has no particular privilege over the writer. He has the same problems, but it's not too likely that the critic would be able to get things better or more straight than the writer. He has no particular advantage, and in that sense criticism is like literature or philosophy. Kant has to use figures of speech to make that little jump. So does the creative writer and so, alas, does the critic. It's not that the critic is arrogating to himself or herself some privilege to be creative but that the critic is no better off, as far as language goes, and probably worse off than the creative writer. There is no special, purified, hygienic language of criticism which is going to avoid all those problems. I don't know whether, if Hartman were here, he'd agree with that, but I assure you that if I could write novels or poems I would do so.

Q: I'd like to comment on two things and I'm speaking as a Marxist. The first is that the name that has been absolutely absent from this whole conversation is Michel Foucault. I think that is interesting and I believe that he's very relevant to many of the topics we're discussing.

But I also wanted to pick up on what you said this morning about resistance. I think that it is the most important difficulty that we face. You specifically said, and I think you're absolutely right, that you encounter a tremendous resistance and that is certainly something that links deconstruction, Marxism and Freudianism: there is a tremendous resistance to all three separately. However, I also feel in all of you a resistance to a holistic interpretation which is very out of fashion right now, and is totalized as a negative abstract. I would insist that Marxism, as I understand it, could and should and must include all four of those groundings. Jameson uses a metaphor similar to the one you were finding in Kant except he calls it the "ultimate bedrock of the signified," a geological metaphor. He talks about the different levels in terms of plate techtonics, and it's interestingly similar to Kant's mole tunnels. What I would suggest is that the way to be truly open to these things is to realize that all of those groundings are, in fact, both real and necessary, and any view that privileges one or the other falsifies and distorts drastically when it does so; that to ignore, as vulgar Marxism does, the linguistic, is absurd. It makes the analysis simplistic, reductionistic.

Sure, for the purpose of analysis you may temporarily foreground one in order to do some thinking about it, but always in the knowledge that it's provisional and that you're bracketing the others temporarily with the plan to bring them forward as well, and thus the goal is a holistic or totalizing understanding. Not a tyrannically totalizing understanding, but a heuristic and open totalizing that encourages us to look for truth wherever we see resistance, and therefore to see these four areas as always affecting each other and as always already grounding whatever we study.

JHM: I've been waiting for someone to say something like that and it hadn't been said, so I gave the answer already, which is that I think what actually happens when you try to do that is that you make a hierarchy out of the four in which you're implicitly making the other three subservient to the fourth. In other words, I'm very dubious about whether what you, in your very generous and open way, are hoping can happen. Maybe that's my own totalizing tendency.

On the question of totalization, it's true that there is another point of difference between Marxism and deconstruction. One of the targets of deconstruction has been the notion of totalization. Perhaps, however, we should all remind ourselves that Marxism as a mode of literary criticism, putting aside Marxism as political economy or something else, is a diverse area. There is a difference between Althusser, Lukács and either of those two and Terry Eagleton, and either of those three and Fred Jameson, so one shouldn't say that there is a single, global Marxism. My understanding is that the notion of totalization is really fundamental in Lukács, and that it is capable of being seen as the inheritance of a Hegelian dialectical way of thinking, just as there is a more naive notion, at least in the Lukács that I've read, of representation than you would find in Jameson or Eagleton. So Marxism is a lot of different things.

Foucault has been in my mind and I was planning on bringing him up because it's often seen now in America as a choice between Derrida and Foucault. You can't have them both together, they are a kind of binary opposition. It's even east coast/west coast since Foucault clearly has a stronger valence or force at the moment in California, at Berkeley with people like Stephen Greenblatt and the journal *Representations*. It was to California that Foucault has gone recently. Of course it's not quite that simple, but I find it interesting: Why California-Foucault, New Haven-Derrida?

I was reading a paper by a graduate student of mine on Foucault recently in which he was talking about recent Foucault interviews but also an early one from 1968, that is to say, right in the middle of '68, which was called "A Response to the Question." In this interview Foucault was asked the question, "Why aren't you out there on the barricades? Why aren't you more politically active?" In the course of his answer what struck me was how close to Derrida the vocabulary he used was. He said, "Well, I want to be very scrupulous and keep myself open for a kind of plural future which will be without the kind of groundings that I fear will occur where we simply substitute one sort of mastery, one sort of traditional metaphysical thinking for another." That sounded to me like a Derrida-sort of answer. A lot of what I read made me want to read further in Foucault. And there were some recent things that I looked at that still sounded to me like Derrida in a lot of ways. However, I tried this thesis out on another graduate student who is probably more of a Foucaultian and he said "Yes, I'm writing an essay on that and I think you're wrong." He insisted that Derrida and Foucault are not the same, are really fundamentally different, and that choosing one rather than the other makes a lot of difference.

I don't know the truth about it, but I think if there is a danger it is in thinking of them as simply another one of those binary oppositions, because I don't think they are. Of course, they are almost absolutely silent about one another for strategic, to use Derrida's word, reasons.

Q: I was recently going through some of the early issues of *Signs* and I noticed that the kind of people that were writing it were very traditional women critics of literature, sociology and so forth, but by about 1977 or '78 there seemed to be a radical change in the language of feminists and feminist criticism, both cultural as well as literary. To what extent do you see deconstruction as affecting a stylistic or rhetorical change in feminist thinking, or do you see such a change?

BJ: I think that change has existed. There was some opposition between a certain kind of politically grounded American feminism and the kind of thing that was starting to come from France, either through French feminists or through the logical extension of deconstruction into feminism on a kind of ad hoc basis. Little by little, through the dialogue or the confrontations that those differences gave rise to, both sides did some rethinking and some changing.

Q: My question is directed primarily to Professor Miller. I appreciated your afterthoughts on genre this morning, and I think that your paper and the discussion we've had this afternoon are very important preparations for discussing a theory of genre. The question I'd like to ask you is this: do you see any progress to be made in a new theory of genre, or do you think that simply reclassifying or using classifications more tentatively is the route? Does the word classification exhaust the meaning of genre or are there other words that perhaps we should begin to use when we want to speak of the effects and the role of genre?

JHM: I don't think we can do without generic terms, but I don't see that anything much is lost in seeing them as, to some degree, artificial or as a result of a classification which was made for convenience. On the other hand, it seems to me still something to be thought and talked about. There may be certain genres that do have a kind of life which is more than simply historical convenience. The only example that I can think of where you could make this argument would be the elegy. If it is true that the process of mourning has a kind of intrinsic rhythm, then the structure of the elegy is not just a historical accident, but is something deeper which has a different sort of ground, in this case it would be a ground in psychology. I'd be happy if I could be persuaded that this was true, because I would then think that the genre of the elegy was not just an artificial classification, but was grounded in something that was more intrinsic and was, in a way, trans-historical. So, it's not just, for example, that Stevens' "Owl and the Sarcophagus" is an elegy because it goes through the same sequence as Whitman's "When Lilacs Last in the Dooryard Bloomed," but for some deeper reason which is not merely artificial or intertextual. But whether you could do that for the other genres I'm not so sure. At least it would be a hypothesis on the basis of which to begin thinking about genres in a way that was not merely negative, not merely saying, "they're just conveniences," "there's no such thing as the novel, and all we do is pour things into this preconception." I think generic considerations are a necessary ingredient in any criticism, if only because it's helpful to know that you are now reading a novel and not a newspaper.

Ronald Schleifer: I'm afraid we've run out of time. Thank you very much.

Part Two
Controversies

Gender Theory and The Yale School

Barbara Johnson
Harvard University

As Harold Bloom puts it in the opening essay of the Yale School's non-manifesto, *Deconstruction and Criticism:* "Reading well is not necessarily a polite process . . . . Only the capacity to wound gives a healing capacity the chance to endure, and so to be heard."[1] I hope, therefore, that my hosts will understand the spirit in which I will use them as the starting point for the depiction of a much larger configuration, and that by the end of this paper I will not have bitten off more of the hand that feeds me than I can chew.

In January of this year, shortly after the death of Paul de Man, I received a call from Robert Con Davis inviting me to attempt the painful and obviously impossible task of replacing de Man in a conference in which Geoffrey Hartman, Hillis Miller, and Paul de Man had been asked to speak about genre theory in relation to their own work. I was invited to speak, however, not about *my* own work but about de Man's. The reasons for this are certainly understandable. I could easily sympathize with the conference organizers' impulse: there is nothing I could wish more than that de Man had not died. But the invitation to appear as de Man's *supplément*—supplemented in turn by a panel of my own choosing—gave me pause. For it falls all too neatly into patterns of female effacement already well established by the phenomenon of the Yale School—and indeed, with rare exceptions, by the phenomenon of the critical "school" as such. Like others of its type, the Yale School has always been a Male School.

Would it have been possible for there to have been a female presence in the Yale School? Interestingly, in Jonathan Culler's bibliography to *On Deconstruction* Shoshana Felman's book *La Folie et la chose littéraire* is described as "a wide-ranging collection of essays by a member of the 'école de Yale.' "[2] Felman, in other words, *was* a member of the Yale School, but only in French. This question of the foreignness of the female language will return, but for now, suffice it to say that there was no reason other than gender why Felman's work—certainly closer to de

Man's and Derrida's than the work of Harold Bloom—should not have been seen as an integral part of the Yale School.

At the time of the publication of *Deconstruction and Criticism*, several of us—Shoshana Felman, Gayatri Spivak, Margaret Ferguson, and I—discussed the possibility of writing a companion volume inscribing female deconstructive protest and affirmation centering not on Shelley's "The Triumph of Life" (as the existing volume was originally slated to do) but on Mary Shelley's *Frankenstein*. That book might truly have illustrated the Girardian progression "from mimetic desire to the monstrous double." Unfortunately, this *Bride of Deconstruction and Criticism* never quite got off the ground, but it is surely no accident that the project was centered around monstrosity. As Derrida puts it in "The Law of Genre"—which is also, of course, a law of gender—"As soon as genre announces itself, one must respect a norm, one must not cross a line of demarcation, one must not risk impurity, anomaly, or monstrosity."[3] After all, Aristotle, the founder of the law of gender as well as of the law of genre, considered the female as the first distortion of the genus "man" en route to becoming a monster. But perhaps it was not *Frankenstein* but rather *The Last Man*, Mary Shelley's grim depiction of the gradual extinction of humanity altogether, that would have made a fit counterpart to "The Triumph of Life." Shelley is entombed in both, along with a certain male fantasy of Romantic universality. The only universality that remains in Mary Shelley's last novel is the plague.

It would be easy to accuse the male Yale School theorists of having avoided the issue of gender entirely. What I intend to do, however, is to demonstrate that they have had quite a lot to say about the issue, often without knowing it. Before moving on to a female version of the Yale School, therefore, I will begin by attempting to extract from the essays in *Deconstruction and Criticism* and related texts an implicit theory of the relations between gender and criticism. For the purposes of this paper, I will focus on the four members of the Yale School who actually teach full time at Yale. Since Derrida, the fifth participant in *Deconstruction and Criticism*, has in contrast consistently and explicitly foregrounded the question of gender, his work would demand far more extensive treatment than is possible here. I will confine myself to the more implicit treatments of the subject detectable in the writings of Bloom, Hartman, Miller, and de Man.

Geoffrey Hartman, ever the master of the throwaway line, has not failed to make some memorable remarks about the genderedness of the reading process. "Much reading," he writes in *The Fate of Reading*, "is indeed, like girl-watching, a simple expense of spirit."[4] And in *Beyond Formalism*, he claims: "Interpretation is like a football game. You spot a hole and you go through. But first you may have to induce that opening."[5]

In his essay in *Deconstruction and Criticism*, Hartman examines a poem in which Wordsworth, suddenly waylaid by a quotation, addresses his daughter Dora with a line from Milton's Samson that harks back to the figure of blind Oedipus being led by his daughter Antigone:

> A Little onward lend thy guiding hand
> To these dark steps, a little further on! (*DC* p. 215)

This is certainly a promising start for an investigation of gender relations. Yet Wordsworth and Hartman combine to curb the step of this budding Delilah and to subsume the daughter under the Wordsworthian category of "child," who, as everyone knows, is *Father* of the man. While the poem works out a power reversal between blind father and guiding daughter, restoring the father to his role of natural leader, the commentary works out its patterns of reversibility between Wordsworth and Milton. "Let me, thy happy guide, now point thy way / And now precede thee . . ." When Wordsworth leads his daughter to the edge of the abyss, it is the abyss of intertextuality.

While brooding on the abyss in *The Fate of Reading*, Hartman looks back at his own precursor self and says:

> In *The Unmediated Vision* the tyranny of sight in the domain of sensory organization is acknowledged, and symbol making is understood as a kind of "therapeutic alliance" between the eye and other senses through the medium of art. I remember how easy it was to put a woman in the landscape, into every eyescape rather; and it struck me that in works of art there were similar centers, depicted or inferred. (p. 6)

Yet the woman in Wordsworth's poemscape is precisely what Hartman does not see. And this may be just what Wordsworth intended. In the short paragraph in which Hartman acknowledges that there may be something Oedipal about this Oedipus figure, he describes the daughter as *barred* by the incest prohibition. The poem would then transmit a disguised desire for the daughter, repressed and deflected into literary structures. Yet might it not also be that Wordsworth so often used incest figures in his poetry as a way, precisely, of barring the reality of the woman as other, a way of keeping the woman in and *only* in the eyescape, making a nun out of a nymph? For the danger here is that the daughter will neither follow nor lead, but simply leave:

> the birds salute
> The cheerful dawn, brightening for me the east;
> For me, thy natural leader, once again
> Impatient to conduct thee, not as erst
> A tottering infant, with compliant stoop
> From flower to flower supported; but to curb
> Thy nymph-like step swift-bounding o'er the lawn,
> Along the loose rocks, or the slippery verge
> Of foaming torrents. . . .

The family romance takes a slightly different form in Hillis Miller's essay, "The Critic as Host." In that essay, Miller discusses Booth's and Abrams' image of deconstructive criticism as "parasitical" on the "obvious or univocal reading" of a text. Miller writes:

> "Parasitical"—the word suggests the image of "the obvious or univocal reading" as the mighty oak, rooted in the solid ground, endangered by the insidious twining around it of deconstructive ivy. That ivy is somehow feminine, secondary, defective, or dependent. It is a clinging vine, able to live in no other way but by drawing the life sap of its host, cutting off its light and air. I think of Hardy's *The Ivy-Wife.* . . .
>   Such sad love stories of a domestic affection which introduces the parasitical into the closed economy of the home no doubt describe well enough the way some people feel about the relation of a "deconstructive" interpretation to "the obvious or univocal reading." The parasite is destroying the host. The alien has invaded the house, perhaps to kill the father of the family in an act which does not look like parricide, but is. Is the "obvious" reading, though, so "obvious" or even so "univocal"? May it not itself be the uncanny alien which is so close that it cannot be seen as strange? (*DC*, p. 218)

It is interesting to note how effortlessly the vegetal metaphor is sexualized in Miller's elaboration of it. If the parasite is the feminine, then the feminine must be recognized as that uncanny alien always already in the house—and in the host. What turns out, in Miller's etymological analysis, to be uncanny about the relation between host and parasite—and by extension between male and female—is that each is already inhabited by the other as a difference from itself. Miller then goes on to describe the parasite as invading virus in the following terms:

> The genetic pattern of the virus is so coded that it can enter a host cell and violently reprogram all the genetic material in that cell, turning the cell into a little factory for manufacturing copies of itself, so destroying it. This is *The Ivy-Wife* with a vengeance. (*DC*, p. 222)

Miller then goes on to ask, "Is this an allegory, and if so, of what?" Perhaps of the gender codes of literature, or of criticism. But this image of cancerous femininity may be less a fear of takeover by women than an extreme version of the desire to deny difference. There is perhaps something reassuring about total annihilation as opposed to precarious survival. The desire to deny difference is in fact, in a euphoric rather than a nightmarish spirit, the central desire dramatized by the Shelley poems Miller analyzes. The obsessive cry for oneness, for sameness, always, however, meets the same fate: it cannot subsume and erase the trace of its own elaboration. The story told, again and again, by Shelley is the story of the failure of the attempt to abolish difference. As Miller points out, difference is rediscovered in the linguistic traces of that failure. But a failed erasure of difference is not the same as a recognition of difference. Unless, as Miller's analysis suggests, difference can only be recognized in the failure of its erasure.

If the parasite is both feminine and parricidal, then the parasite can only be a daughter. Miller does not follow up on the implications of a parricidal daughter, but Harold Bloom, whose critical system is itself a garden of parricidal delights, gives us a clue to what would be at stake for him in such an idea. In *The Map of Misreading* he writes:

> Nor are there Muses, nymphs who *know*, still available to tell us the secrets of continuity, for the nymphs certainly are now departing. I prophesy though that the first true break with literary continuity will be brought about in generations to come, if the burgeoning religion of Liberated Woman spreads from its clusters of enthusiasts to dominate the West. Homer will cease to be the inevitable precursor, and the rhetoric and forms of our literature then may break at last from tradition.[6]

In Bloom's prophetic vision of the breaking of tradition through the liberation of woman, it is as though the Yale School were in danger of becoming a Jael School.[7]

The dependence of Bloom's revisionary ratios upon a linear patriarchal filiation has been pointed out often enough—particularly in the groundbreaking work of Sandra Gilbert and Susan Gubar—that there is no need to belabor it here. I will therefore, instead, analyze the opening lines of Bloom's essay "The Breaking of Form" as a strong misreading of the question of sexual difference. The essay begins:

> The word *meaning* goes back to a root that signifies "opinion" or "intention," and is closely related to the word *moaning*. A poem's meaning is a poem's

complaint, its version of Keats' Belle Dame, who looked *as if* she loved, and
made sweet moan. Poems instruct us in how they break form to bring about
meaning, so as to utter a complaint, a moaning intended to be all their own.

(DC, p. 1)

If the relation between the reader and the poem is analogous to the
relation between the knight-at-arms and the Belle Dame, things are
considerably more complicated than they appear. For the encounter
between male and female in Keats' poem is a perfectly ambiguous
disaster:

LA BELLE DAME SANS MERCI
A Ballad

I
O what can ail thee, knight-at-arms,
  Alone and palely loitering?
The sedge has withered from the lake,
  And no birds sing.

II
O what can ail thee, knight-at-arms,
  So haggard and so woebegone?
The squirrel's granary is full,
  And the harvest's done.

III
I see a lily on thy brow,
  With anguish moist and fever dew,
And on thy cheeks a fading rose
  Fast withereth too.

IV
I met a lady in the meads,
  Full beautiful—a fairy's child,
Her hair was long, her foot was light,
  And her eyes were wild.

V
I made a garland for her head,
  And bracelets too, and fragrant zone;
She looked at me as she did love,
  And made sweet moan.

VI
I set her on my pacing steed,
  And nothing else saw all day long,

For sidelong would she bend, and sing
  A fairy's song.

VII

She found me roots of relish sweet,
  And honey wild, and manna dew,
And sure in language strange she said—
  "I love thee true."

VIII

She took me to her elfin grot,
  And there she wept, and sighed full sore,
And there I shut her wild wild eyes
  With kisses four.

IX

And there she lullèd me asleep,
  And there I dreamed—Ah! woe betide!
The latest dream I ever dreamed
  On the cold hillside.

X

I saw pale kings and princes too,
  Pale warriors, death-pale were they all;
They cried—"La Belle Dame sans Merci
  Hath thee in thrall!"

XI

I saw their starved lips in the gloam,
  With horrid warning gapèd wide,
And I awoke and found me here,
  On the cold hill's side.

XII

And this is why I sojourn here,
  Alone and palely loitering,
Though the sedge has withered from the lake,
  And no birds sing.

Rather than a clear "as if," Keats writes: "She looked at me *as* she did love, / And made sweet moan." Suspicion of the woman is not planted quite so clearly, nor quite so early. In changing "as" to "as if," Bloom has removed from the poem the possibility of reading this first mention of the woman's feelings as straight description. "As she did love" would still be the knight's own interpretation, but it would be an interpretation that does not recognize itself as such. Perhaps Bloom is here demonstrating what he says elsewhere about the study of poetry being "the study of what Stevens called 'the intricate evasions of as.' " By the end of the poem, it becomes impossible to know whether one has read a story of a knight enthralled by a witch or of a woman seduced and abandoned by a male hysteric. And the fine balance of that undecidability depends on the "as."

If the poem, like the woman, "makes sweet moan," then there is considerable doubt about the reader's capacity to read it. This becomes all the more explicit in the knight's second interpretive assessment of the woman's feelings: "And sure in language strange she said— / 'I love thee true.' " The problem of understanding the woman is here a problem of translation. Even her name can only be expressed in another tongue. The sexes stand in relation to each other not as two distinct entities but as two foreign languages. The drama of male hysteria is a drama of premature assurance of understanding followed by premature panic at the intimation of otherness. Is she mine, asks the knight, or am I hers? If these are the only two possibilities, the foreignness of the languages cannot be respected. What Bloom demonstrates, perhaps without knowing it, is that if reading is the gendered activity he paints it as, the reading process is less a love story than a story of failed translation.

That the question of gender is a question of language becomes even more explicit in an essay by Paul de Man entitled "The Epistemology of Metaphor."[8] Translation is at issue in that essay as well, in the very derivation of the word "metaphor." "It is no mere play of words," writes de Man, "that 'translate' is translated in German as '*übersetzen*' which itself translates the Greek '*meta phorein*' or metaphor." (p. 17) In all three words, what is described is a motion from one place to another. As we shall see, the question of the relation between gender and figure will have a great deal to do with this notion of *place*.

De Man's essay begins as follows:

Metaphors, tropes, and figural language in general have been a perennial problem and, at times, a recognized source of embarrassment for philosophical discourse and, by extension, for all discursive uses of language including historiography and literary analysis. It appears that philosophy either has to give up its own constitutive claim to rigor in order to come to terms with the figurality of its language or that it has to free itself from figuration altogether. And if the latter is considered impossible, philosophy could at least learn to control figuration by keeping it, so to speak, in its place, by delimiting the boundaries of its influence and thus restricting the epistemological damage that it may cause. (p. 13)

This opening paragraph echoes, in its own rhetoric, a passage which occurs later in the essay in which de Man is commenting on a long quotation from Locke. Locke concludes his discussion of the perils of figuration as follows:

> Eloquence, like the fair sex, has too prevailing beauties in it to suffer itself ever to be spoken against. And it is in vain to find fault with those arts of deceiving wherein men find pleasure to be deceived. (p. 15)

De Man glosses the Locke passage as follows:

> Nothing could be more eloquent than this denunciation of eloquence. It is clear that rhetoric is something one can decorously indulge in as long as one knows where it belongs. Like a woman, which it resembles ("like the fair sex"), it is a fine thing as long as it is kept in its proper place. Out of place, among the serious affairs of men ("if we would speak of things as they are"), it is a disruptive scandal—like the appearance of a real woman in a gentleman's club where it would only be tolerated as a picture, preferably naked (like the image of Truth), framed and hung on the wall. (pp. 15–16)

Following this succinct tongue-in-cheek description of the philosphical tradition as a men's club, de Man goes on to claim that there is "little epistemological risk in a flowery, witty passage about wit like this one," that things only begin to get serious when the plumber must be called in, but the epistemological damage may already have been done. For the question of language in Locke quickly comes to be centered on the question, "What essence is the proper of man?" This is no idle question, in fact, because what is at stake in the answer is what sort of monstrous births it is permissible to kill. Even in the discussion of Condillac and Kant, the question of sexual difference lurks, as when de Man describes Condillac's discussion of abstractions as bearing a close resemblance to a novel by Ann Radcliffe or Mary Shelley, or when Kant is said to think that rhetoric can be rehabilitated by some "tidy critical housekeeping." De Man's conclusion can be read as applying to the epistemological damage caused as much by gender as by figure:

> In each case, it turns out to be impossible to maintain a clear line of distinction between rhetoric, abstraction, symbol, and all other forms of language. In each case, the resulting undecidability is due to the asymmetry of the binary model that opposes the figural to the proper meaning of the figure. (p. 28)

The philosopher's place is always within, not outside, the asymmetrical structures of language and of gender, but that place can never, in the final analysis, be proper. It may be impossible to know whether it is the gender question that is determined by rhetoric or rhetoric by gender difference, but it does seem as though these are the terms in which it might be fruitful to pursue the question.

In order to end with a meditation on a possible female version of the Yale School, I would like now to turn to the work of a Yale daughter. For this purpose I have chosen to focus on *The Critical Difference* by Barbara Johnson.[9] What happens when one raises Mary Jacobus' question—"Is there a woman in this text?" The answer is rather surprising. For no book produced by the Yale School seems to have excluded women as effectively as *The Critical Difference*. No women authors are studied. Almost no women critics are cited. And, what is even more surprising, there are almost no female characters in any of the stories analyzed. *Billy Budd*, however triangulated, is a tale of three *men* in a boat. Balzac's *Sarrasine* is the story of a woman who turns out to be a castrated man. And in Johnson's analysis of "The Purloined Letter," the story of Oedipal triangularity is transformed into an endlessly repeated chain of fraternal rivalries. In a book that announces itself as a study of difference, the place of the woman is constantly being erased.

This does not mean, however, that the question of sexual difference does not haunt the book from the beginning. In place of a dedication, *The Critical Difference* opens with a quotation from Paul de Man in which difference is dramatized as a scene of exasperated instruction between Archie Bunker and his wife:

> Asked by his wife whether he wants to have his bowling shoes laced over or laced under, Archie Bunker answers with a question: "What's the difference?" Being a reader of sublime simplicity, his wife replies by patiently explaining the difference between lacing over and lacing under, whatever this may be, but provokes only ire. "What's the difference?" did not ask for difference but means instead "I don't give a damn what the difference is." The same grammatical pattern engenders two meanings that are mutually exclusive: the literal meaning asks for the concept (difference) whose existence is denied by the figurative meaning. As long as we are talking about bowling shoes, the consequences are relatively trivial; Archie Bunker, who is a great believer in the authority of origins (as long, of course, as they are the right origins) muddles along in a world where literal and figurative meanings get in each other's way, though not without discomforts. But suppose that it is a *de*-bunker rather than a "Bunker," and a de-bunker of the arche (or origin), an archie Debunker such as Nietzsche or Jacques Derrida, for instance, who asks the question "What is the Difference?"—and we cannot even tell from his

grammar whether he "really" wants to know "what" difference is or is just telling us that we shouldn't even try to find out. Confronted with the question of the difference between grammar and rhetoric, grammar allows us to ask the question, but the sentence by means of which we ask it may deny the very possibility of asking. For what is the use of asking, I ask, when we cannot even authoritatively decide whether a question asks or doesn't ask?

Whatever the rhetorical twists of this magnificent passage, the fact that it is framed as an intersexual dialogue is not irrelevant.

Another essay in *The Critical Difference*, a study of Mallarmé's prose poem "The White Waterlily," offers an even more promising depiction of the rhetoric of sexual difference. The essay begins:

If human beings were not divided into two biological sexes, there would probably be no need for literature. And if literature could truly say what the relations between the sexes are, we would doubtless not need much of it then, either. Somehow, however, it is not simply a question of literature's ability to say or not to say the truth of sexuality. For from the moment literature begins to try to set things straight on that score, literature itself becomes inextricable from the sexuality it seeks to comprehend. It is not the life of sexuality that literature cannot capture; it is literature that inhabits the very heart of what makes sexuality problematic for us speaking animals. Literature is not only a thwarted investigator but also an incorrigible perpetrator of the problem of sexuality. (p. 13)

But the prose poem in question ends up dramatizing an inability to know whether the woman one is expecting to encounter has ever truly been present or not. It is as though *The Critical Difference* could describe only the escape of the difference it attempts to analyze. This is even more true of the essay subtitled "What the Gypsy Knew." With such a title, one would expect to encounter at last something about female knowledge. But the point of the analysis is precisely that the poem does not tell us what the gypsy knew. Her prophecy is lost in the ambiguities of Apollinaire's syntax.

There may, however, be something accurate about this repeated dramatization of woman as simulacrum, erasure, or silence. For it would not be easy to assert that the the existence and knowledge of the female subject could simply be produced, without difficulty or epistemological damage, within the existing patterns of culture and language. *The Critical Difference* may here be unwittingly pointing to "woman" as one of the things "we do not know we do not know." Johnson concludes her preface with some remarks about ignorance that apply ironically well to her book's own demonstration of an ignorance that pervades Western discourse as a whole:

> What literature often seems to tell us is the consequences of the way in which what is not known is not *seen* as unknown. It is not, in the final analysis, what you don't know that can or cannot hurt you. It is what you don't *know* you don't know that spins out and entangles "that perpetual error we call life." (p. xii)

It is not enough to be a woman writing in order to resist the naturalness of female effacement in the subtly male pseudo-genderlessness of language. It would be no easy task, however, to undertake the effort of re-inflection or translation required to retrieve the lost knowledge of the gypsy, or to learn to listen with re-trained ears to Edith Bunker's patient elaboration of an answer to the question, "What *is* the difference?"

NOTES

1. "The Breaking of Form," in *Deconstruction and Criticism* (New York: The Seabury press, 1979), pp. 6, 5. Further references to this and other essays in the volume will be indicated in the text by the abbreviation *DC* followed by a page number.

2. Jonathan Culler, *On Deconstruction* (Ithaca, NY: Cornell University Press, 1982), p. 289.

3. *Glyph*, 7 (Baltimore: The Johns Hopkins University Press, 1980), pp. 203–04.

4. *The Fate of Reading* (Chicago: University of Chicago Press, 1975), p. 248.

5. *Beyond Formalism* (New Haven: Yale University Press, 1970), p. 351.

6. *A Map of Misreading* (New York: Oxford University Press, 1975), p. 33. I would like to thank Susan Suleiman for calling my attention to this quotation.

7. The story of Jael is found in Judges 4. Jael invites Sisera, the commander of the Canaanite army, into her tent, gives him a drink of milk, and then, when he has fallen asleep, drives a tent peg through his head and kills him. (I would like to thank Sima Godfrey for this pun.)

8. *Critical Inquiry*, 5 (1978).

9. Baltimore: The Johns Hopkins University Press, 1980.

The Politics of Deconstruction

Barbara Foley
Northwestern University

It is by now something of a commonplace that, despite its adversarial rhetoric, deconstruction possesses questionable value as a radical political *praxis*. Gerald Graff, for example, has argued that deconstruction's posture of rebelliousness is readily assimilable to the imperatives of advanced capitalist society, which in fact thrives off of verbal opposition.[1] Frank Lentricchia proposes that the poststructuralist project reinforces rather than subverts the reification to which it opposes itself; it is an "activity of textual privatization, the critic's doomed attempt to retreat from a social landscape of fragmentation and alienation." Deconstruction, he concludes, "does not isolate [the critic] from the mainstream conditions of modern society, but rather constitutes an academic elaboration of them."[2] Edward Said asserts that deconstruction fails as a political *praxis* because it lacks a political analysis. "Contemporary 'Left' criticism," he complains, "is vitally concerned with various problems stemming out of authority," but "nowhere in all this will one encounter a serious study of what authority is."[3] Terry Eagleton, who offers the sharpest political insights about Derridean deconstruction, argues that deconstruction actually rejects an oppositional politics, for it "provides you with all the risks of a radical politics while cancelling the subject who might be summoned to become an agent of them."[4]

While these and other critics have advanced some very useful arguments about the dead-endedness of the deconstructionist project in terms of politics, deconstruction has not yet been exposed in its full political bankruptcy. There are two main reasons for this. First, a number of critics argue that there are in effect two Derridas: a "false" Derrida who has been contaminated by conservative misappropriations, and a "real" Derrida who bears the torch of a truly liberatory program. Lentricchia, for instance, notes that "the fundamental aspects of Derrida's writing do not sanction a new formalism or a new hedonism," but that "the Yale Derrideans will not in the long run threaten every partisan of traditionalism, because they will turn out to be traditionalism's last formalist buttress."[5] Gayatri Spivak and Michael Ryan, as we shall see, argue that Derrida's bourgeois followers have simply ignored the radical—indeed, Marxist—implications of his project.

A successful critique of deconstruction's adversarial posture, I propose, would have to delineate the continuity between Derrida and his American disciples and demonstrate that Derrida's implied politics are essentially as supportive of the status quo as are theirs. This critique would also have to point out that any "Marxism" claiming to enlist deconstruction on its side is itself a highly dubious proposition, bearing more resemblance to a left pluralism than to a program for proletarian revolution. Second, deconstruction has not yet been routed from its lair because those critics who take exception to its propositions and implications have not provided adequate historical foundations for their ideological analyses. Deconstruction is chided for its separation from practice, its shallow conception of "opposition," its eradication of a purposive subject, its celebration of impotence—all very valid points. But most of these arguments operate from the assumption that deconstruction is an exclusively philosophical and literary-critical phenomenon and has not itself arisen from political practice. A historical materialist examination of the politics of deconstruction would have to locate deconstruction within the principal political movements and debates of our era—specifically, within the context of the notions of liberation and opposition generated by New Left theory and practice. We need not take seriously the claims of deconstructive politics, but we should understand their origins and take seriously their existence.

I shall not attempt a discussion of deconstruction's relation to the New Left in this brief essay, but I shall set forth an ideological critique that should prove useful to more extended historical analyses. First, I shall briefly examine the politics implicit in the critical perspective of the Yale School of deconstruction; I shall argue that this viewpoint signals not merely a patrician disregard for the world beyond literary discourse, but in fact a highly developed cluster of essentially conservative social attitudes. Next, I shall set forth the claims to oppositional status—both rhetorical and substantive—that are articulated in the work of Derrida. In this context, I shall also discuss the arguments of those who hold that Derrida's project is compatible with—or even supersedes—that of Marx. Then I shall refute the notion that Derrida's position is in any important sense "radical" and shall propose that his perspective is not so remote from that of the Yale critics as it might first appear. I shall suggest, finally, that Derrida's politics are assimilable only to an essentially revisionist and antirevolutionary reading of Marx—in other words, to a fundamental misreading of the Marxist text rooted in an antipathy to a Leninist epistemology and politics.

I recognize that, in much of what follows, I depart from a conventionally "literary" discussion of deconstruction and raise considerations and arguments that are not frequently found in critical writing. I focus my discussion as I do not because I find the literary applications and procedures of deconstruction unworthy of commentary, but because there is an urgent necessity for literary critics to examine more closely the concept of the "political" as it applies to our investigations. We are quite willing these days to admit that all discursive activity is in some sense political, but we are ordinarily quite imprecise, even naive, when actual political questions arise. In the case of deconstruction this kind of conceptual fuzziness is particularly unpardonable, since deconstruction poses itself as in some sense a radical, if not a revolutionary, practice, carrying implications far beyond the narrow domain of textual exegesis. It is the purpose of this essay to offer some interpretations of this "in some sense," and more generally, to clarify the relation between literary and political spheres of discourse and practice.

i

In an essay entitled "Criticism, Indeterminacy, Irony," Geoffrey Hartman sets forth a series of theses that can, I believe, be taken as paradigmatic of the political perspective implicit in the textual maneuverings of the Yale School. Indeterminacy, Hartman argues, constitutes delay, and

> the delay is intrinsic: from a certain point of view it is thoughtfulness itself, Keats's "negative capability," a labor that aims not to overcome the negative or indeterminate but to stay within it as long as is necessary. . . .
>
> Indeterminacy resists formally the complicity with closure implied by the wish to be understood or the communication-compulsion associated with it. Criteria of correctness or correspondence (of *truth*) may be caught up in this complicity. Indeterminacy functions as a bar separating understanding and truth. Understanding is not disabled but is forced back on the conditions of its truth: for example, the legitimacy of its dependence of texts.[6]

Indeterminacy necessitates, therefore, a "radical perspective" on "semiliterate" culture that has lost itself in a Babel of competing (mis)representations.

Every statement, idiom or idiolect has now its rights; and this situation of *surnomie*, where there are too many styles, terms, interpretations, leads to a low-grade *anomie* that is expressed in TV sitcom. . . .

There is no presence; there is only representation and, worse, representations. The crisis focuses on that, not on language as such. It is a crisis of *evidentiality*. How do we save phenomena that cannot save themselves?

Hartman therefore calls for "resistance . . . to conversion of representation into presence," a resistance that presumably will be conducted under the aegis of deconstruction. He concludes,

No wonder some are scared witless by a mode of thinking that seems to offer no decidability, no resolution. Yet the perplexity that art arouses in careful readers and writers is hardly licentious. It is the reality: it is only as strange as truth. It recalls the prevalence of propaganda, both in open societies that depend on conversation, jawboning, advertising, bargaining, and in controlled societies that become sinister and inquisitorial, adding to their torture chambers the subtlest brainwashing and conditioning devices without giving up the brazen and reiterated lie. Can any hermeneutics of indeterminacy, any irony however deeply practiced and nurtured by aesthetic experience, withstand either society while they are still distinguishable?

We may note a few things about this passage. To begin with, its rhetoric is emphatically liberatory. Indeterminacy furnishes a "radical" perspective. It is "labor" that will hold out "as long as is necessary" against an instrumentalist reductionism. It "resists" the "complicity with closure" of a naive logocentrism; moreover, rather than "licentious-[ness]" it is "thoughtfulness itself." It proposes an unabashed willingness to confront the open-endedness necessary for critical thought, even though the less courageous are "scared witless" by a "mode of thinking that seems to offer no decidability, no resolution." Deconstruction stands forth, indeed, as the only sane discourse amidst the Philistine "jawboning" of bourgeois society, as the final ironic gesture of resistance against the torture chambers of countries behind the Iron Curtain.

A liberatory program, indeed, one that would presume to rescue us from various and sundry kinds of reification and oppression in the modern world. But what substantive social analysis underlies this apocalyptic claim? To begin with it appears that the "crisis in evidentiality" in late capitalist culture, epitomized by the *"anomie* . . . expressed in TV sitcom,"* is attributable to a state of widespread popular "semiliteracy," in which—horrors—"every statement, idiom or idiolect now has its rights." It is odd that an advocate of a "radical perspective" should object so strenously to the extension of "rights" to different linguistic communities: one ought rather to expect that a proponent of textual freeplay would welcome any diversity that would call into question the logocentric models enforced by the dominant linguistic order. In this attack on *surnomie* and *anomie*, Hartman may well wish to target the organs of propaganda in consumer culture; but his criticism of the media converges in a telling way with a revulsion against the consumers of mass culture themselves, who are presumably accountable for the low quality of the communications they receive from New York and Hollywood. Indeed, we might note, to the extent that Hartman sets himself in opposition to the late capitalist social formation at all, he focuses exclusively on its characteristic mode of exchange—the modern form of the "cash nexus"—and on the linguistic conventions that accompany this mode of exchange. Hartman does not seem much concerned with the forms of production and distribution that undergird the contemporary system of exchange: his is essentially a formalistic argument, reflecting on a mode of intercourse—or on those who engage in that intercourse— rather than upon real relations of class and power.

Moreover, we should not slough over the fact that Hartman articulates a simple old-fashioned anti-communism in his assignation of a liberatory posture to the deconstructive project. One does not need to be an advocate of Soviet or Eastern European forms of government (I certainly am not) to see the speciousness of the assumption that he posits as "original" and "present" grounds for his argument—e.g., his opposition of "open" and "controlled" societies. One might question the "radicalism" of a perspective that so complacently assumes that American society is "open" for all its inhabitants. Finally, we should note that, in traditionally elitist fashion, Hartman places his hopes for the future on the class of literary intellectuals, who, as possessors of a critical "irony practiced and nurtured by aesthetic experience," are the only ones capable of "resisting" or "withstanding" the totalitarian tendencies of twentieth-century mass cultures. While this statement clearly expresses a patrician bias, it does so in a particularly significant manner. The intractability of social reality is assumed in advance, and the intellectual's freedom therefore consists in his or her occupation of a position on the margins that entails little or no concrete social responsibility.

I have quoted and then criticized Hartman's statement at some length because it is necessary, I believe, to go beyond the commonly held estimate that the Yale Derrideans are simply somewhat removed from more urgent social realities. Gayatri Spivak articulates this estimate when she argues for a disjunction between Derrida and his American disciples and invokes as an analogy Walter Benjamin's distinction between Brecht's alienation techniques and those of the Romantic Ironists. "All that [Romantic Irony] demonstrates," declared Benjamin, "is the philosophical sophistication of the author, who, while writing his plays, always has at the back of his mind the notion that the world may, after all, be just a stage."[7] The judgment carried by this parallel does not go nearly far enough: the conviction that all the world is a stage necessitates, in Hartman's case at least, an unmistakable disdain toward the people who are stuck with the job of actor. Besides, the American deconstructionists would probably be happy enough to grant Spivak's parallel with the Romantic Ironists, merely adding that their strategy of indeterminacy entails not "licentious[ness]," but "thoughtfulness itself." In other words, it is important to realize that the Yale critics' conservatism is hardly restricted to critical and literary matters alone, for they are perfectly willing to admit to a "traditional" stance in this sphere. As J. Hillis Miller has stated, "My instincts are strongly preservative and conservative. I believe in the established canon of English and American literature and in the validity of the concept of privileged texts."[8] We must recognize that the concept of "privileged texts" goes hand in hand with the concept of privileged people, and that the Yale formulation of undecidability can be interpreted to facilitate positions that are distinctly anti-working class, anti-communist, and even racist.

ii

But what can be said of Derrida himself? Can it be charged that he subscribes to the same cluster of attitudes that I have attributed to Hartman? In order to answer these questions, we must examine the grounds on which Derridean deconstruction makes its claim to oppositional status. In what follows, I do not, of course, propose anything like an exhaustive account, or even a comprehensive summary, of the deconstructionist program. I simply attempt to isolate what I see as being deconstruction's most significant claims to a liberatory philosophical method.

Before I undertake an inquiry into the substance of Derrida's argument, however, I would like to note that Derrida's rhetoric, even more than Hartman's, is characterized by an idiom of adventurousness and subversion. If words could kill, the last vestiges of Western metaphysics would now be six feet under. In his early essay "Structure, Sign and Play in the Discourse of the Human Sciences" Derrida threw down the gauntlet. The deconstructive practitioner, he boasted, must relinquish all longing for presence, "play the game without security," and engage in an "affirmation of a world of signs" that "determines the non-center otherwise than as the loss of center."[9] In "Différance," he continued, "in the delineation of deconstruction everything is strategic and adventurous. Strategic because no transcendent truth present outside the field of writing can govern theologically the totality of the field. Adventurous because this strategy is not a simple strategy in the sense that strategy orients tactics according to a final goal, a *telos* or theme of domination, a mastery and ultimate reappropriation of the field."[10] In "Living On: Border Lines," he proposed that "all organized narration is 'a matter of the police,' " insofar as it posits a "narratorial voice [that] is the voice of a subject recounting something, reinventing an event or a historical sequence, knowing who he is, where he is, and what he is talking about."[11] In *Positions*, where he clarified and defined the essential terms of deconstructive practice, Derrida claimed that the strategy of binary opposition characteristic of all Western metaphysics entails not "the peaceful coexistence of a *vis-à-vis*," but a "violent hierarchy." It is the goal of deconstruction, accordingly, to "overturn," "displace," and "transgress" this hierarchy; its strategy of undecidability "resists" and "disorganizes" binary opposition. And, unlike "representation," which simply "castrates," and even "polysemia," which remains committed to a "teleological and totalizing dialectics," dissemination "marks an irreducible and *generative* multiplicity."[12] Even if one did not follow the details of Derrida's argument, it would be difficult to miss its emancipatory—indeed, messianic—tone.

I shall in a moment return to Derrida's language, for its explosive rhetoric is, I think, not an incidental feature, but rather a constitutive part of Derrida's characteristic mode of argument. Derrida's claim to a disruptive and oppositional stance rests, it seems to me, on three propositions that are closely interrelated. To begin with, he posits that binary opposition is not merely a linguistic phenomenon, but in fact a strategy necessary to class rule: language is never innocent of the relations of power in which it is enmeshed. Binary oppositions such as internal/external, center/margins, fiction/nonfiction, male/female, West/Third-World—the list is virtually endless—are encoded in social realities. A political act of exclusion or subordination masks itself as a feature neutrally present in language (and representation) itself. Deconstruction seeks to counter this hegemony not by "constituting a third term" or "abolishing" the opposition, but by exposing its internal contradictions: any other strategy, Derrida argues, would end up "resurrecting" the very exclusionary mode of thought that it seeks to vanquish. Deconstruction is therefore a "technique of trouble,"[13] aiming not to substitute one authority for another, but rather to undermine the epistemological grounds upon which any authority presumes to rest. It "sounds the knell of the classicum,"[14] revealing that boundaries—whether generic or otherwise—denote property relations in a textualized terrain.

In keeping with this assault upon the power relations encoded in language, deconstruction calls into question the premises both of naming and of arguments based upon naming, pointing out that term which posits itself as the "origin" of a logical chain is in fact the product of a whole process of prior textualization, a process that is inevitably political. The presumption of a "referent" that is transparently "present" through language is a strategy characteristic of Western metaphysical thought in all its modes, declares Derrida. A deconstructive recuperation of discourse, by contrast, reveals that "presence" is not the "absolutely central form of Being but . . . a 'determination' and . . . an 'effect.' " Accordingly,

> the present becomes the sign of the sign, the trace of the trace. It is no longer what every reference refers to in the last analysis. It becomes a function in a structure of generalized reference. It is a trace, and a trace of the measure of the trace.
>
> Thereby the text of metaphysics is *comprehended*. Still legible; and to be read.[15]

Not only binary opposition, then, but also the logocentrism of the "longing for presence," that operates as the logical premise to binary opposition, is exposed in its complicity with existing institutions of power. Placing the "text of metaphysics" *sous rature*, deconstruction exposes the text's contradictory nature—not by negation, but by "différance." Indeed, Derrida claims, this technique is much more dangerous to bourgeois hegemony than is any "revolutionary" discourse that unproblematically assumes its capacity to represent itself by means of inherited linguistic formulations. Speaking of the "politico-institutional problem of the University," he declares:

> What this institution cannot bear, is for anyone to tamper with . . . language, meaning *both* the *national* language *and*, paradoxically, an ideal of translatability that neutralizes this national language. It can bear more

readily the most apparently revolutionary ideological sorts of "content," if only that content does not touch the borders of language . . . and of all the jurido-political contracts that it guarantees. [16]

Indeed, Derrida argues, logocentrism is "the matrix of idealism. Idealism is its most direct representation, the most constantly dominant force." Accordingly, "if matter . . . designates . . . radical alterity (I will specify: in relation to philosophical oppositions), then what I write can be considered 'materialist.' "[17] While, as we shall see shortly, Derrida has carefully steered clear of a confrontation with "the text of Marx," he lays claim to an enlightened epistemological position on grounds similar to those invoked by Marx.

Derrida ordinarily carries out his project of deconstructing Western metaphysics on a fairly high level of abstraction, but occasionally he articulates the more concrete political implications of his project. In "The Ends of Man"—delivered, he is careful to note, amidst the events of May, 1968—he pointed to the correspondences between the violence of the West's "linguistic" relationship to the rest of the globe and its "ethnological, economic, political, military relationships." He stated that a "radical trembling can only come from the *outside*," meaning, presumably, the "other" of the West—the oppressed nations and peoples of color—and urged that the task of those "inside" is, meanwhile, to engage in the dual deconstructive activity of overturning and transgressing. [18] In "The White Mythology," he expanded upon the racist and imperialist implications of the strategy of binary opposition:

> Metaphysics—the white mythology which reassembles and reflects the culture of the West: the white man takes his own mythology, Indo-European mythology, his own *logos*, that is, the *mythos* of his idiom, for the universal form of thought he must still wish to call Reason . . . White mythology—metaphysics has erased within itself the fabulous scene that has produced it, the scene that nevertheless remains active and stirring, inscribed in white ink, an invisible design covered over in the palimpsest. [19]

Like Roland Barthes' *Mythologies*, which unmasks the ideological representations justifying colonial and neocolonial rule, Derrida's text aligns itself—at least rhetorically—with liberation movements against European and American hegemony.

Derrida proposes, in short, that the deconstructive project is not self-indulgent word-play, but an epistemological practice possessing the capacity to expose and disrupt the ideological stratagems by which advanced capitalist society legitimates itself. He has therefore been careful to point out the various misconstruals of deconstruction that might end up divesting his project of its radically adversary quality. He has frowned, for example, upon those American uses of deconstruction that produce "an institutional closure"[20] stabilizing current power relations. He has argued, moreover, that traditional liberal freedom of speech should not be allowed to represent itself as freedom from domination. "It would be illusory," he declares,

> to believe that political innocence has been restored, and evil complicities undone, when opposition to them can be expressed in the country itself, not only through the voices of its own citizens but also those of foreign citizens, and that henceforth diversities, i.e. oppositions, freely and discursively relate to one another. That a declaration of opposition to some official policy is authorized, and authorized by the authorities, also shows, precisely and to that extent, that the declaration does not upset the given order, is not *bothersome*.[21]

It is clear that Derrida has a much more sophisticated understanding than Hartman of the strategy of liberal co-optation. He has insisted, in addition, that deconstruction aspires not simply to "neutralize the binary oppositions of metaphysics [by] residing within the closed field of these oppositions, thereby confirming it," but instead to "overturn" and "transgress" and "displace" in a double gesture that is simultaneously negative and positive.[22]

Reading Derrida along the lines I have set forth here, Gayatri Spivak and Michael Ryan have argued that Derrida's methodology is eminently compatible with that of Marx and in fact supplements and buttresses Marx's work on ideology in important ways. Spivak, in a review of Derrida's *Limited Inc. abc*, describes deconstruction as

> a practically fractured yet persistent critique of the hidden agenda of ethico-political exclusion; a sustained though necessarily fragmented stand against the vanguardism of theory; and, most importantly, a call to attend to the ever-askew "other" of the traditional disciplines; the need persistently to analyze that "confrontation," to figure out and act upon that "something like a relationship" between "ideology" and "social production" which, non-self-identical, will not keep us locked in varieties of isomorphism. These are enabling principles far more than a constant cleaning-up (or messing-up) of the language of philosophy, although the importance of this latter is not to be underestimated. If the "other that is not quite the other" were to be conceived of as political practice, pedagogy, or feminism—simply to mention my regional commitments—one might indeed look for "revolutions that as yet have no model."[23]

The effect of the deconstructionist project, Spivak concludes, goes "rather further than a new school of literary–philosophical criticism, or even a mere transformation of consciousness. Presumably, according to Spivak, deconstruction can aid in the transformation of that materiality upon which transformed consciousness will operate.

Spivak is, we should note, by no means oblivious to the weaknesses to which many literary deconstructors are prone. Participating in the Cérisy seminar dedicated to an examination of "la politique" and "le politique" in the work of Derrida—the seminar significantly entitled *Les Fins de l'homme*, after Derrida's apocalyptic text of 1968—she decried the tendency of deconstruction to "marginalize" the question of political economy and to place philosophical discourse at the center, thus practicing the very exclusionary operation against which Derrida has warned. She also noted that more than discourse is at stake where questions of power are concerned: "Le corps du travail, bien qu'il soit un texte, n'est certainement pas un texte parmi d'autres."[24] The challenge facing deconstruction, she argued, is to incorporate the concerns of Marx, who, in his defetishization of the mysteries surrounding exchange value, undertook "une confrontation massive de la philosophie et de son autre complice. Philosophiquement parlant, il y a là une belle aporie, à partir de laquelle une lecteur subtile pourrait montrer un Marx deconstructeur avant la lettre." Were deconstruction to take on this task, she concluded, it could become "un instrument politique puissant," directed "vers les femmes, vers le monde non-occidentale, vers les victimes du capitalisme." Even though, she concedes, the Derrida who in 1968 called for an "ébranlement radical" "n'invoke plus ce project," nonetheless his methodology makes possible—indeed, she implies, necessitates—such a *rapprochement* between the texts of Marx and Derrida.

Ryan's *Marxism and Deconstruction: A Critical Articulation*—which is dedicated to Spivak—attempts to articulate the terms of such a *rapproachement*. The central revolutionary feature of Marx's thought, Ryan proclaims, consists in its capacity to decenter the "originary" presuppositions of bourgeois ideology. Thus in his assault upon classical political economy's attempts to naturalize and fetishize such historical products as property, wage labor, rent, and capital, Marx enacted a methodological deconstruction profoundly akin to the epistemological rupture contained in Derrida's formulations of "différance" and undecidability. Indeed, Ryan argues, Marx and Derrida deploy very similar strategies in their critiques of positivism, idealism, naturalism, and objectivism. By contrast, Ryan argues, the theory and practice of Leninism is founded in a logocentric paradigm that equates meaning with the vanguard party, thereby eliminating that play of difference which consitutes the essence of revolutionary activity. Leninism, he contends, is "exclusive, elitist, hierarchical, [and] disciplinarian."[25] A truly radical appropriation of Marxism, Ryan argues, would abandon the totalitarian epistemology implicit in the Leninist program and pursue a "radical democracy" that would retain bourgeois democratic freedoms and "displac[e] and defus[e] . . . power relations." For Ryan, Marx's discourse is privileged to subvert the logocentrism not only of bourgeois rule but also of Leninist and post-Leninist socialism. In place of the authoritarian category of "representation," it proposes the radical discursive mode of "metaphor," which, Ryan claims, always denies definitive (and therefore totalitarian) closure to the propositions it entertains.

While Spivak and Ryan argue that deconstruction's oppositional posture consists largely in its alignment with Marxism, it is important to point out that other theorists have used the categories of deconstruction to propose a—presumably radical and liberatory—deconstruction of Marxism itself. Stanley Aronowitz, for example—in an essay significantly entitled "Towards a New Strategy of Liberation" in his *The Crisis in Historical Materialism*—deploys a Derridean vocabulary in his critique not only of bourgeois strategies of hegemony but also of Marxism's presumed failure to subvert that hegemony. Speaking of the antirevolutionary role played in recent decades by both Western and Eastern European Communist parties, Aronowitz argues, "The left, because of its claim to a master discourse—its 'scientific' claims—becomes the most indefatigable enemy of the opposition in those countries where it 'represents' the masses within the state."[26] In other words, the revisionist policies of the Eurocommunist parties are, for Aronowitz, traceable not to class-collaborationism within the working-class movement, but to a fundamental error in Marxism's claim to totalize the dialectic of historical development by positing the primacy of the class contradiction. "Marxism's economic *logocentricity* has constituted its major weakness, both theoretically and politically," he declares. In working out a "new strategy of liberation," then, the left must fashion a "new historic bloc" built upon "the micropolitics of autonomous oppositional movements" rather than upon the notion of class. This "new historic bloc" would have to "become anti-hegemonic as a political and social principle, recognizing the *permanence* of difference." While Aronowitz's differences with Spivak and Ryan are obvious—they see Marx as a protodeconstructionist, while he sees Marx as wedded to the "bourgeois rationalist order"—it is nonetheless suggestive that all three invoke the language of undecidability and rupture in their prognostications for social change.

iii

If Derrida has been so careful to disavow any connection with those critical appropriations that would tame the disruptive character of the deconstructive project, and if his leftist adherents have deployed Derridean concepts in their critiques of racism, imperialism, and sexism, can Derridean deconstruction be dismissed as inassimilable to a radical politics? Can one assert that Derrida's continuity with the Yale School is more significant than his affinity with a radical analysis of modern capitalist social relations? I believe that one can—and should—still argue that the political implication of Derrida's project is fundamentally anti-progressive—but that in order to make this argument, one must pursue the critique of Derrida beyond the usual sorts of objections that are made to deconstruction's solipsism or its denial of objective reality. For example, M. H. Abrams' complaint that a deconstructive reading is "parasitical" on an "obvious or univocal" reading[27] is itself highly vulnerable to a deconstructive "overturning," since it posits as "original" an authoritative textual appropriation that is necessarily constituted by dominant critical conventions. A humanist or positivist critique of Derrida's project is not sufficient. If one seeks to understand the political bankruptcy of deconstruction, I believe, one must grant its occasional value as an instrument of ideological exposé and must admit that its denial of self-evidence is not necessarily tantamount to a subjectivist relativism. But then one must confront the essential flaw in Derrida's project—namely, its fundamental antipathy to centralism, an antipathy that is shared by all Derrida's supporters on the left and that, in my view, finally vitiates their liberatory postures as well as his. If my endorsement of Leninist politics brings down on me the disapproval of some who might otherwise agree with my critical description of deconstruction, so be it: it is high time that a critique of deconstruction undertaken from a Marxist-Leninist perspective be distinguished from one mounted from the vantage point of liberalism.

Before confronting directly the substance of Derrida's claims to oppositional status, however, I would again like to come back to the question of style. For the messianic overtones of Derrida's rhetoric raise real problems for his claim to have superceded the metaphysical operations of binary opposition. Derrida's language—which, he would be the first to admit, can hardly be neutral in its procedures of reference, however much it may self-critically circle back on itself—implies a profoundly dualistic view of philosophical debate. Indeed, Derrida's entire universe is essentially Manichean, for it is characterized by an incessant battle between the two sides of its Force. The bad side of the Force comprises such oppressive operations as domination, mastery, appropriation and reappropriation, presence, representation, telos, totality, fixity, castration, and above all—the evil Emperor— logocentrism. On the good side of the Force are rallied such friendly creatures as rupture, différance, trace, heterogeneity, dispersal, autonomy, dissemination, refusal of mastery, and—the blond, blue-eyed Luke Skywalker—undecidability. While Derrida proposes to overturn and transgress binary opposition, it is difficult to see how the rhetorical operations generated by such a dualism can do anything other than perpetuate the linguistic adjudication of a real, privileged interior, in contradistinction to a false, derivative exterior. The margins have simply taken over the role of the center.

If the rhetoric of Derrida's prose leads us to wonder whether there might not be a logical contradition in his strategy of argument, a closer scrutiny of its substance only confirms this suspicion. For, *pace* Spivak and Ryan, I would argue that there is little radical utility in a program that hypostatizes its refusal of mastery and militates against the formulation of any "third term" that would articulate and concretize its supression of the exclusionary operations of metaphysical thought. While I would not choose to argue that, in its specific propositions, Derrida's argument is as complacent and elitist as that of the Yale critics, I would assert that his methodology leads logically enough to the kind of criticism that they practice.

I would propose, first, that Derrida's refusal to "transcend" binary opposition leads to a re-fetishization of the very metaphysical pain to operations that it has taken such pains to defetishize. While Spivak and Ryan argue quite emphatically that Marx's procedures of critique are essentially comparable to those of Derridean deconstruction, they are, I believe, fundamentally wrong. Consider the strategy of defetishization deployed in the following excerpt from the *Grundrisse*:

> The conditions and presuppositions of the *becoming*, of the *arising*, of capital presuppose precisely that it is not yet in being but merely in *becoming*; they therefore disappear as real capital arises, capital which itself, on the basis of its

own reality, posits the conditions for its realization. Thus e.g. while the process in which money or value for itself originally becomes capital presupposes on the part of the capitalism an accumulation—perhaps by means of savings garnered from products and values created by his own labour etc., which he has undertaken as a *non-capitalist*, i.e., while the pre-suppositions under which money becomes capital appear as given, external *presuppositions* for the arising of capital—neverthe[less], as soon as capital has become capital as such, it creates its own presuppositions, i.e. the possession of the real conditions of the creation of new values *without exchange*—by means of its own production process. These presuppositions, which originally appeared as conditions of its becoming—and hence could not spring from its *action as capital*—now appear as results of its own realization, reality, as *posited by it*—*not as conditions of its arising, but as results of its presence.*[28]

Here Marx dissects the self-evidence of the binary opposition wage-labor/capital, revealing that these terms, rather than serving as "origins" of a scientific discussion of political economy, are themselves products of an extensive prior textualization. Recognition of process, for Marx, defetishizes "presence"; "becoming" is the key to "presence." He demonstrates at length in *Capital* that this opposition is a function of a historical specific process of proletarianization—specifically, the wresting of the peasantry from the land—rather than an eternal truth of the human condition, as the political economists of his time would have it.

But Marx was a dialectician, not a deconstructionist. He described the historical roots of the opposition, wage-labor/capital, not simply in order to demonstrate its historicity as the negation of feudal social relations, but in order to supercede it with a "third term"—communism—that would serve as the negation of that negation. Oppositions are, for Marx, dialectical rather than static: the bourgeoisie may be at present the principal aspect of the opposition bourgeoisie/proletariat, but in time the proletariat becomes the principal aspect of the contradiction, because of a motion internal to the contradiction—i.e., class struggle—that enables it to produce its own "third term." For Marx, in other words, dialectical oppositions produce their own synthesis: "[The] integument is burst asunder. The knell of capitalist private property sounds. The expropriators are expropriated. . . . Capitalist production begets, with the inexorability of a law of Nature, its own negation."[29] The knell that Marx sounds is not the knell of the classicum, but the knell of a mode of production; the agent of this process is not deconstructive discourse, but a historically specific class-subject. And the historical opposition that the revolutionary proletariat negates is not a metaphysical product of ideological domination but a *real* opposition: Marx proposes to overturn and transgress the binary opposition wage-labor/capital not because it is a binary opposition, but because it is a binary opposition that prohibits the historical development of human potentiality. It will, presumably, be replaced by another binary opposition, such as the contradiction between humanity and nature, or between consciousness and materiality. His critique is therefore substantive rather than formalistic. Marx takes to task not the existence of opposed categories *qua* categories, but their historically specific contents.

Despite some superficial resemblances between the procedures of defetishization and deconstruction, then, I would assert that Marx's project is very different indeed from that of Derrida. For Derridean deconstruction extracts binary oppositions from their historical moment, formalizes and hypostatizes contradiction, and elevates undecidability to the status of the historical subject. In our determination of the political relationship between Derrida and his American disciples, then, the central question we debate should not be whether or not undecidability has become a third term, a new metaphysics, in the hands of less subtle practitioners. There is, to my mind, no doubt that Derrida's argument avoids much of the self-satisfied conservatism that attends the discourse of the Yale critics. The awareness of the racist implications of hegemonic discourse that is manifested in "The White Mythology" is clearly at variance with the horror at cultural diversity that is implicit in Hartman's discussion of indeterminacy. And Derrida's insistence that deconstruction entails a conscious *procedure* is very different from J. Hillis Miller's complacent contention that literary discourse "perform[s] on itself the act of deconstruction"[30] with critic and author alike serving as amanuenses of language's inevitable and natural procedures of self-annihilation.

But this difference, while noteworthy, is not as far-reaching as Derrida's leftist adherents would have us believe. For the real issue at stake is deconstruction's valorization of the refusal of mastery—its insistence that the strategy of placing exclusionary oppositions *sous rature* constitutes a viable mode of political *praxis*. On this question, I believe, Derrida and the Yale critics present a solid united front. It was, after all, Derrida, not Geoffrey Hartman, who declared, "I do not believe in decisive ruptures, in an unequivocal 'epistemological break,' as it is called today. Breaks are always, and fatally, reinscribed in an old cloth that must continually, interminably be undone."[31] Whether it is practiced in Paris or New Haven, deconstruction cannot—will not—provide the grounds for a rupture that is, finally, anything more than discursive. For to engage in an oppositional *praxis* based upon a determinate analysis and pursuing determinate results would be to grant that binary oppositions are dialectical, rather than static—historical rather than epistemological. And this is an admission that deconstruction cannot make. Marx was willing to accept the eventuality that any negation would carry with it multiple traces of what it had negated: he knew that the new would always be fashioned out of the cloth of the old. But deconstruction does not envision any process—let alone progress—arising from any clash *within* binary opposition. If there is to be a "radical trembling," we will recall, it will come exclusively from the marginalized "other" of the West, and not from any dialectical interaction between the margins and the center. Hence the only activity possible for a deconstructor of good conscience is to adopt a hygienic position that will avoid any contaminating contact with the moldy cloth of history. (We also note here, by the way, a curious re-entry into Derrida's text of a racist attitude that his methodology of difference would seem to have banished. The notion that progressive-minded Europeans and Americans should restrict themselves to philosophical inquiry while they await the eruption of oppressed nations and races suggests a particularly unfair division of responsibility in the world-historical task of overturning and transgressing bourgeois hegemony.) The fatal flaw of deconstruction—as it is practiced on both sides of the Atlantic, I would argue—is that it is not so much ahistorical as it is anti-historical. It desires to freeze in time (or, better, to hold in suspended animation) its act of epistemological transgression and actively to block the possibility of resolution or synthesis. Deconstruction's polemic against Hegelian dialectics—which it terms "telelogical" and "totalizing"—is in essence a polemic against any *praxis* that would attempt to transform social relations by means of a plan on the one hand and power on the other: "totalizing" becomes tantamount to "totalitarian."

What this fetishization of the refusal of mastery amounts to, I believe, is that the deconstructionist critic's antipathy to totalization and synthesis is, finally, greater than his or her antipathy to capitalism. And what this bedrock assumption leads to, in terms of actual political practices, is little more than a rewarmed liberal pluralism. There is, of course, a significant difference between old-fashioned liberal pluralism and its deconstructionist variant, insofar as the classical formulations posit a collocation of discrete subjectivities, each of which possesses a knowledge of "who he is, where he is, and what he is talking about." Deconstructionist pluralism, by contrast, posits a subject who eschews such metaphysical certainties. The deconstructive subject inhabits a distinctly reified late-capitalist world, in which, as Jean-Francois Lyotard puts it, discourse "is dispersed into clouds of linguistic particles—narrative ones, but also denotative, prescriptive, descriptive, etc., each with its own pragmatic valence. Today, each of us lives in the vicinity of many of these. We do not necessarily form stable linguistic communities, and the properties of those we form are not necessarily communicable."[32] Nonetheless, I would contend, the fundamental unit of the liberal pluralist program remains unaltered: the sovereign (or not-so sovereign) ego, seeking freedom from authoritarian constraints and entering into social relations (whether communicable or not) on the premise that its autonomy will remain inviolate. Liberal pluralism is an essentially formalistic ethos, positing the equivalence of all forms of power and domination—except, of course, those with which it happens to agree or within which it happens to be enmeshed. While Derrida does not invoke Hartman's heavily loaded opposition of "controlled" and "open" societies, then, his valorization of dispersal and heterogeneity implies a tacit assent with the political premises of liberalism—argue as he may that his methodology poses a greater threat to the bourgeois order than does any "apparently revolutionary ideological sort of 'content.' "

I can at this point anticipate two objections that might be raised. First, one might ask, what of the celebrated "*lacunae*" in Derrida's writings with reference to Marx? Is it fair to assert the incompatability of Derrida's methodology with that of Marx when Derrida himself admits that these *lacunae* "mark the sites of a theoretical elaboration which remains, *for me*, at least, *still to come*"?[33] I shall certainly be interested to see Derrida's confrontation with the text of Marx, if and when it should appear, but I do not anticipate that Derrida will find much there to endorse—at least not in terms of an implied political *praxis*. While Derrida would like to consider himself a materialist "if *material* means radical alterity," this conditional statement is, I think, something of a hedge. Clearly materialism must entail, in some sense, the determination of consciousness by social being: alterity comes in as a useful epistemological tool for understanding the nature of the mediation between the two categories, but not as a basis for subverting the categories themselves. For all its claim to constitute the definitive criticism of logocentric idealism, then, deconstruction itself qualifies more as an idealism than as a materialism, insofar as it deprives the investigatory of any epistemological grounds for finally distinguishing between materiality and consciousness.

What is more, while Derrida claims not to have abandoned history, but to have endorsed a " 'monumental, stratified, contradictory' " history (he quotes Sollers), he also makes it clear that anything resembling "linear" history is, for him, "metaphysical." Where he requires a "history that . . . implies a new logic of *repetition* and the *trace*," he decries the history derived from Hegelian tradition as "not only linked to linearity, but to an entire system of implications (teleology, eschatology, . . . accumulation of meaning, a certain type of traditionality, a certain conception of continuity, of truth, etc.)."[34] Marx may have jettisoned a good deal of what he learned from Hegel, but what he kept—Hegel's dialectic "turned right side up"[35]—is exactly the aspect of Hegel to which Derrida so strenuously objects. *The Eighteenth Brumaire* and *Capital* may be constituted by a lively awareness of trace and repetition, but they also posit a conception of historical process that is unequivocally linear, through hardly mechanistic or monocausal.

But what of the arguments of Spivak and Ryan? it might be asked. After all, both these critics disavow any association with liberal pluralism and maintain that Derridean deconstruction provides a powerful tool for oppositional political movements of a leftist character. To their assertions I would respond, first, with my critique of deconstruction's valorization of the refusal of mastery, adding that Marx's defetishization of political economy sets forth a model for other procedures of defetishization philosophical, literary, and historical—and does not need any supplementation by deconstructive undecidability. But I would go further and assert that Spivak's and Ryan's Marxism itself emerges as somewhat suspect in the light of its unproblematic assimilation to deconstruction. Despite their readiness to identify themselves with the interests of actual oppressed people, I would note, both critics are quite ambiguous about their relation to the principal category of a Marxist social analysis—namely, the concept of class. Spivak expresses her concern about women, the non-Western world, and even the victims of capitalism (whoever precisely they may be), but she remains notably silent about how these groups' rebellious practices could relate to the agenda of proletarian revolution—or, indeed, about whether such an agenda is in order at all. What is more, she refers to her own political activities as "regional commitments"—a telling phrase, for it suggests that her own activities are part of a larger (pluralistic) terrain, in which different individuals, acting on the prompting of their different consciences, stake out their own activist turfs. Each commitment possesses its own "pragmatic valence" (to recall Lyotard), and none is guided by an overall (totalizing) strategy or plan adjudicating whether some activities are more necessary than others to the movement toward a general human liberation.

Ryan develops an argument that reveals even more clearly the fundamental affinity between "leftist" deconstruction and liberal pluralism. For Ryan's Marx is a peculiar creature who demonstrates his compatibility with Derrida by making manifest his incompatibility with Lenin. In a quite remarkable misreading of Marx's writings on the Paris commune and of Lenin's writings on the state, Ryan attempts to depict Marx as an advocate of dispersal and heterogeneity "avant la lettre," with Lenin playing the role of a positivist authoritarian irrevocably bound to an oppressive and—you guessed it—logocentric conception of the party. In contradistinction to the Leninist strategy, Ryan holds up the example of Antonio Negri's "autonomist" movement—which seeks to establish democracy in the workplace without fundamentally altering property relations—and of the socialist women's movement—which seeks the realization of women's demands through a decentralized network that eschews assimilation to the master (male) network of traditional Marxism.

I would propose, in sum, that the hidden text behind Spivak's and Ryan's radicalism is an antipathy to centralism of all kinds—the democratic centralism of a communist movement equally as much as the various forms of domination characterizing bourgeois hegemony. This formalistic anarchism will find precious little support in the writings of Marx, who vigorously organized the International as an articulation of unified proletarian identity and who declared, in the 1872 preface to *The Communist Manifesto*, that the main lesson taught by the Paris Commune was the necessity of smashing altogether the existing state apparatus. Boiled down to its essentials (a supremely antideconstructionist maneuver and metaphor, I am aware), the Marxism of Spivak and Ryan constitutes a kind of leftist pluralism, one that finds its natural expression in local organizing and at times, coalition politics. (Coalitions, after all, place a primacy upon autonomy and heterogeneity and posit any broader unity as temporary and provisional.) Now, doubtless some will find this program perfectly satisfactory and will wonder at my discontent. Unfortunately, I do not have the opportunity here to argue the merits of Leninist revolutionism over piecemeal reformism. My main point, however, is that Spivak and Ryan find an affinity between Marx and Derrida only by stripping Marx of his commitment to revolutionary practice; he is a "deconstructeur avant la lettre" only if his text can be construed as a refusal to master—in practice—the text of capitalist domination.

While I find Aronowitz's political outlook to be even less congenial than that of Spivak and Ryan, then, I would propose that, in a curious way, he has made a more fitting political use of Derrida's methodology. For Aronowitz's deployment of a deconstructive rhetoric is unabashedly anti-Marxist *and* anti-Leninist: he faults Marx for his forumulation of a third term—Aronowitz calls it Marx's "economic logocentricity"—and criticizes the entire Leninist tradition for its authoritarian imposition of this "master discourse." Rather than purporting to formulate a coherent politics based upon deconstruction, then, he uses Derridean terms primarily to deconstruct inherited notions of the political.[36] To the extent that he does propose a "new strategy for liberation," he introduces a patently anarchistic perspective. The enemy, he asserts, is the "bourgeois rationalist order" (one might say, Western metaphysics). His preferred strategy entails a "micropolitics of autonomous oppositional movements" that eschews the "master discourse" of Marxism, acknowledges the "unknowable" as a "property of nature itself,"[37] and recognizes the "permanence of difference." Certainly anything so decisive as the seizure of state power would be a violation of such a politics of undecidability. What remains, then, in terms of a concrete political practice—not only for Aronowitz, but, as I have tried to show, for the whole Derridean, deconstructionist project—is a willfully fragmented movement, of which dispersal and hetergeneity constitute both the promise and the goal. Marxism has been finally banished from the scene, this time with a vengeance.

NOTES

1. Gerald Graff, *Literature Against Itself: Literary Ideas in Modern Society* (Chicago: University of Chicago Press, 1979).

2. Frank Lentricchia, *After the New Criticism* (Chicago: University of Chicago Press, 1980), p. 186.

3. Edward W. Said, "Reflections on Recent American 'Left' Criticism," in *The Question of Textuality: Strategies of Reading in Contemporary American Criticism* (Bloomington: Indiana University Press, 1982), p. 24.

4. Terry Eagleton, *Walter Benjamin, or Towards a Revolutionary Criticism* (London: NLB, 1981), p. 109.

5. Lentricchia, p. 169.

6. Geoffrey Hartman, "Criticism, Indeterminacy, Irony," in *Criticism in the Wilderness: The Study of Literature Today* (New Haven: Yale University Press, 1980), pp. 270, 271–72. The following quotations are from pp. 282 and 283.

7. Gayatri Spivak, "Revolutions That As Yet Have No Model: Derrida's *Limited INC*," *Diacritics*, 10 (Winter, 1980), 47–48.

8. J. Hillis Miller, "The Function of Rhetorical Study at the Present Time," *ADE Bulletin*, 62 (September–November, 1979), 12.

9. Jacques Derrida, "Structure, Sign and Play in the Discourse of the Human Sciences," in *The Structuralist Controversy*, eds. Richard Macksey and Eugenio Donato (Baltimore: Johns Hopkins University Press, 1972), p. 264.

10. Derrida, "Différance," in *Margins of Philosophy*, trans. Alan Bass (Chicago: University of Chicago Press, 1982), p. 7.

11. Derrida, "Living On: Border Lines," in *Deconstruction and Criticism* (New York: Continuum Books, 1979), pp. 105, 104.

12. Derrida, *Positions*, trans. Alan Bass (Chicago: University of Chicago Press, 1981), pp. 41, 43, 66, 45.

13. Quoted in Lentricchia, p. 172.

14. Derrida, "The Law of Genre," quoted in Michael Ryan, *Marxism and Deconstruction: A Critical Articulation* (Baltimore: Johns Hopkins University Press, 1982), p. 19.

15. Derrida, *Margins of Philosophy*, pp. 16, 24.

16. Derrida, "Living On," pp. 94–95.

17. Derrida, *Positions*, pp. 51, 64.

18. Derrida, *Margins of Philosophy*, pp. 134–35.

19. *Ibid*, p. 213.

20. Quoted in Eagleton, *Literary Theory: An Introduction* (Minneapolis: University of Minnesota Press, 1983), p. 148.

21. Derrida, *Margins of Philosophy*, p. 114.

22. Derrida, *Positions*, pp. 41, 66.

23. Spivak, "Revolutions," pp. 46–47. The quotation below is from p. 49.

24. Spivak, "Il Faut s'y prendre en s'en prenant a elles," in *Les Fins de l'homme: a partir du travail de —Jacques Derrida* (Paris: Editions Galilee, 1981), p. 511. The quotations below are from pp. 511 and 513.

25. Ryan, p. xiv, et passim.

26. Stanley Aronowitz, *The Crisis in Historical Materialism: Class, Politics and Culture in Marxist Theory* (South Hadley: J. F. Bergin, 1981), p. 124. The quotations below are from pp. 127, 128 and 133.

27. Quoted in Miller, "The Critic as Host," in *Deconstruction and Criticism*, p. 217.

28. Karl Marx, *The Grundrisse: Foundations of the Critique of Political Economy*, trans. Martin Nicolaus (New York: Vintage Books, 1973), pp. 459–60.

29. Marx, *Capital: A Critique of Political Economy* (New York: International Publishers, 1967), I, 763.

30. Miller, "Deconstructing the Deconstructors," *Diacritics*, 5 (Summer 1978), 31.

31. Derrida, *Positions*, p. 24.

32. Jean-François Lyotard, quoted in Craig Owens, "The Discourse of Others: Feminists and Postmodernism," in *The Anti-Aesthetic: Essays on Postmodern Culture*, ed. Hal Foster (Port Townsend, WA: Bay Press, 1983), p. 64.

33. Derrida, *Positions*, p. 62.

34. *Ibid.*, pp. 56–57.

35. Marx, "Afterword to the Second German Edition," *Capital*, I, 20.

36. I owe this formulation to Nancy Fraser's essay, "The French Derrideans: Politicizing Deconstruction or Deconstructing the Political?" forthcoming in *New German Critique*.

37. Aronowitz, p. 130. I wish to thank my friend and colleague Gregory Meyerson for the many discussions that have helped me to formulate my ideas in this essay.

Error at Yale:
Geoffrey Hartman, Psychoanalysis, and Deconstruction

Robert Con Davis
University of Oklahoma

> Human life, like a poetical figure, is an indeterminate middle between
> overspecified poles always threatening to collapse it. The poles may be birth
> and death, father and mother, mother and wife, love and judgment, heaven
> and earth, first things and last things. Art narrates that middle region and
> charts it like a purgatory, for only if it exists can life exist; only if the
> imagination presses against the poles are *error* and life and illusion—all those
> things which Shelley called "generous superstitions"—possible.
>
> —Geoffrey Hartman

> With respect to its own specificity (that is, an existing entity susceptible to
> historical description), literature exists at the same time in the modes of error
> and truth; it both betrays and obeys its own mode of being.
>
> —Paul de Man

> *Les non-dupes errent.*
>
> —Jacques Lacan

Geoffrey Hartman's essay "Psychoanalysis: The French Connection"
shows the divided response to psychoanalysis typical of deconstruction.
Like Jacques Derrida (also J. Hillis Miller, Paul de Man, and Harold
Bloom) Hartman is skeptical of and deeply attached to Freud—both
drawn to the figure that Bloom calls the "strongest Poet" of the twentieth century and repulsed by the one that Derrida shows to be
phallogocentric. Hartman's focus in this essay is on a principal conflict
between Freud and Derrida—psychoanalysis' status as "cure," as an
illuminating corrective for people or for literature, a "healing" supplement. Psychoanalysis is, of course, the "talking cure" and is supposed to
rehabilitate and heal. As Hartman reminds us, ". . . the [psycho-]
analytic situation is linked [in fact] to its representational character:
something is acted out here-and-now to *cure* the here-and-now."[1]
However, questions about whether psychoanalysis "cures" anything,
what "cure" means, and exactly what is being "cured" lead in the

direction where Freudian thought is most vulnerable. In literary criticism the same questions seem to arise. Psychoanalytic criticism, and
perhaps all criticism, tries to "cure" the literary here-and-now of critical
misrecognition and error, to make literature "well" through interpretration.

In Hartman's reading, Jacques Derrida challenges this idea of "cure"
as another instance of Freud's (and Heidegger's) "jargon of authenticity," the attempt to posit a therapeutic or ontological movement from
disease to health, inauthentic to authentic, absence to presence, copy to
original, error to truth—a movement predicated on the existence of
complete "health" or masterable Truth. Particularly wary of such psychoanalytic attempts to view language as "a 'cause' that cures" (p. 110),
Derrida says that no such transformation is possible through language or
the various privileged oppositions it underwrites. There is "no [linguis-
tic] triumph of the therapeutic," as language "is itself infected by a
sickness unto death" (p. 110).

Hartman grants much of Derrida's critique, yet in his essay tries to
intervene between Freud and Derrida in order to salvage some aspect of
the literary "cure" and, therein, to safeguard and bolster what supposedly is made well, the "text." In this attempt to mediate between the old
"talking cure" and the new "science of writing," Hartman makes
psychoanalysis into a corrective, a "cure," for deconstruction. Along the
way, his strategy requires reformulation for the concepts of "cure" and
"disease" in literature. And these concepts, in turn, as he implies, are
defined by the broader concept of "error" in language and literature
generally. Hartman intends these discriminations to be part of his
project to "save the text," to safeguard it from deconstructive reversals
and losses of meaning. What Hartman *can* save of it and what he cannot
reveal much about the "health" (and dis-ease) of American formalist
criticism, particularly in its encounter with deconstruction. In this essay
I will attempt to follow this encounter in Hartman (and metonymically
in American criticism) by following Hartman's examination of psychoanalysis in his and my own readings of Lacan, Derrida and, in wider
contexts, Nietzsche, Miller, de Man, and Shoshana Felman. My central
focus will be on figures of disease and health and the seemingly nonfigu-
ral opposition of error and corresponding truth.

i

Hartman begins his meditation on "cure" by reading Jacques Lacan
against Jacques Derrida. Lacan's psychoanalysis, too, is the "talking

cure," therapy, but Hartman self-consciously interprets it in somewhat Derridean terms—at first more in relation to language than literature. In a very broad theory of language's "origin," for example, he describes a Lacanian "cure" as a kind of linguistic ripening process, the way in which language gradually comes into being. Hartman posits a mythic "primal scene" of language in which two strong psychic forces, depicted as "fantasies," move into a "discourse." The first (with imagery drawn from Derrida's *Glas*) is the "fantasy" of "l'imago du nom propre" (the image of a proper name); the second is that of the "corps morcelé" (the cut-up body). In Hartman's explanation, these fantasies confront each other in a pre-linguistic (pre-"mind") "event" that evolves as a "discourse" or set of relations with each other. The complete failure to relate word and body (as expressed in the fantasies) is a fatal linguistic disease, a failed cure. By the "image of a proper name" here he does not mean a word as such but an ideally pure "name," a potential for language in which meaning and expression are perfectly aligned in a "truth," utterly without ambiguity or vagueness. Then, the "cut-up body" (a castrated body) is pure physicality without meaning, merely carnage and desiccation. The first is a fantasy of complete *substantial* identity, a "true" name, an un-compromised linguistic essence, whereas the second fantasy is corporeal insubstantiality and the radical failure of signification.

These phantoms of word and body haunt Lacanian psychoanalysis and also (as Hartman knows) the discourses, in their intertextuality, of Freud/Derrida/Hegel/Genet, and others. In Lacan's thought, Hartman sees these powerful forces related first in a standoff, a structural dimension of all language that Lacan calls "imaginary." This is a static relationship, the set of all either/or, absence/presence oppositions, a dimension in which signifiers stand in binary stasis in relation to each other but *not* to themselves. The "nonsymbolic" signifier in the imaginary is necessarily self-cancelling and even in itself nonlinguistic (or not yet linguistic) in that it is void of any mediated or articulable opposition. The "corps morcelé," the grim sign of vanquished desire beyond reparation, and the "l'imago du nom propre," a linguistic plenitude and concentration of all the "corps" lacks, stand in this relationship as complements.

As the "ripening" or cure continues, these fantasies become what Lacan calls "symbolic"—language per se—when they stand in relation to themselves, when they become signifiers and have both a function and an identity. This comes about through a principle of difference arising through repetition, the "nom-du-père." The "name-of-the-father" divides the signifier into a function and (a deferred) identity. This occurs (although Hartman does not say this) when the play of imaginary oppositions is extended temporally as a difference in a series, when the "imaginary," in effect, enters history. The "imaginary" in time, serialized, with the gaps (or spacings) of difference, is in fact none other than the "symbolic." Here the "nom-du-père" has a transformative function as an "Aufhebung" or movement ("sublation") of imaginary, self-canceling oppositions into the series of linguistic-oppositions-in-time: into language.[2] With this "sublation" through difference, which splits the signifier into a function and a meaning, imaginary oppositions are henceforth distinguished by the split or "gap" that constitutes them, the split becoming, so to speak, "significative."

In this linguistic "ripening," further, these gaps are the openings between the "nom propre" and the "corps morcelé," even the "wounds" that mark the "corps morcelé" as a divided signifier. Each "blessure" (wound), in enabling the signifier to exist, is also a "blessing"—(in Lacan's words) the "symptom that acts out whatever is human in it" (p. 99). In the symbolic realm, and along the path of these "wounds," an "other" discourse takes place. "Language" begins to operate. It is as if the "nom propre" summons or *calls* the "corps morcelé" into range for the hearing of "true" speech, the language of the unconscious, the systematic splitting and operation of these signifiers. Shoshana Felman explains this "curing" of the "speaking body" as a breakdown of "the domain of the 'mental' and the domain of the 'physical' . . . the oppositions between body and spirit, between matter and language."[3] The "other" (the unconscious) figuratively "speaks" with its own "voice" in the operations made possible by the "symbolic" split between function and meaning. The symbolic "discourse" in this "scene of nomination" (Hartman's term) suggests Jean Genet's description, as it also does for Derrida in *Glas*, of "the world . . . turned inside out like a glove. It happens that I am the glove and I understand at last that on the day of judgment God will call me with my own voice: 'Jean, Jean' " (p. 109). This calling, this "other" nominating voice, belongs as Lacan says, to language itself as a signifying system. Lacan says that "[in the symbolic] the Word always subjectively includes its own reply. . . . What I seek in the word is the response to the other [of language]. . . . In order to find him, I call him by a name which he must assume or refuse in order to reply to me" (p. 109).

This ability to nominate and "call"—somewhat romantic in tone—describes language as a psychoanalytic "cure" effecting the movement from "imaginary" to "symbolic." Thus, in Hartman's version of Freud/ Lacan, language elevates and lifts (as in the "Aufhebung") the signifier from binary oblivion into a stable orbit of linguistic change and oscillation, from ontological nothingness to linguistic "absence"—into what Hartman calls the "contagious orbit" of an "epidemic of soul(un)making" (p. 99). Whereas the "nom propre" and the "corps morcelé" oppose one another in the *imaginary*, in the *symbolic* they are "positions" marking the terrain of speech, in Hartman's terms, agents in the "scene of nomination." Hartman argues, in short, that language itself is "cured" into being by the agency of the "nom-du-père," of *difference*. Exactly how this linguistic healing relates to actual texts, however, is not yet clear.

We do know that nominational "curing" is identified in the Western tradition with the concentrated language of poetry. Through catachresis generally, poetry *names* as a kind of healing. In intensifying the effects of ordinary language, as J. Hillis Miller says in quoting Wallace Stevens, "Poetry [itself] is a health,"[4] both the healer and the namer of the thing healed. "Poetry," as Stevens says, is "a cure of the mind" (p. 7), a "cure beyond forgetfulness" (p. 9). That is, poetry does not aim to destroy experience in repression, but to name it and to alter it. In doing this, poetry "must be," Miller goes on, "a cure not subject to the periodic cycles of annihilation revealing the illusion to be illusion and so negating it" (p. 9). Attempting such a cure, poetry and—presumably— psychoanalysis are trying to cure the "ground" of experience by naming it, covering over its wounds and nurturing it. Psychoanalysis, or any "critical text," "prolongs, extends, reveals, covers, in short, cures, the literary text in the same way that the literary text attempts to cure the ground [of experience]. If poetry is the impossible cure of the ground, criticism is the impossible cure of literature" (p. 331).

The issue of a psychoanalytic "cure" in criticism raises the more basic question of whether *any* cure takes place at all in literature. Miller interrogates contemporary criticism on this point and uses his answers as the basis for describing critics as "canny" or "uncanny." The "canny" are those "Socratic critics" committed to the "rational ordering of literary study" (p. 335), to a "cure." They believe that logic, in Nietzsche's words, "can penetrate the deepest abysses of being, and that thought is capable not only of knowing but even of correcting (*corrigiren*) it" (p. 335). Gérard Genette, Roland Barthes, Roman Jakobson, A. J. Greimas, Tzvetan Todorov, and many Marxist and Freudian critics fit this category to some degree. By contrast, the "uncanny" critics see in literary studies prominent "regions which are alogical, absurd" (p. 336).

For them "logic fails" at the moment of "deepest penetration into the actual nature of literary language" (p. 338). In their analyses "sooner or later there is the encounter with an 'aporia,' or impasse. The bottom drops out, or there is an 'abyssing' " (p. 338). Paul de Man, Jacques Derrida, Sarah Kofman, Barbara Johnson, Miller himself, and many deconstructionists generally fit this category. Whereas the Socratic critics believe ultimately that they can, in Nietzsche's phrase, "heal the eternal wound of existence" (p. 347), fix things right, the uncanny critics have "the uncomfortable feeling that [they] cannot quite hold what is being said in [the] mind or make it all fit" (pp. 337–38), and they instead wrestle with "the aporia between trope and persuasion" (p. 339)—the aporia of language itself.

Where Lacanian psychoanalysis fits in these categories is, strangely enough, and as I will show later, not easy to decide. Any claimant to the true cure is "canny," a healer of the "eternal wound." And surely psychoanalysis claims to heal psychic/literary wounds. As we inquire further, however, the division between "canny" and "uncanny" is itself problematic. Can the two be distinguished from each other at all? Miller admits to a difficulty here, namely that "Socratic procedures will ultimately lead, if they are carried far enough," to uncanny conclusions (p. 338) . This qualification establishes that there are only degrees or gradations of uncanny criticism and that possibly no such thing as canny criticism even exists. In fact, it now seems that *all* critics are uncanny, more or less.[5] At what point the *quasi*-uncanny critic moves over to true uncanniness is hard to determine. While the "canny" vanishes into the "uncanny," the broad range of the "uncanny" signals the need for additional distinctions. The degree of uncanniness marks a commitment to recognizing the aporia and helps to situate this inquiry, but we still need to know exactly what needs curing in actual texts.

We know, though, that the metaphor of "cure" and "healing" does presuppose the existence of contamination or infection. Disease or infection subverts a body and makes it act an "other" part, as if from the "outside" or foreign. Disease, too, is an exception (a violation) in the body's regular effects, a veering in a corporeal "mistake," an "erring" of flesh. In the realm of ideas, this notion of "error" extends easily as a veering of thought to major, traditional cases of misapprehension. Socratic error, for instance, is ignorance, negative "contamination" as a lack of information and appropriate reasoning—an error that is fully correctable. Platonic error, more clearly epistemological, is flawed mundane experience itself, life other than that in the Ideal Forms. It can be only partially remedied. Christian error is sin, a veering from the transcendental (divine) self and the source of love. The complete cure, of course, comes in divine redemption. Marxist error is "false consciousness," ideology that blocks revolution, and the correction is a successful revolution. In each case the swerving of error can be depicted in two ways: metonymically as an imbalance of contiguous relationships or internal "parts," or metaphorically as a substituion of the invading "infection" for the interior substance. Socratic misunderstanding, for example, suggests the imbalance of contiguous relationships in ignorance or forgetfulness, that is, metonymic error, but it also substitutes falsehood for truth in metaphoric error. Likewise, Christian error substitutes sin for grace in metaphoric erring. Yet it, too, includes metonymic error in the varying relationship of doubt and faith, and so on.

Likewise, for the literary body error is a text's veering from itself so that it, or part of it, is not itself but somehow acts an "other" part—in "error" in relation to the rest. Paul de Man's idea of a text's deconstructive economy manifests just such vicissitudes whereby the text is radically disjunctive. Key to his notion is the manner in which a text *says* one thing and *does* another. To show this de Man (following Charles Sanders Peirce) opposes "rhetoric" to "grammar," "pure rhetoric" being an interpretive swerving or "deflection" of meaning, a mode of error. On the other hand, "pure grammar . . . postualtes the possibility of unproblematic, dyadic meaning."[6] De Man then postulates a move deconstructing the opposition between rhetoric and grammar wherein a text has a "meaning," a given and somewhat static indication of significance, and also "asserts" or "performs" that meaning to produce a quite different statement, actually a different "text" and one not consistent with the first. This "discrepancy between meaning and assertion" in the same "text," de Man says, "is a constitutive part of their logic," one could say of the "text's" logic.[7] The text, in effect, swerves from meaning to assertion, from "blindness" to "insight," from falsehood to truth, and the gap between terms in each case de Man calls "error," not the "mere error" of jumbled facts, a "mistake," but a constituent of textuality ("Rhetoric of Blindness," p. 109). This is error generated specifically by a text's inability to *say* what it *does*, to meld saying with doing—by its (in Ortega y Gasset's term) *constitutive instability*.

De Man gives a practical illustration of textual error in "Semiology and Rhetoric" when he quotes the passage from Proust's *Swan's Way* in which young Marcel sits reading on a summer's day in the "dark coolness" of his room. He takes in only "a glimmer of daylight" through "almost closed blinds" and hears the distant "hammering [of] dusty crates" outside.[8] He also hears "flies executing their little concert, the chamber music of summer" (p. 13). This last impression turns out to be a "necessary link" to his imagined total impression of the day, one that (as the passage argues) is superior in its unity to the fragmented impressions Marcel would have if he were actually outside. De Man identifies the imagined day as metaphorical; that is, through the "necessary link" of "the flies executing their little concert," one experience is substituted for another. On the other hand, the empirical (actual) experience of the day is metonymic, constituted by a series of impressions related in fragments, in contiguity. By fostering this arrangement, as de Man points out, the "passage [rhetorically] is *about* the aesthetic superiority of metaphor over metonymy" (p. 14), the superiority of the imagined day over the real one. However, as de Man also shows, "the text does not practice what it preaches. A rhetorical reading of the passage reveals that the figural praxis and the metafigural theory do not converge and that the mastery of metaphor over metonymy owes its persuasive power to the use of metonymic structures" (p. 15). In sum, the text uses metonymy to argue for metaphor and, thereby, necessarily undercuts the conclusion about metaphor's superiority. The text in this way advances, *reads itself* one might say, from meaning to assertion to a new meaning—from blindness to insight to new blindness, and so on. The text each time swerves from what it said previously, veers from its own meaning, in order to posit a new meaning, which in turn will be decentered, and so on. Such swerving, in time and in series, obliges the text to be continually *different* from itself.

The Lacanian concepts that seemed distant from literature in Hartman's essay now are showing up in the deconstructive text. In particular, de Man's text shows traces of the unconscious discourse of language. In textual error, for example, is a breaching of language like the gaps of the "corps morcelé," an unreifiable linguistic absence—the "blessure," the wound or gap that is also (for what it enables) a "blessing." This suggests the nonsubstantial nature of the text. Also, the repetitive inscription of error as difference is a version of Lacan's "nom-du-père." The "sublation" through this *difference*, for Lacan and for Miller, is simultaneously a failure to transform the signifier; that is, each swerving leads out to other swervings in a chain of such gaps. These gaps or traces of another discourse demonstrate, too, that just as other versions of error are cast as metonymic or metaphoric veerings, so textual error is a gliding (*glisse-*

ment) of signifiers past each other in two directions. The text errs in the metaphoric substitution of a new meaning for an old one. And it also errs as meaning (blindness) is resituated metonymically in the assertion (insight) of yet a new reading. In this way, de Man's text, not a substantial thing, is constituted by the error (or gap) that opens repeatedly within it. The text cannot contain, incorporate, or nullify this error because it, like the "nom-du-père," situates the text without becoming a part of it. The deconstructive text manifests the *constitutive instability* that Lacan and Miller designate as deriving from a text's function, particularly its *failure* to function. On this account—the swerving of literature in textual error—we are enabled to talk at least about the psychoanalytic corrective or cure Hartman mentions, a strategy, even if an impossible one, for making literature well.

ii

I will return to Hartman shortly, but here it is helpful briefly to follow de Man's envisionings of textuality for their connections with psychoanalysis, which will return us to Hartman. In his career de Man increasingly imagined the text to be a speech-act, a "literary" speech-act taking place within a grammatical and rhetorical (textual) context. The speech-act is governed by rules articulated as strategies, and it fails or succeeds at accomplishing aims that may be described in "situational" terms. In this appropriation of ordinary-language theory to deconstruction, de Man's conception of textual "meaning" is recast as J. L. Austin's "constative" use of language—"cognitive" statements about the world that may be judged as accurate or inaccurate, true or false. De Man's "assertion" becomes "performative" language, speech as an *act* within a situation, not language in the ideal as testable for truth value, but language in the act of doing something. Such an act, like the pronouncement "I do" in a marriage ceremony, is to be judged as either accomplishing an aim or "misfiring," that is, doing something *un*-intended. Any instance of language has at least some constative function, a "given" or "referential" quality, just as every use of language is to some degree performative, producing not purely a cognitive significance but also a linguistic activity. In that an unclosable gap exists between the constative and performative, every speech-act as a "completed" activity (to an important degree) fails—is in error. Thus, the speech-act perspective intensifies an already strong sense in de Man's work of the error-ridden and virtually "impossible" dilemma of textuality and reading. De

Man, of course, can imagine the performative capability of language, as can Austin, but "impossibility" is a structural necessity in language itself—an inherent instability that drives language on to be different in its own self-elaboration.

Shoshana Felman, along the same lines as de Man, has sought to extend this rapprochement of speech-act theory and deconstruction in terms of the error-ridden nature of language. In a meditation on "le scandale du corps parlant," a scandal seen in light of the convergence of deconstruction, speech-act theory, and psychoanalysis, she also sees the *failure* of language as principally indicating its constitution and gives due credit to speech-act theory for highlighting the importance of such error. Also like de Man, she views language's function, while disjunctive, as yet being primarily self-referential. In this language is guilty, she says, of "referring to itself and at the same time of missing its own self-referentiality."[9] This doubleness of language, referential and always failing at referentiality, is the very scandal of "corps parlant," of language radically in error. Emergent in Felman's meditation on language scandal and referentiality is an important extension of de Man's thinking about error in literature. She also wants, rather boldly, as we will also see, to situate deconstruction and speech-act theory within psychoanalytic discourse.

Felman theatricalizes this "scandal" in various ways, but primarily in her staged meetings between Don Juan-the-lover and J. L. Austin-the-language-philosopher—the man-of-pleasure and the man-of-knowledge. The drama of this encounter lies in the ability of each figure to be the other, or at least to *enact* each other's part in regard to language. For example, Molière's *Don Juan* is a play, in Felman's reading, about promising—the very model of a performative event. At issue in the play is the meaning and meeting of constative and performative views of language. She shows that Don Juan's "antagonists and victims" in the play tend to hold the constative view of language as "an instrument for transmitting *truth*, that is, an instrument of knowledge, a means of *knowing* reality" (p. 26). This conception of language, as Charles Sanders Peirce said, is "grammar," an unproblematic instrument of communication—language conceived purely for its *saying*, for its "cognitive" representation. Set against this view is Don Juan's performative theory of language. As Felman explains,

saying, for him, is in no case tantamount to knowing, but rather to *doing*: *acting* on the interlocutor, modifying the situation and the interplay of forces within it. Language, for Don Juan, is performative and not informative; it is a field of enjoyment, not of knowledge. As such, it cannot be qualified as true or false, but rather quite specifically as *felicitous* or *infelicitous*, successful or unsuccessful. (p. 27)

Here the activity of language as a *doing* nearly obliterates the validity of *saying*. Don Juan promises ad infinitum but never has to *act* in a marriage ceremony. Theoretically, of course, Don Juan must say *and* do in order to speak at all, as must his victims, but the dramatization of extremes illustrates Molière's particular concern with the nature of promising (and failed promising)—of performative language in general. Thus, Felman concludes, the " 'theory of Donjuanism' . . . [is essentially] a speech-act theory" (p. 30).

J. L. Austin is a Don Juan, too, in that his "fundamental gesture, like Don Juan's, consists in substituting, with respect to utterances of the language, the criterion of *satisfaction* for the criterion of *truth*" (p. 61). This Donjuanism is enacted in Austin's abandoning of his early constative/performative distinction in favor of a performance theory based on the generalized notion of *illocutionary force*. Such a move, in effect, substitutes satisfaction, or performance, for truth, or the constative. In his later theory, where "constative" and "performative" are the interweavings, or overlapping dimensions, of a broad performative theory of language, Austin is a performer (linguistically) like Don Juan.

More germane to Austin's Donjuanism is his handling of the issue of referentiality. An important tenet of speech-act theory is its insistence upon language's referential quality—the necessary referential context of a speech-act. In Austin's revised theory emphasizing performance, reference is self-reference because the performative act (by definition) refers directly to its own doing; " 'the act,' " as Felman quotes Emile Benveniste as saying, " 'is identical to the referent' " (p. 79). *Identity*, however, is not the same as *symmetry* because the "utterance" (doing) of a performative also exceeds its "statement" (meaning)—all of which owes to the textual error that de Man describes. Perforce there is a "referential excess" in the speech act, "an excess on the basis of which the real leaves its trace of meaning" (p. 80). Language "refers," therefore, to one of its own effects, and this *referential excess* escapes and remains available for an other, subsequent speech act. The "excess" may be called "specular" in that its positioning creates the illusion of its being a "substantial" and "real" referent. Regarding this referent, Don Juan's actions parallel Austin's: "if Don Juan abuses the performative by exploiting the self-referential capacity of language in order to produce referential illusions by means of self-referentiality, the very act of producing referential illusions itself overflows and reaches toward referentiality" (p. 80). Ultimately, Don Juan depends on the illusion of linguistic specularity to seduce others into believing in language's constative "truth" value while he takes his pleasures in linguistic performance. Don Juan, in this way, is a speech-actor, an "Austin," and Austin-as-language-philosopher is a "Don Juan," an exploiter of language's illusory capability to be specular or "real."

The principal "scene" showing Austin's Donjuanism takes place in regard to the "infelicity" of speech acts, or the way in which Austin, like Don Juan, founders in error and fails to keep his word, to deliver on his promises. The promise of Austin's performative, of course, is the actual completion of an act; the whole of speech-act theory rests on the fact of this accomplishment. What Austin enacts, though, is the very *failure* to reach this goal, to deliver on performative efficacy. A performative action such as saying "I do" in a marriage ceremony is completely successful or "felicitous" only so long as its aims are met, the central of which is the match-up or symmetrical relationship of utterance and statement. But, as Austin shows, the inevitable excess of utterance over statement, the manner in which a doing always overshoots its intention, dictates that "infelicity is an ill to which *all* acts are heir . . ." (p. 105). No performance escapes error. Far from being an empty paradox, this notion of perennial "infelicity" (performative error) points up the productive error or imbalance in language, a dynamic principle that continually drives language toward a repetition of difference. The very infelicity of speech is instrumental to language operation. The stress on infelicity also casts Austin as an errant promiser, a Don Juan who plays with meanings but never (because of the nature of speech) can fulfill his promises completely in action.

This reading of the importance of "infelicity" in speech-act theory enriches de Man's idea of error in literature and postulates textual error as a function, ultimately, of all narrative—literary and nonliterary. It also positions the text within psychoanalysis (as does Hartman) and, specifically, within the linguistic discourse of Lacan. The argument here is simply that the scandal of the "speaking body" is truly a psychoanalytic concern, for only psychoanalysis addresses the terms of word and body, of a language-producing body—of a being, as Paul Claudel says, who continually makes a "promise that cannot be kept," a being who lives necessarily in linguistic/bodily scandal. Further, the breach between saying and doing in speech-act theory is located already in the gap between word and body, "nom propre" and "corps morcelé"—in psychoanalysis. More specifically, the structural asymmetry of "constative" and "performative" as functions generates a discourse "other" than what can be represented as a unified text. The nonsubstantial discourse here is the "unconscious," a differential system functioning in two sites simultaneously and leaving its trace in the breaching, difference, between sites—the gap between constative and performative, saying and doing. This differential system, the repetition of a breaching of word and body, is an enabler of a sort (an origin *manqué*) for the articulations of language.

iii

In retrospect, Hartman's view of literature and cure is confirmed by de Man's and Felman's close readings. Whereas Hartman discusses the problematics of difference in textuality, de Man talks about the "impossibility" of reading and the disruption of texts. Felman speaks of linguistic failure and bodily scandal. Out of this three-way colloquy emerges a distinct view of literary cure and disease—particularly cast in the dynamics of textual error. But there are important differences of tone and substance among the three. De Man is serene in his overview of textual discontents and philosophical problematics—even authoritative. Felman is committed and sure in her articulation of Lacanian deconstruction—confident enough to enjoy the good "fun" of being seduced by *and* of seducing Lacan/Austin/Don Juan. By contrast, the Hartman of "Psychoanalysis: The French Connection" is tentative and halting. He addresses psychoanalysis and then moves to deconstruction and religion, and on further to Jean Genet and Walter Benjamin, and back to religion—moving around but always looking back toward (as he says elsewhere) the "boa-deconstructor," Jacques Derrida. Even in Hartman's own discourse on Freudian criticism, Derrida looms large and threatens to obscure Freud/Lacan and to undo Hartman's essay. The threat here is that if deconstruction dismantles logocentrism and can fit Lacan into the Western "metaphysics of presence," then psychoanalysis itself (as Hartman seems to fear) will be denatured and its impact lost to literature. If this happens, the text that psychoanalysis attempts to cure could then vanish in the dissemination of error, in the textual veerings that "cannot be economized . . . a telling that is merely that of time, whose wasting becomes a tolling: *Glas*" (Hartman, p. 111). Hartman responds to this deconstructive threat with a project for "saving the text," "saving" in the specific sense that "curing" (as in "curing" food) preserves and guards something from contamination and degeneration. In effect, he wagers the text on the fortunes of psychoanalysis—on Lacan and the curing that may forestall literature's "wasting."

In Hartman's view, Derrida threatens Lacan most directly by attacking the "nom-du-père." Hartman's explanation is that "the phallus or the body part . . . 'represents' the sexual foundation of otherness . . . ," and in the "differential yet substitutive (compensatory) mechanisms" of this representation, "acceptance of the (absent) phallus, or of the (absent) father, or, basically, of the mediacy of words, allows a genuine recognition of difference" (p. 100). This "recognition" implies (postulates) a "subject" who does the "recognizing," and also a site of difference and recognition, the "text." The "nom-du-père" in this view actually underwrites subjectivity and textuality—in a sense, unlocks or beckons them as if from confinement or sleep. In short, while not in any way a "thing," the "nom-du-père" yet facilitates and guarantees meaning. Now, Derrida objects to virtually all of this as illusion, sleight-of-hand. He shows that in reality "the phallus is always 'winged,' 'plumy' or 'disseminated' . . . and cannot be used in the manner of a key to lock or unlock a subject" (p. 107). No signifier can so uniformly be a thing, and there is no such symbolic agency to intervene in dissemination or to forestall the "tolling" or the "wasting" of signifiers. In sum, there is no "nom-du-père" as such. Derrida grants that there is difference and recognizes its *traces* in discourse. But difference is not confinable as a concept or principle, and the *trace* is itself another name for dissemination and so by definition is nonrecuperable. At issue in this dispute over the nature of language is Derrida's claim that Lacan reifies and substantializes difference—tries to turn it into a symbol, a "thing."

This damaging critique strikes directly at Hartman's conception of discourse as a play of images or "phantoms," "scenes" in literature like the "nom propre," "corps morcelé," "scéne familiale," "scene of nomination," and "scene of recognition." Each one is a staged moment of textuality, "a repetition of the specular name [that] gives rise to texts . . ." (p. 102). As responses to deconstruction, these claims move Hartman into a cul de sac. For example, he asserts that each "scene," itself a mechanism of narration, actually orients literary discourse within the Judeo-Christian tradition. Each is a participant in (as Jean Paul Sartre termed it) "la grande affaire," "the scandal of theological survivals in even the most secular" thought (p. 99). Each scene is a link to tradition, though possibly through a circuitous route, and a connection (however strained and troubled) with cultural origins—a link Hartman calls the "Eden connection" (p. 117). Now, as theoretical assertions, these claims for narrative specularity do not survive deconstruction. It can be shown that each "scene" is chosen arbitrarily and carries with it much ideological baggage. These scenes can be quickly dismantled and reinscribed interminably in an open series of differences, the very process of dissemination that Hartman is attempting to forestall.

Hartman, however, brings his "scenes" together anyway into a "coherent" textual model, using as his example Walter Benjamin's autobiographical fragment *"Agesilaus Santander"*—in Hartman's words "a particularly revealing example of how autobiography is determined by the idea of a hidden—spectral or specular—name" (p. 112). In this text Benjamin relates how his parents "gave me in addition to the name by which I was called . . . two further, exceptional ones, from which it couldn't be perceived either that a Jew bore them or that they belonged to him as first names . . ." (p. 112). He then explains the Jewish tradition of having a secret "additional name" which parents reveal to children only when they are grown (p. 112). Benjamin's secret name gets conferred in a "scene of nomination": "In the room I occupied in Berlin, before he [the giver of the name] stepped—armed and encased—out of my name into the light, he fixed his picture on the wall: New Angel" (p. 112).[10]

Hartman's reading of this fragment shows that the textual "scenes" are concentrated as if to form a hard-to-read but unified palimpsest. Hartman implies that the make-up of this autobiographical fragment and the manner in which he interprets it constitute virtually empirical evidence for the existence of such narratological "scenes." These claims, again, however, are easily undone by deconstruction, particularly since Hartman's approach suggests an "archetypal" reliance on the specular very like Northrop Frye's. He does caution that his assuming "that literature is the elaboration of a specular name" is not intended "to encourage a new substantialism of the word" (p. 111). His interpretation, though, does encourage precisely a specular substantialism through its use of predetermined "scenes." Hartman, of course, *knows* this, too, yet is not daunted in his specular reading of Benjamin.

With Hartman's insistence on specularity we arrive at a genuine impasse in his text, a moment in which Hartman insists on a literary formalism that he cannot be responsible for—which he cannot shield from his own version of deconstruction, and which, apparently, he cannot back away from. This is a telling moment in American criticism, a dramatic instance in which an impasse—like a recurring dream or an old trauma—can gradually shift angles and yield up something hitherto withheld. Hence, it is important not to "solve" this dilemma too quickly, somehow remove it, detour around it, or cover it over—cure it in the wrong way. We need here, as de Man and Miller would advise (echoing Nietzsche), a "slow reading," what would be involved, for example, if de Man entered this discussion, insisting on a "slow reading" of what Hartman's essay actually *says*, its cognitive (or constative) dimension. In the essay's title, for instance, we can read that psychoanalysis is a "drug" connection, a supplier, the "French Connection" between American (literary) users and the French (philosophic) producers, between American college professor-critics and Derrida. In this transaction, psychoanalysis (like most pushers) is both a supplier and dilutor of the drug, a seller and a contaminator. From Hartman's viewpoint, however, the effects of this French drug must somehow be lessened, and the psychoanalytic "dilution" cuts the drug's harshness. Because of their consumer mentality (their pragmatic and anti-theoretical leanings), the Americans will take the French drug in any event, so it is left up to psychoanalysis—the "French Connection"—to supply the drug and "cut" it, as Hartman hopes, in order (inadvertently) to diminish its power.

Along this line, de Man would slowly read (and want us to read) the psychoanalytic cure in Hartman's essay rhetorically, in its metaphoric and metonymic dimensions. For example, in Hartman's essay deconstruction is a disease invading the body of American criticism from the outside; it substitutes for the healthy (formalist) criticism it displaces. Psychoanalysis is then a metaphoric cure because it substitutes for the deconstructive infection. On the other hand, in that psychoanalysis is similar to deconstruction in its undermining of the subject and logocentrism, but supposedly less severe, it merely alters relationships already present within the deconstructive infection, merely shifts the interior balance within the disease and, thus, within the body. In this way the psychoanalytic cure is metonymic. However—and this point is crucial—this metonymic dilution (cure) of deconstruction, if it succeeds in saving the text from dissemination, could open the way to a more powerful cure, one more decidedly metaphoric and long-term in effect. The "grande affaire" in the mixing of psychoanalytic and religious concerns opens exactly this possibility—in retrospect, of *substituting* religious scenes and icons (like the "New Angel") for the ungrounded figures of deconstructive rhetoric. Religion could cure deconstruction.

In other words, through the mediation of psychoanalysis, deconstruction (much as has happened for René Girard) could give way to religious ritual, visions of divine unity, and a sacred "source."

Hartman shows here, much as Proust does in *Swan's Way*, that in the correction of error metaphor is superior to metonymy. Religion, in other words, is superior to Freud—and Lacan and Derrida. However, de Man would want to step in here and point out that this text "does not practice what it preaches. A rhetorical reading [of Hartman's essay] reveals that the figural praxis and the metafigural theory do not converge and that the mastery of metaphor over metonymy owes its persuasive power to the use of metonymic structures" ("Semiology and Rhetoric," p. 15). This objection, of course, is right: religion and Freud are not easily hierarchichalized. And it points up that Hartman's essay misreads itself (has a blindness) in its constative dimension and that a gap opens between what this essay says and does.

We can see, too, that Hartman misreads his own version of Lacan. For example, when Hartman quotes Derrida on the "winged," "plumy," and "disseminated" phallus that "cannot be used in the manner of a key to lock or unlock a subject: that is, fix a person's truth or identity-theme, or found it in a drive like the libido" (p. 107), he then goes on to conclude that "psychoanalysis remains, according to Derrida, logocentric" (p. 107). This is Derrida's critique, as I discussed earlier, of the substantialism of the "nom-du-père," and Hartman lends support to it by attributing the notion of the "identity-theme" to Lacan (in reality, Norman Holland's concept). However, the substantiality of the "nom-du-père," as Felman shows, is

a misunderstanding that frequently arises in the usual interpretation of Lacanian theory. The notion of "lack" is often hypostasized as being central to Lacan's thought; it is believed that, for Lacan, the referent is the "lack," which to some observers links Lacanian theory, by a simple specular reversal, to the traditional conception of the referent as substance, to the "metaphysics" of presence.

But in reality this common interpretation itself misses the dimension of the "lack," or rather of "failure" [*manquement*] in Lacan. The comparison with Austin is particularly enlightening: for no more than Austin does Lacan deal with the *lack*, but rather with the *act of lacking* or *missing* (failing, misfiring, falling short . . .), which is entirely different from the "lack." (p. 83)

Neither one a cure or a disease in this regard, Lacanian discourse and deconstruction are equally unable (*or* able) to save the text as they have a similar view of the signifier's dissemination. Thus, Lacan would seem to be an unlikely corrective or cure for Derrida.

Hartman also misreads Derrida. We see this in the way Hartman's project to "save the text" is predicated the absolute threat of uncontrollable dissemination, the endless "tolling" that, without a "center" or "subject," is purely a "wasting" of all meaning and significance—possibly a sliding away of civilization and history into an "otherness" completely beyond human grasp. Derrida may be and sometimes is read this way, and certainly he has written diverse things. But on the issue of the "center" and the "subject," and on the aim of his deconstructive project, he is at his most direct:

> First of all, I didn't say that there was no center, that we could get along without the center. I believe that the center is a function, not a being—a reality, but a function. And this function is absolutely indispensable. The subject is absolutely indispensable. I don't destroy the subject; I situate it. That is to say, I believe that at a certain level both of experience and of philosophical and scientific discourse one cannot get along without the notion of subject. It is a question of knowing where it comes from and how it functions. Therefore I keep the concept of center, which I explained was indispensable, as well as that of subject. . . .[11]

The point here is that Hartman does his own version or "voice" of Derrida—Derrida as the police—and the *doing* of this essay (its performative dimension) continually contradicts Hartman's *saying*, misses the mark and shows something different from what Hartman claims. Hartman's text reads itself blindly, and only in performance, in reading/interpretation, do its insights come about.

The "errors" of Hartman's essay constitute exactly the textual error that de Man speaks of. Hartman's essay, like all speech, cannot collapse its own saying and doing into a single text, a unity. This is true, but it is not the whole story. In the particular swervings of Hartman's essay we can also read another pattern, that of American formalism facing the spectre of its own threatening "other"—formalism confronting its own morcellation and destruction in deconstruction. The impasse in Hartman's text belongs as well to a certain dimension of American criticism which is unable to enter a discourse with deconstruction. In the view presented in Hartman's essay, American formalism had "foreclosed" any possibility of mediation between form and dissemination and, instead, hallucinates a scene of castration and violence. The *performance* of Hartman's essay (not what Hartman *says*) shows a fully substantial formalism being desiccated grotesquely by a meaning-denying (infinitely corrosive) deconstruction. This scenario, as I have shown, belongs to Hartman's text, but it also, as I want to suggest now, is part of American criticism's response to Jacques Derrida.

iv

I want to be clear that I am very taken with Hartman's essay and with Hartman. As an American critic, I appreciate the honesty of his dilemma: his Donjuanism, his efforts to domesticate deconstruction, and particularly his attempt to mediate among formalism, psychoanalysis, and deconstruction—all Herculean tasks. Less comfortably, I also enjoy his nervous fun in darting from waiting chamber to lion's den and back again—first looking the deconstructive lion in the face and then scrambling back to supposed (formalist) safety. This is exactly the situation of much of the American literary establishment: Hartman is testing and then retreating from the dangers of deconstruction—as many of us are doing, too. Finally, I admire the looseness of "Psychoanalysis: The French Connection," its constant reminders that it is merely weighing and assaying and not proclaiming, wagering what it has to play, and not attempting to tighten the game's rules into certitude or pomposity. This is, I think, an especially valuable mode of literary criticism and theory—a "disciplined" willingness to take chances critically and *play*. What all of this *does*, in its convolutions and errantry, is provide valuable turning room, a little play, perhaps an instant of specularity, in which an aspect of American criticism can see the reflection of its own performance—view the function of American criticism at the present time. This "seeing" is not a purely critical and highly rigorous act, and Geoffrey Hartman is not the whole of American criticism, but his critical dilemmas—measured in self-awareness and performed in honest, broad gestures—assist us incalculably in reflecting on some of the dilemmas of American criticism in an increasingly theoretical and deconstructive age. Hartman—with his honesty and daring—provides a text in which American formalism can read (an allegory of) itself, and this is no small event.

What is true of Hartman in this regard is true in various degrees of the "Yale" critics as a group. Harold Bloom has moved from New Critical and historical readings of Romanticism to experiments in understanding the "ratios" of literary "influence," the "anxieties" of literary production. Miller has moved from graduate studies in Kenneth Burke to phenomenological reading and then to deconstruction—at each point reorchestrating literary discourse in a different key. Each of these careers parallels the development of post-World War II literary criticism. The development in each case, though, is not an unbroken arch of progress, a smooth, curved line. The appropriate figure, rather, is that of a broken Ariadne's thread—each break the trace of a sudden swerving away from an intended goal, a movement in error in relation to what came before. Each of these critics, as it turns out, has a tremendous capacity (in their own estimation) for being wrong, for advancing a criticism continuallly different from itself—for being critically in error. This propensity for error, posited in part as the willingness repeatedly "to make it new," is a de Manian accounting of the tremendous productivity (and importance) of these critics.

But it is de Man, however, more than any other post-World War II theorist, whose career is aligned with the productive veerings of literary "error" and to a rethinking of formalism. He has done more than anyone to rethink literary criticism in relation to deconstruction, and to philosophical/linguistic discourse generally. And the radicality of de Man's thinking about error is clearly one of the most difficult aspects of his work for American critics to understand and accept. This textual breach de Man ultimately calls *irony*, a schism absolute and unrecuperable, a loss extending beyond literature and moving through all "texts" humanly intelligible. Juliet MacCannell reports de Man's comment, as he faced his last year of life and mused about the end, that "*death interests me.*" This remark, surely, is a critical restatement about and a fitting continuation of de Manian "reading," of "reading" as an activity profoundly interested in and committed to the poetics of "error" (of loss)— "reading" (as he continually reiterated very seriously) of "language infected with a sickness unto death."

In discussing de Man and the Yale critics in this way, I am deliberately trying to evoke the "uncanny" atmosphere that sets them apart in American criticism. In a manner largely alien to the tradition of American optimism and pragmatism, the Yale critics have tried to bring the "plague" to American scholarship and teaching. The history of criticism, of course, is a history of such imports and exports, some more unsettling than others, but the Yale importation of deconstruction is an "uncanniness" calculated to "plague" American formalism (whether New Critical, archetypal, or reader-response) with the irony and undecidability so completely foreign and "other" to it. More than any other feature, it is this deliberate introduction of irony (of death absolutely—

not New Critical irony) that has alarmed many American academics and has brought about the charge that current theory turns "literature against itself." Unwittingly, of course, this charge is exactly right. As de Man shows (virtually *enacts* in his criticism), language/literature is irrevocably divided against itself—is at each moment different from itself, turned against itself in the folds of error and irony. This mode of recognition and reading runs against the American tradition (not necessarily the whole of the American tradition) of philosophical pragmatism and temperamental optimism—against the native impulse to focus all of experience as an openness in the "light of common day," within the sleep of empiricism. It is against this native tradition that the Yale critics have wagered the Derridean-plague.

Perhaps no amount of pressure on the text will overcome the resistance of American formalism. We might ask whether an American, self-reliant and optimistic, can ever read deconstructively. The answer is not yet clear, but it is in the context of these difficulties—what George Steiner calls "tactical" and "ontological" difficulties—that Hartman's discourse should be read. His is a theatrical assaying, a sympathetic enactment of the invasion of the plague (or the French "drug"), of the ills and attempted cures for American criticism at the present time. The "failure" of Hartman's essay to know more than it does is but an instance of literary "error" within the text of American formalism, the example of literature swerving away from itself that we have been inquiring after all along. Moreover, Hartman's doing the "voices" of American formalism, psychoanalysis, and deconstruction makes for the therapeutic theater that is necessary to criticism and literature, not so much as a cure but as an interminable *curing*—a repeated commitment to the poetics of error and difference.

NOTES

1. (emphasis added) "Psychoanalysis: The French Connection," *Saving the Text: Literature/Derrida/Philosophy* (Baltimore and London: The Johns Hopkins Univ. Press, 1981), p. 98. Subsequent page references to this essay will be noted in the text.
2. Ronald Schleifer argues persuasively for the temporal "spacing" of narration in "The Space and Dialogue of Desire: Lacan, Greimas, and Narrative Temporality," *MLN* 98, 5 (1983), 871–90.
3. *The Literary Speech-Act: Don Juan with J. L. Austin, or Seduction in Two Languages*, trans. Catherine Porter (Ithaca: Cornell Univ. Press, 1983), p. 94.
4. J. Hillis Miller, "Stevens' Rock and Criticism as Cure" (I and II), *Georgia Review*, 30 (1976), 7. Subsequent page references to this article will be noted in the text.
5. Behind Miller's "uncanny" and "canny" are Claude Lévi-Strauss' "bricoleur" and "engineer," an opposition which Derrida deconstructs. See Lévi-Strauss' *The Savage Mind* (Chicago: Univ. of Chicago Press, 1966).

6. "Semiology and Rhetoric," *Allegories of Reading: Figural Language in Rousseau, Nietzsche, Rilke, and Proust* (New Haven and London: Yale Univ. Press, 1979), p. 9.

7. "The Rhetoric of Blindness: Jacques Derrida's Reading of Rousseau," *Blindness and Insight: Essays in the Rhetoric of Contemporary Criticism*, Second Edition, Revised. Intro. Wlad Godzich (Minneapolis: Univ. of Minnesota Press, 1983), p. 110.

8. "Semiology and Rhetoric," p. 13. Subsequent page references to this essay will be noted in the text.

9. *The Literary Speech-Act*, p. 92. Subsequent page references to this work will be noted in the text.

10. The "New Angel" is a complex symbol for Benjamin connected with Paul Klee's painting *Angelus Novus*, which, Hartman tells us, Benjamin owned. For a full discussion of this painting and Benjamin's "calling," see Geoffrey Hartman, "The Sacred Jungle 2: Walter Benjamin," *Criticism in the Wilderness: The Study of Literature Today* (New Haven and London: Yale Univ. Press, 1980).

11. Jacques Derrida, "Structure, Sign, and Play in the Discourse of the Human Sciences," *The Structuralist Controversy* (Baltimore and London: The Johns Hopkins Univ. Press, 1972), pp. 271–72.

Part Three
Theory and Practice

Geoffrey Hartman and the Spell of Sounds

Herman Rapaport
University of Iowa

We are in the realm of the passions, perhaps of their tenuous sublimation; and it is the stricken ear rather than stricken eye that leads us there. . . .
—Geoffrey Hartman, "Words, Wish, Worth: Wordsworth."

One might say that human consciousness possesses a series of inner genres for seeing and conceptualizing reality.
—P.N. Medvedev/M. Bakhtin, *The Formal Method in Literary Scholarship*

i

In a paper delivered at Ann Arbor in 1978, Roman Jakobson talked about the sound shapes of language and pointed out that for the child the sound of words is already a transitional substance in D. W. Winnicott's sense: a phatic buffer, separating psyche from world, self from other. The sound shapes of language are redundantly spread out in sentences, Jakobson said, because it is sound itself which is the matter of the text, but also the protective envelope within which the subject comes to be and through which the subject can penetrate the world while never leaving what is one's coverlet of words. [1] In the sound shapes of language, the subject finds a safe berth, and it is to this safety that the subject will later return, a safety that like the Heideggerian house of Being (*Sprache*) will have restorative possibilities. Although Jakobson was talking about a subject, it is clear that this subject is itself not something that idealistically precedes language; rather, the subject is itself constituted within the linguistic, since it is, as Jacques Lacan has pointed out, structured like a language. For Lacan, as for Jakobson, the crucial condition for language is that signs are not merely fixed as in a society of bees but that they are *expressed*. Lacan has said, in this regard, "As language becomes more functional, it becomes improper for speech, and as it becomes too particular to us, it loses its function as language." For Lacan and Jakobson, speech (*Parole*) or language cannot be considered apart from the inevitable recognition of the role of enunciation.

What I seek in speech is the response of the other. What constitutes me as subject is my question. In order to be recognized by the other, I utter what was only in view of what will be. In order to find him, I call him by a name that he must assume or refuse in order to reply to me. [. . .] If I now place myself in front of the other to question him, there is no cybernetic computer imaginable that can make a reaction out of what the response will be.[2]

In such passages it is evident that language is not an autonomous system of signs but speech, and the subject is constituted in the appeal or evocation of this speech, this communication whose horizons are, as Jakobson pointed out, addressor and addressee, or, *destinateur* and *destinataire*. Julia Kristeva in *Semiotikà: Recherches Pour Une Sémanalyse* calls these poles *sujet* and *destinataire*, preserving some psychoanalytic resonances, and calls it a dialogic relation in so far as the "code" transmitted in the "message" never belongs to the *sujet* or *destinataire* but is appropriated from what Mikhail Bakhtin would call the polyglossia of linguistic formations in culture.[3] The sound shapes of language are themselves part of this polyglossia, and if they are used by the subject as a phatic buffer or shelter, it is a protective covering which is always already part of the speech of an other, a covering which is identified with the voices others have spoken. To quote Lacan, "The function of language is not to inform but to evoke."[4]

When Sigmund Freud moved from the practice of hypnosis to that of analysis, it was by means of discovering that in place of working directly with the primary processes in hypnosis, one could work more effectively through the resistances the patient encountered with words in a more conscious state. That is, Freud noticed in the diachronic analysis of the analysand's relation to words a dialogue with the unconscious marked by impasses, intolerances, inhibitions, and, too, sudden revelations. Through the sound shapes of language, the analysand breaks down and establishes particular defenses, thereby discovering in the coverlet of words both traumatic and therapeutic dimensions. In analysis the sound shapes of words articulate a relation between *sujet/destinataire* which is protective as well as destructive, and thus ambivalence is detected in what for analysis becomes a text/context relation. This is most evident in Serge Leclaire's case study, "Le rêve à la licorne," in which slippages between the name, Liliane, and *licorne* (unicorn) take precedence.[5] Without recounting the whole case history, let me just say that the dream of the unicorn defends against a trauma, that of a phobia concerning sand, and the sound shape *li* helps to constitute an address between the *sujet* (Phi*li*ppe) and the *destinataire* (*Lili*) as mediated by the *li*corne. These *li* sounds allow Philippe to articulate the phrase "j'ai soif" ("I'm thirsty") evoked by the figure of Lili. In this way, "Philippe, j'ai soif" becomes an ambivalent phrase which thanks to the sound slippages traverses the *sujet* and *destinataire* in two directions: Philippe saying, I'm thirsty, and Lili mocking him by saying, you, Philippe, who are always saying I'm thirsty, I dub you, "Philippe, j'ai soif." Yet, as Leclaire is quick to point out, "Philippe, j'ai soif" also means that Lili is saying, "Philippe, I want you, I'm thirsty for you." In "Le rêve à la licorne," which is a very complex rebus going far beyond what has been related here, the sound shapes allow the subject to seek shelter in a wish and a phantasm while at the same time marking the trajectory or series of traumatic instances of which one is the perimeter of a phobia. Indeed, if one reads Leclaire's analysis, it is evident that during the composition of the study, Leclaire is often moving back and forth between the axis of *sujet/destinataire* and that of text/context (dream/past experiences/family relations), axes whose articulation *vis-à-vis* one another is maintained by the clues disclosed by the sound shapes themselves. These sound shapes are like passwords which establish the channel between addressor and addressee and in doing so situate the subject in a dialogic relation which is not logocentric or egocentric but rather one that is articulated in the errancy of sound slippages. This is a "radical ambiguity of the letter" which requires that "any attitude of psychoanalytic listening seeks to be 'free-floating.' "[6] Certainly, what Leclaire notices in the dream of the unicorn is that a major role of the sound shapes is to allow the dreamer to keep on sleeping through his thirst. Yet no one can say that the dreamer is sleeping well. Masud Kahn has argued in "Dreams and the Analytic Situation" that dreams are already a wish for a cure and that the aim of analysis should be to allow the patient to sleep well.[7] This means, from our perspective, that in the sound shapes of dream language both trauma and a defense or attempt for a cure are at issue, a desire to sleep well.

Geoffrey Hartman has, of course, been very sensitive to the sound shapes of language and particularly in terms of psychological defense formations. He recognizes with respect to the "timely utterance" of Wordsworth that such poetry absorbs thoughts which could unbalance the mind. In "Words, Wish, Worth: Wordsworth," Hartman explores the wish-work of a poet who speaks with the voices of his predecessors, searching for safe poetic attachments in order to gain access to his own voice. It is as if Wordsworth were looking for a shelter in the words of others.

Wordsworth's antiphonal style—his version of 'ecchoing song'—limits by quotation or self-institutionalizing commentary a potentially endless descent into the phantom ear of memory.

Wordsworth wants not be capsized or swamped by the phantom ear of memory, to be overwhelmed by the superfluidity of the voices. Yet,

Wordsworth's voice has lost, or is always losing, its lyric momentum; formally it is hesitant, disjunctive, 'dark steps' over places in nature or scripture aware of the 'abrupt abyss' that may, again, open up.[8]

Perhaps this is why William Wordsworth makes an abrupt appeal to Dorothy, his sister, in *Tintern Abbey*, saying, "in thy voice I catch / The language of my former heart, and read / My former pleasures in the shooting lights of thy wild eyes." The emphasis is upon the recognition of the sister's voice as that medium in which movement to a happier and more protected state is facilitated. This is not so far removed from Serge Leclaire's case study, "Le rêve à la licorne," because there, too, Liliane (Lili [a cousin] and Anne [a sister]) marks the voice or sound shape of a relative through whom one finds shelter and protection. Similarly, in *Tintern Abbey* voice assuages pain. Just as Philippe is voice dependent on Lili, William is voice dependent upon Dorothy. And he speaks by way of a curious appropriation of her voice in which his own seeks shelter. It is what one might call the activity of a therapeutic consciousness. Indeed, if J. Hillis Miller has written about textual parasitism and Harold Bloom has talked about the anxiety of strong precursors, through Hartman we appreciate in the wish for words an intervocative worth and an intertextual or dialogic blessing. As Hartman writes concerning "timely utterances," "Lyric is a speech act between vowel and passionate wish," and this suggests an intertextuality greatly indebted to the "surround of sound."[9]

Of course, not all texts are blessed by the sound shapes of language. For if the sound shapes of language facilitate a restoration of the self in some literary contexts, such as those of Wordsworth, they also have the potential for trauma. In "Wordsworth and Goethe in Literary History," Hartman asks, "what does voice want? What is the point or hidden intent of the supposed narrative? Why does it haunt this place?"[10] Voice is not located in the subject but around the subject, and, moreover, these voices traverse, suddenly call out, summon or evoke. In Goethe's *Erlkönig* this summoning is particularly ominous. It marks not the assuaging of pain but its ghostly and ghastly penetration in a *mise en scène*, one reminiscent of that moment in Freud's *Interpretation of Dreams* when a voice calls out, "Father, Can't You See That I Am Burning?" In Goethe, of course, the child asks its father "Mein Vater, mein Vater, und hörest du nicht, / Was Erlenkönig mir leise verspricht?" Here the voice doesn't console; rather, it terrifies the paternal ear through the prattle of the child.

In "Wordsworth and Goethe" Hartman has gone so far as to make two crucial suggestions for literary theory. The first is that through an analysis of the intervocative in literature one can uncover oppositions which go beyond traditional genre differences. "I have tried to uncover an opposition which goes deeper than that between lyric and narrative," Hartman says. The second point is,

> But just as we have used poetry to analyze the notions of 'voice' and 'character,' so we could use it to analyze the notion of 'psyche.' A psychoanalysis should emerge from this more adequate to art than any so far devised; and these concepts of voice, character, and psyche may then allow us to explore the history of the poets: the relation between the works of an artist and the role he plays or desires to play in literary history.[11]

These points complement a very important insight made by Julia Kristeva in *Semiotikà* when she argues that we can read literature in terms of a synchronic or text/context relation emphasizing ambivalence and a diachronic or *sujet/destinataire* relation emphasizing what she calls the dialogic. Indeed, *chora, polylogue*,[12] or voice is situated on the register of the *sujet/destinataire*, that register of the psychoanalytic, and it is here that certain linguistic formations infiltrate a spectrum of cultural genres with which we are familiar on the axis on the synchronic: tragedy, comedy, lyric, novel, essay, etc. In the passages above from Hartman's "Wordsworth and Goethe," it appears that like Kristeva he is interested in pursuing an intertextual, intersubjective, or dialogic system(s) of linguistic formations which cuts through traditional genre forms and, in fact, disarticulates them in so far as they can be considered to be reified structures. In that sense, Hartman seeks oppositions through the analysis of the sound shapes of language which go beyond distinctions like the lyric and the narrative. Furthermore, through reading literature with an emphasis on the *sujet/destinataire* relation—one that is always prominent in Hartman's analysis of Wordsworth, but which he considers with respect to Derrida, as well, in *Saving the Text*—and through uncovering linguistic formations which invalidate genre structures posed simply on a text/context model of conventional and formal features, Hartman demonstrates that by way of the dialogic one may arrive at a psychoanalysis which he terms the "psychoesthetic." Such an analysis will lead to what appears a psychohistory through which one might be able to discern specific types of dialogic formations which reveal the psychic defenses as particularly important for an historical understanding. Already with respect to Goethe and Wordsworth, Hartman suggests he has uncovered in the analysis of voice some distinctions which would allow one to begin a psycho-historic research, one in which the axis of *sujet/destinataire* is stressed.

ii

In this essay, I wish to offer four examples in which we can begin to see how psychological defense formations are part of a dialectics between the dialogic or diachronic axis and the formal or synchronic axis of Kristeva's model. We will begin to notice how psychological defense formations can be organized such that we distinguish works in which words succeed in bringing about a felicitous defense from those works in which words or sounds fail to protect the subject from an overspillage of trauma. The works I will discuss are Virginia Woolf's *To the Lighthouse*, Herman Melville's *Moby-Dick*, James Joyce's *Finnegans Wake*, and Alban Berg's *Violin Concerto*. In none of these works will we find unambiguous sources for psychological typing in the same sense that no analysand is unambiguous. However, one can try to initiate a comparative analysis of psychological defense formations as they are disclosed in the spell of sounds. What will be of interest is not so much a saving of the text as cultural artifact, but a saving of consciousness as the performance and behavior of *chora*, a saving we will find more troubled as we proceed. For certainly by the time we consider Alban Berg, the performance or behavior of sound will be a performance of the composer's dying. What is saved or treasured up is sound, a saving that in Berg is a symptom of a sickness or abscess in being by means of which he finds melodic completion in his own passing. This is very different from the consolations of voice in Woolf where the melodies of the dead can still comfort and heal, however precariously.

We recall that in *To the Lighthouse* Lily Briscoe is asking what the voice of Mrs. Ramsay wants. The novel is a texture of leitmotifs which in large part pair emotionally aggressive statements like "No going to the lighthouse," or, "Someone blundered" with defensive and therapeutic ones. "But it may be fine tomorrow," Mrs. Ramsay said, "I expect it will be fine." Here a little boy is spoken to and the sound shapes defend and ward off the inevitable truth which Mr. Ramsay wants his children to know, that "it won't be fine." The whole novel, it seems to me, is a struggle with this defensive voice of Mrs. Ramsay, that is, the wish that she may be right after all. James wishes nothing more than to prove his mother correct, a wish later fulfilled in the father's guilty completion of a ritual which speaks to him from the grave. The voice is ghostly, a mixture of memory and desire for a restitution which history and quotidian time denies. Mrs. Ramsay's voice or voices speak from the grave in order to mark that wish for a return to childhood or a past when words could still console even in the teeth of a threatening storm out of the West. In the last section of the novel everyone returns to Mrs. Ramsay's wish that it should be fine, and this is the novel's great vision as well as its transcendental lie.

> 'Mrs. Ramsay!' Lily cried, 'Mrs. Ramsay!' But nothing happened. The pain increased. That anguish could reduce one to such a pitch of imbecility, she thought![13]

In this last section of To the Lighthouse words fail Lily Briscoe, and she feels terribly cheated. In their place she paints and wonders what that voice of Mrs. Ramsay really meant. This is, of course, the dark side of feminine consciousness, the feeling that there are not enough shelters in which a feminine consciousness may seek protection, that there is perhaps no feminine voice or only very few which speak truly, only the empty defenses of so many manic housewives catering to philosophically obstreperous blockheads. In calling out the name, "Mrs. Ramsay," Lily expects some answer, some presence, some sign. But there is nothing. And yet, there is the scene in which reconciliation takes place, in which Lily has her vision when James, Cam, and Mr. Ramsay, a man now in his seventies, reach the lighthouse. Suddenly the voices become vision, the painting of Lily a "touching compulsion" of the eye, that symbolic articulation fixing what Kristeva calls the chora. And still, Lily's feeling that the painting will rot in an attic suggests that even here we feel the obverse side of an anxiety of influence: the sense that the voices may inevitably fail us.

To the Lighthouse is filled with melody and accompanyments, as the characters themselves notice, and this offsets the dark premonitions, fills in for the lack that Mrs. Ramsay and Lily Briscoe feel so poignantly and pointedly. Moreover, this melodic structure in which phrases take on the resonance of motifs—one thinks of "Minta's glow" or "the athiest Tansley"—quickly sound themselves out as an ambience for reverie. Surely, it is in the melody of the text, its chora, that thought is supported, carried forward, pushed to associative crescendos which coincide with the crashing of the waves. At one point Mrs. Ramsay says, reflecting on some lines of poetry recited by her husband,

> The words (she was looking at the window) sounded as if they were floating like flowers on water out there, cut off from them all, as if no one had said them, but they had come into existence of themselves. [14]

Here, too, there is profound awareness that voice may fail us, though perhaps not wholly. For the words, the sounds, do come into existence of themselves. These words are homeless, restless, their existence saturated with loss, with what Lily and Mrs. Ramsay both understand as the alien habitat in which feminine consciousness finds little support, and yet they come into existence, they precipitate, for they are of the sea and its soundings, its melodious roar. It is this roar, these sound shapes, which fill the novel with the bass of being, as Irving Massey might put it, the soundings, tissue, or woof within which the textually sonorous interlacings establish themselves as homes for reverie and dream. It is in this sound-space, this timbre, that the novel replicates an analytic situation to the degree that these sounds allow the agents of voice to come to terms with their resistances, disappointments, repressions and fears.

> Always, Mrs. Ramsay felt, one helped oneself out of solitude reluctantly by laying hold of some little odd or end, some sound, some sight. She listened, but it was all very still; cricket was over; the children were in their baths; there was only the sound of the sea. [15]

The intervocative is strong in Woolf, and Hartman calls it the antiphonal in Wordsworth when he sights it there. I think that in Woolf's novel the antiphonal allows for a fragile and tenuous reconciliation between *sujet* and *destinataire*, that the restorative properties of voice are saturated with the knowledge that we must accept what blessings we can, that finally there is a consolation and great beauty of vision, however tenuous and momentary. Here voice opens onto symbolization or thematization in which a restoration of the self is possible while homage to the dead is paid. It is a symbolization which facilitates the capacity to dream well, and, perhaps, to sleep knowing that the voices protect and save us.

In *Moby-Dick*, a much more strident work, the defenses of voice are handled differently. We recall Pip who after having watched the sailors interpret the hieroglyphs on the Ecuadorian doubloon, says only, "I look, you look, he looks; we look, ye look, they look." Stubb, the second mate, remarks, "Upon my soul, he's been studying Murray's Grammar. Improving his mind, poor fellow!" It is a Jakobsonian comment in that Stubb acknowledges grammar is not independent of the sound shapes, that syntax and voice are intimately related. Stubb's comment also implies that sound shapes improve the mind, and this is reinforced by his comment, "here's the ship's navel, this doubloon here," a navel that is most accurately described by Pip's grammatical recitations. [16] This is, I would suppose, an anticipation of Freud's notion of the navel of the dream. And in Pip's slippage of the pronoun, as well as within the pun, navel, Lacan would almost certainly have noticed the production of a *logique du fantasme*, that articulation which Freud notices in the transforms of "a child is being beaten," a phrase which in itself reminds one of Pip.

But this is only a small instance of the sound shapes of language in *Moby-Dick*, the residue of one who has been capsized and driven mad in the infinity of the sea. There is also the intensity of the parodic, as G. Genette would notice, the weaving of many discourses: scripture, science, navigation, geography, history, anthropology, folklore, and much else. When Ahab speaks we hear a parody of King Lear and Hamlet. Similarly the cetology chapters mimic sources well known to specialists concerned with the "try-works" of the novel. Indeed, the "try-work" of the book is an attempt to appropriate these discourses in order to break away from a fixation, to drown out the trauma of Moby Dick (that Mrs. Ramsay of Melville's text) by means of speaking about whaling and whales generally. Like Lily Briscoe, Melville's narrator is painting pictures in order to make voice visible, something that has been taken to extremes in the Arion Press Edition of Melville's text. Here the antiphonal is somewhat anti-phonic, perhaps a defense against drowning in the streaming of voice. Still, the antiphonal and the anti-phonic repeat an appointment with the cataclysm that is Moby Dick, one we see in the painting Ishmael sees of a whale impaled by a ship's masts, or, in Chapter 45—"The Affidavit"—the numerous accounts of the stoving in of boats by whales, and, again, the various accounts by passing vessels of encounters with the phantom-like whale of which the story of the Town Ho is most chilling. In all these examples, the voices or antiphonal play points to a desire to escape trauma, a primal scene, while at the same time meeting it head on. Here restoration implies destruction.

An emblem for this condition is Jonah sleeping below the water line while storms toss the ship. In part, Jonah represents someone who finds a safe berth in words, who allows the spell of sounds to transport him to a land of calm. But in another sense, Jonah also represents the sleeper who journeys to the navel of the dream and enters it. He returns to the womb of words, and not only once, but twice: first in the ship, second in the whale. It is a troubled passage, because Jonah's descent is a defensive tactic countering the call of God's words—escaping the prophetic history of Nineveh—while striking it head on by entering God's watery temple. This is a "complex," as some have called it, which struggles between acceptance and rejection of the voice. It is not so much that a dialectics is at work but that within the defensive appropriation of the sound shapes, that covering which allows Jonah to sleep, there is revealed the trauma. At issue, then, is not so much the failure of voice, that nothingness which Lily Briscoe intuits in *To The Lighthouse*, but the Otherness of words which makes itself known from a fixation which is that fixation's very appearance.

The sound shapes of language provide a home, however troubled, for consciousness in which a wish-work can be conducted, an "analysis" undertaken. And in *Moby-Dick*, as in Woolf's novel, the water is not so much an image, merely, but a cascading of sound as well as a topos for wishing. As Melville puts it, men are drawn to the sea because "meditation and water are wedded forever." Melville calls the sea a "wonder world," meaning both an astonishing medium as well as a topos where we read "signs and wonders." It is here that Ahab wishes to slay the trauma, that Pip intuits his own madness in the infinite watery plain, that Ishmael wishes for deliverance, Queequig for wisdom, and so on. The sea, one could say, has therapeutic elements. Even little Pip is delivered from his cowardice or fear and is safely berthed in the sound shapes of words. Starbuck says of Pip, "in this strange sweetness of his lunacy, [he] brings heavenly vouchers of all our heavenly homes."[17]

In "Christopher Smart's *Magnificat*" Hartman writes, "Yet Smart's anxiety about 'tongues' may have produced too good a poetic defense mechanism."[18] Here is the suggestion that poetic language may well be pathological, and it is a point I want to develop further with respect to James Joyce's *Finnegans Wake*. A psychoanalyst would have little trouble noticing that in the *Wake* the voice marks a destabilization of ego formations and the overrunning of the primary processes. The *Wake* is indeed more like what one might expect in hypnosis than in analysis, since under hypnosis the analysand is directly involved in the over-spillings of suggestion. We notice too in sections like the "Study Chapter" that *Finnegans Wake* is similar to *Moby-Dick* in that we have again a "try-works" aimed at triangulating a traumatic zone, a "try-works" which is marked by the intertextual collision of many discursive systems: geometry, science, anthropology, etc. In part the trauma of *Finnegans Wake* concerns the vagina of A.L.P. which is, if one thinks about it, but another watery berth. However, in the *Wake* this kind of fixated symbol has been more or less successfully desymbolized in the overspillings of suggestion whose medium is the channel or current of the sound shapes of many blended languages. Here the anxiety has been channeled into sound and has produced what many readers would call "too good a poetic defense mechanism."

This defense mechanism follows the psychopathology of everyday life, which Margot Norris has focused on in her study, *The Decentered Universe of Finnegans Wake*.[19] But the poetic defense mechanism is also highly developed in terms of Joyce's sexual inhibitions which Mark Shechner has documented from a clinical perspective in *Joyce in Nighttown*. At one point, Shechner relates that these inhibitions were accompanied with elaborate fantasies written out at length in letters to Nora when Joyce was far away from her but that they were converted into something more like sleep when he was with her. "I am so tired after all I have done here," Joyce wrote, "that I think when I reach Via Scussa I will just creep into bed, kiss you tenderly on the forehead, curl myself up in the blankets and sleep, sleep, sleep."[20] In *Finnegans Wake* the spell of sounds is perhaps the expression of a sleep wish that at the same time supports sexual fantasies akin to what Shechner documents as part of Joyce's sexual life. This is especially relevant in terms of the water imagery of the *Wake*.

Joyce invokes water with respect to Anna Livia Plurabelle, and it is this watery invocation which supports a sexual fantasy while drowning it in sleep. In doing so a disarticulation of a *mise en scène* takes place which is recovered as a spell or hush of sounds, a therapeutic current which at the end of the Anna Livia Plurabelle chapter, for example, assuages what Margot Norris sees as the trauma of the text: the fault of the father as primal scene. In the passage which follows, there is a fading effected by sound as the scandals of the text are diluted and washed away by the blessed water that is woman.

Can't hear with the waters of. The chittering waters of. Flittering bats, fieldmice bawk talk. Ho! Are you not gone ahome? What Thom Malone? Can't hear with bawk of bats, all thim liffeying waters of. Ho, talk save us! My foos won't moos. I feel as old as yonder elm. A tale told of Shaun and Shem? All Livia's daughter-sons. Dark hawks hear us. Night! Night! My ho head halls. I feel as heavy as yonder stone. Tell me of John or Shaun? Who were Shem and Shaun the living sons or daughters of? Night now! Tell me,

tell me, tell me, elm! Night night! Telmetale of stem or stone. Beside the
rivering waters of, hitherandthithering waters of. Night![21]

Two washerwomen are speaking from bank to bank on the river Liffey,
and as the dusk darkens, they turn into stem and stone. And between
flows the stream of words, the anti-phonal of textual confluences and the
dissipation of voice into voices and sounds, a plurality of narrative
residues reclaimed in the power of sleep, the wish to dissolve into the
debris and droplets of mothery wit. But too there is a wish to stay awake
and entertain lascivious fantasies, to keep the dirty gossip going about
the daughter and sons of A.L.P. The washerwomen, who clean the dirty
linen of these "daughter-sons" (the phrase suggests incest), turn into
stem and stone (the tools for cleaning laundry), become the stuff out of
which dreams are made, and yet not unlike children they resist sleep by
asking for more narrative. It is as if parents are saying "night, night"
while the children play "tell me a tale." As in Woolf, there is the fear that
voices may fail us, that the spell of sounds is the charm preventing us
from liquidation or dissipation.

In the quoted passage there is a fine balance between sounds determining what appears as represented and the representation determining the
course of sounds. The spell sustains the course or chorus of voice but also
sedates and allows these sounds to suggest metamorphic distortions in
which agencies of voice turn into visible or concrete things, not to
mention, a framed *mise en scène* of the river Liffey at dusk. In themselves
these things, so much like ghostly mutterings, become sonorous densi-
ties which later take on identities as the Mookse and the Gripes, Glugg
and Chuff, St. Patrick and the Archdruid. Here the ambivalence of
text/context comes into play, just as it does when we realize the allusions
of "Night! Night!" remind us of T.S. Eliot's bar closing scene in *The
Wasteland*, a poem in which water also plays an important role. But there
is also the dialogic relation of *sujet/destinataire* in the movement of a
disarticulating relation between enunciation and the enunciated, a relation in which the agent of voice fades into vocal stammerings, natter-
ings, or sonorous glides into the silence. In part, passages such as the one
quoted do not raise so much what voices mean—for example, the relation
of "Night! Night!" in the *Wake* to "good night, sweet ladies, good
night, good night" in *The Wasteland*—or even how they present the very
trauma they wish to flee—the primal scene—but a defensive means of
desymbolization, depersonalization, and desexualization made possible
through the syntax, rhyme, leitmotif, crescendo, retard, voicings, and

resting of antiphonal tonalities, this texture of sounds in whose vocative tracings we can appreciate ghostly effects of the intervocative medley of sound shapes, ghostly effects which Lacan notices everywhere in the unconscious.

When Hartman writes that Christopher Smart produced too good a poetic defense mechanism, he suggested that the spell of sound was the medium where the symptoms of madness infiltrated the aesthetic and vice versa. Similarly, Harriet Weaver believed that *Finnegans Wake* was symptomatic of Joyce's madness, and Clive Hart has asserted that this charge has been all too easily dismissed. Hart argues there may, in fact, be some truth to it.[22] According to this view, Joyce's text marks a serious failure in artistic communication since the poetic defense mechanism worked all too well. Moreover, Joyce's madness, such as it was, can be seen in terms of a fetishistic investment of emotions in sound. As Hart notes, Joyce had a magical theory concerning sound and this worked in favor of a desymbolization which many Joyceans have never seriously considered. It is a desymbolization which Masud Kahn would see as typical of what he calls "alienation in perversion," that is, the maintenance of fantasy structures in the service of depersonalization. If Lacan has noted that Joyce "stuffed the signifier," meaning that words became thinglike—sound as matter, word as object, etc.—Masud Kahn allows us to see the relevance of this assessment. In perversions, he says,

> The object occupies an intermediary position: it is not-self and yet subjective
> . . . it is needed as an actual existent not-self being and yet coerced into
> complying with the exigent subjective need to *invent* it.[23]

Although this may sound like a definition of literature in general, we must bear in mind that in perversion Kahn says the relationship to the object is marked with an incapacity to relate to the object and that this failure is compensated for by magical investments and the kinds of regressive identifications typical of the passage cited from the *Wake* above. Here the magical investments mark what is, in fact, the failure of a poetic voice. And sound becomes a perverse object.

Hartman acknowledges such a condition in "Christopher Smart's *Magnificat*" when he says,

> Should we feel that words are defective, or else that we are defective *vis-à-vis*
> them (words becoming the other, as is not unusual in poets who have a
> magnified regard for a great precursor or tradition), then a complex psychic
> situation arises. It is fair to assume, however, that the distance between self
> and other is always disturbed, or being disturbed; that there is always some

difficulty of self-presentation in us; and that, therefore, we are obliged to fall back on a form of 'representation.'[24]

It is clear that in the *Wake* sounds concern a wish and a wound, a wish to repair the defectiveness of words, that wound which distances or alienates the author. The difficulty concerns, then, a self-presentation or re-presentation which is suppressed on the level of text/context and compensated for by that polylogue on the diachronic register of the *sujet* and *destinataire* in which a certain disarticulation has occurred.

My last example concerns the vanishing of words and the sustaining of the sound shapes themselves. Since I have discussed the precarious relations which the spell of sounds articulate, especially with respect to psychic defense, I will consider an example of how sound prepares the artist, still in his prime, for a premature and mysterious death. The Alban Berg *Violin Concerto* was written and dedicated to the passing of Manon Gropius, a beautiful young woman who lay in bed for about a year with polio. The *Violin Concerto* was begun before Manon died and Berg finished it rather quickly upon learning from the mother, Alma Mahler Gropius, that an angel had passed away. Not long after the piece was completed, Berg himself died. He never returned to completing his opera, *Lulu*, which had been suspended for the sake of the *Violin Concerto*. As we know, music has its affiliations with death; the Dies Irae, Requiems, Funeral Marches, and so on are all prominent in the repertoire. Berg's *Violin Concerto* is not any of these, which is to say, it is not distanced in terms of a specific musical genre appropriate for mourning. Rather, the *Violin Concerto* is an unmediated vision, the reflection of a severely depressed consciousness which strains against melody. Indeed, the death of Manon is investigated in the initial playing of open fifths in the violin and harp parts, a series of pitches which pose as so much tuning up on an instrument at the outset. It is a tuning which ordinarily would come between silence and performance, a transitional object, perhaps, carrying one from the inarticulate to the articulate, though not without resistances. For these open fifths are merely sound shapes, a kind of found musical object. The *Violin Concerto* fixes on this object as something belonging rather distinctly to the musical portrait of the girl, to the beauty of an association between a child and her practicing, her beginning to play. The pitches of the fifths suggest a *mise en scène*, then, of someone learning music or of someone starting to play. These notes also outline a Romantic direction taken within the atonal sequences or rows which Berg develops, as if the *Violin Concerto* were stuffed into the sound shapes of the fifths. Thus it is out of these notes, this raw sounding on the violin, so suggestive of a ghostly presence, that a *Trauermusik* is born, a music in which the composer does not, as figures do in Woolf and Melville, find a safe berth in sound. For Berg contemplates death in the margins of the music, in that spell of sound not yet music, though in every sense, music proper.

It is from these margins climaxing into sweeping chords based on the interval of the fifth that Berg attempts to bring Manon back from the dead even as this passionate reach takes account of itself as a groping in the margins where music ends and silence begins—this land of the dead. Indeed, Manon slips into the darkness, is reclaimed by the low woody timbres of the clarinets which in the Adagio play a Lutheran chorale, "Es ist genug." Musicologists never cease to be amazed with what rapidity Berg worked the chorale into the *Violin Concerto*, not much unlike an afterthought which, it seems, was always already intended. Even the shape of the chorale's melody curiously fit exactly into part of Berg's main tone row which was, oddly enough, its last four notes. "It is Enough . . ." In the sounding out of the chorale there is the desire to end, the wish-work of the sounds to die, of the composer to lie down and be himself claimed by the afterworld.

"O Ewigkeit, Du Donnerwort," J. S. Bach entitled his *Cantata 60* from which Berg borrowed the chorale. "Oh Eternity, You Thunderous Word." In the *Violin Concerto* the word of the eternal thunders in the climaxes of the second movement, though it is never far from the structure of the open fifths, that sustaining agency of the concerto. Indeed, the fifths maintain the illusion that in music the voices will not fail us, and yet Berg's composition reminds us that the voicings and voices are, in fact, failing, fracturing, breaking off. The open fifths testify that the music threatens to turn into mere sound shapes or noise and the atonal rows struggle abrasively against their harmonic contexts marking a dissonance indicating that in this piece music is in trouble. Even if the last bars offer a restatement of the fifths as a ray of hope, it is a reconciliation tainted with soft bitter dissonances, a reconciliation haunted by the memory of Manon, by that *mis en scène* of a child's tuning on the violin, a tuning, *Stimmung, Trauermusik* in whose disillusioned scale or clime the composer expresses his wish to leave off, to quietly end where the tuning stops and the hush which follows the thunder starts. The music is no longer a defense against death but an acquiescence to it. The composer has, in a word, wrecked. He has, to recall a leitmotif from Woolf, "Perished . . ." "Alone . . ."

iii

These examples form a brief introduction, then, to the study of discursive formations which come together at the level of the diachronic *sujet/destinataire* axis of Kristeva's model in *Semiotikà*. It is a question here of the psychological or attitudinal aspects relative to the sound shapes as they are interpreted from a perspective of psychological defense, what Roman Jakobson saw in 1978 to be a determining factor in the understanding of sound with respect to sense. We are moving toward an intertextual understanding of generic affiliations which include, among much else, the infiltration of dialogic elements which in this case are the psychological defense formations that are a part of artistic expression. But as has been pointed out earlier, this dialogic strain can be viewed in terms of not only "analysis"—that is, psycho-analysis as the relation of *sujet* to *destinataire* or Lacan's $-A—but also in terms of a classification along a synchronic axis which we see in Roy Schafer's *A New Language for Psychoanalysis* when he finds genres of attitudinal styles expressed by the analysand during analysis.[25] Indeed, in the examples above, we can already see our way from the diachronic to the synchronic. This movement is not contradictory, establishing but a new formalism, but consistent with a dialectical understanding of linguistic formations in which diachrony and synchrony interpenetrate. Certainly, my stress has been on the diachronic migration of discursive formations across or through specific formations, and, as Jakobson has noted, it is the sound shape which serves as a convenient conveyance for such a movement.

By way of a dialogic approach, we have been able, not unlike Hartman, to ally psychoanalytic criticism with a reading that touches on some aspects of phenomenological interpretration that is somewhat reminiscent of the Geneva critics whose influence on the Yale school has been greater than is usually assumed. For it is clear that psychic defense has not only been discussed from the perspective of the sound shapes but also in terms of the imagery of water, the figure of woman, the meditation on death, and the listening to melodic structures. In this way, thematism as part of the embalming spirit of a criticism of conventions is avoided and a more sensitive interrogation in terms of a phenomenological "intention" opens the way for an understanding of theme within various dialogic and psychoanalytic relations. Whereas some phenomenologically oriented critics have restricted "intentionality" to a more or less ego oriented criticism, we have, following Geoffrey Hartman, but also Julia Kristeva, pursued intertextuality as an intersubjectivity while not completely turning away from the idea of a particular consciousness as it is reflected in the psychological formations of defense, an approach we also find in Hartman's readings of Wordsworth as well as in Kristeva's readings of Louis-Ferdinand Céline.

In *Saving the Text*, Hartman says, "I return to language in its relation to the conscious ear." He suggests that no investigation of *écriture* can wholly escape accountability in the recognition of an ear-fear.

> I return to my initial hypothesis, that the ear is vulnerable, or passes through phases of vulnerability. Its vulnerability is linked—the actual causes being obscure—to real or fantasied words, to an ear-fear connected with overhearing, or to the word as inherently untrustworthy, equivocal, betraying its promise of immediacy or intimacy.[26]

It is this intimacy of language which Hartman reads in Shakespeare, Goethe, Keats, Wordsworth, Melville, Baudelaire, Joyce, and Genet, but also in the philosophers, Nietzsche, Heidegger, and, too, Derrida. In *Saving the Text*, Hartman's *magnum opus*, the ear fear of Derrida is interrogated from the perspective of the sound shapes of language. "For many readers *Glas* does emanate an incomprehensible or intolerable music. 'Klang und nicht Sprache' is the wound attributed by Hegel to Memnon's colossus."[27] And yet, for Hartman this music is decipherable in the slippages of verbal sounds, in the intimate sonorities heard in the echoland of psychic defense sensitive to that awful vulnerability of the ear.

This defensiveness is itself revealed most brutally by Derrida in "Limited Inc abc . . ." in which the name of John Searle is molested with the power of a curse, hence impugning the credibility of the author's claim to his own thoughts, that imaginative copyright transmitted via the voice through the text. Derrida calls him "Sarle": "société à responsabilité limitée." In "Limited Inc abc" Sarle snarles. And Derrida asks in a similar tone, "And how do the 'common,' 'generic' elements, which always exist even in a proper name, withstand contamination in and by foreign languages?"[28] Which is to say, how can the ear decide the *translinguistic*? How can the ear not deconstruct the signature of a snarling opponent whose words participate in a collective slandering of the name, Derrida, of not a restricted but an unrestrained and general attack mounted through collegeal mutterings, those frantic and heated telecommunications between academic "friends"? Who is real? Who fantasied? What is the *genre* of this transmission, these words, this essay, this signature, this muttering, this debate, this writing? As Hartman so rightfully notes in *Saving the Text*, deconstruction is trapped in this labyrinth of the ear, in this genre of hearing that goes *beyond genre*. And it is in sympathy with such a deconstruction that he bids us to listen to the sonorities and seductions of that "Klang" in "Sprache," to those slips of the tongue which molest the certainties of a generic imperative for whom the sound shapes of language can never be much more than a lyric impulse chained to the labor of form.

NOTES

1. Also see Roman Jakobson and Linda R. Waugh, *The Sound Shape of Language* (Bloomington: Indiana University Press, 1979). Unfortunately, this study says almost nothing about psychological defense formations, nor does it discuss transitional phenomena and split brain studies, something Jakobson talked about at length at a semiotics conference at the University of Michigan in May, 1978.

2. Jacques Lacan, "Function and Field of Speech and Language" in *Écrits*, trans. Alan Sheridan (New York: Norton, 1977), pp. 85, 86.

3. Julia Kristeva, *Semiotikà: Recherches Pour Une Sémanalyse* (Paris: Seuil, 1969), pp. 145–54.

4. Jacques Lacan, p. 86.

5. Serge Leclaire, *Psychanalyser* (Paris: Seuil, 1968), pp. 99–117.

6. Serge Leclaire and Jean Laplanche, "The Unconscious: A Psychoanalytic Study," *Yale French Studies*, 48 (1973). In this paper, Leclaire's case history of Philippe is summarized.

7. Masud Kahn, *The Privacy of the Self* (New York: International Universities Press, 1974), pp. 27–42.

8. *Deconstruction and Criticism* (New York: Seabury, 1979), pp. 193, 194.

9. See Hartman's paper in this volume.

10. *The Fate of Reading* (Chicago: Chicago University Press, 1975), p. 190.

11. *The Fate of Reading*, pp. 195, 196.

12. Kristeva uses the terms "polylogue" and "chora" in a later study, *Polylogue* (Paris: Seuil, 1977), but it is clear she already has such notions in mind earlier in the 1960s. These terms are cousins to Mikhail Bakhtin's terms "polyglossia" and "heteroglossia," though Kristeva's psychoanalytically inclined analyses go much further in allying such ideas with the pre-Oedipal in which the *chora* takes on maternal, unconscious, and fluid characteristics.

"La *chora* . . . désigne un réceptacle mobile de mélange, de contradiction et de mouvement, nécessaire au fonctionnement de la nature avant l'intervention téléologique de Dieu, et correspondant à la mère . . . La *chora* est le *lieu* d'un *chaos* qui *est* et qui *devient*, préalable à la constitution des premiers corps mesurables. [. . .] La notion que nous essayons d'en former concerne la disposition d'un procès qui, pour être celui du sujet, traverse la coupure unaire qui l'installe et fait intervenir dans son topos la lutte des pulsions qui le met en mouvement et en danger. [. . .] La voix que nous empruntons consiste à ne pas localiser la *chora* dans quelque corps que ce soit, fût-il celui de sa mère, qui précisément représente, pour l'ontologie sexuelle infantile . . ." (p. 57.). The "discourse polylogue" implies a multiple, stratified, heteronomous enunciation. Speaking of Sollers' novel, *H*, Kristeva writes, "*H* produit ce transfini de la langue: ni monologue phrastique ni dialogue allocutoire, mais élévation du sens phrastique (monologique *ou* dialogique) à la puissance d'une infinité ouverte pour autant que sont ouvertes les postures possibles du sujet vis-à-vis de son dire." (p. 187.) Crucial to these concepts is the recognition of literature as akin to music, particularly pieces like Karlheinz Stockhausen's *Hymnen*.

13. Virginia Woolf, *To the Lighthouse* (New York: Harcourt Brace, 1927), p. 269. A passage worth developing in a more detailed account of the novel would be the moment when Mrs. Ramsay covers the pig's skull with her shawl while putting Cam to bed. Here the defenses against death are overtly thematized with respect to vocal and visual allayings of fears. " 'But think, Cam, it's only an old pig,' said Mrs. Ramsay, 'a nice black pig like the pigs at the farm.' But Cam thought it was a horrid thing, branching at her all over the room. 'Well then,' said Mrs. Ramsay, 'we will cover it up . . .' " (p. 172).

15. *To the Lighthouse*, p. 99.

16. Herman Melville, *Moby-Dick; Or, The Whale* (Berkeley: University of California Press, 1979), p. 445.

17. *Moby-Dick*, p. 488–89.

18. *The Fate of Reading*, p. 90.

19. Margot Norris, *The Decentered Universe of Finnegans Wake* (Baltimore: Johns Hopkins University Press, 1977).

20. Mark Shechner, *Joyce in Nighttown* (Berkeley: University of California Press, 1974), p. 92.

21. James Joyce, *Finnegans Wake* (New York: Viking, 1939), pp. 215–16.

22. Clive Hart, "*Finnegans Wake* in Perspective," *James Joyce Today: Essays on the Major Works*, ed. T. F. Staley (Bloomington: University of Indiana Press, 1966), pp. 135–65.

23. Masud Kahn, *Alienation in Perversions* (New York: International Universities Press, 1979), p. 21. Elsewhere, Kahn says, "In my clinical experience perverts are not persons who impress one with being endowed with a biologically high or intense natural sexual appetite and drive. [. . .] It is all programmed in the head and then instinctual apparatuses and functions are zealously exploited in the service of programmed sexuality." (p. 15.)

24. *The Fate of Reading*, p. 74.

25. Roy Schafer, *A New Language for Psychoanalysis* (New Haven: Yale University Press, 1976). See pages 22–56.

26. *Saving the Text* (Baltimore: Johns Hopkins University Press, 1981), pp. 157, 143.

27. *Saving the Text*, p. 72.

28. Jacques Derrida, "Limited Inc abc. . . ," *Glyph* 2 (Baltimore: Johns Hopkins University Press, 1977), p. 167.

Tristram Shandy and "Narrative Middles": Hillis Miller and the Style of Deconstructive Criticism

Robert Markley
Texas Tech University

In 1978 J. Hillis Miller published an article in *Genre* (the first in a special section, "Strategies of Interpretation") entitled "Narrative Middles: A Preliminary Outline." Devoted, among other matters, to *Tristram Shandy*, the essay apparently has been ignored by just about everyone. J. Douglas Atkins, Vincent Leitch, William Cain, and Donald Pease do not mention it in their studies of Miller's role in contemporary American criticism; it also escapes the attention of Melvyn New in his often acerbic review essay of Sterne scholarship in the seventies—a particularly ironic oversight because New take Sterne's critics to task for failing to come to terms with contemporary literary theory.[1] One reason for the obscurity of "Narrative Middles" may be that its ostensible subject—eighteenth-century fiction—lies outside Miller's historical periods of specialization, the nineteenth and twentieth centuries. And Miller's own subtitle, "A Preliminary Outline," seems to relegate the essay to the status of a rough draft, or perhaps an extended footnote to both his earlier (*The Form of Victorian Fiction*) and later (*Fiction and Repetition*) works. In at least three senses, then, "Narrative Middles" is a marginal work: marginal to commentators on the Yale School seeking to explain deconstruction to the uninitiated (the word "deconstruction" appears in the article exactly once); marginal to traditional Sterne scholars (like New); and marginal to what his colleagues consider Miller's historical interests in the problems of faith and belief in nineteenth and twentieth-century literature.

Yet as most readers of contemporary theory (particularly of Derrida's *Margins of Philosophy*) will recognize, the notion of marginality is one of things that deconstructive criticism sets out to deconstruct. If "Narrative Middles" exists on the margins of Hillis Miller's critical discourse, its "preliminary" status, its position as an "introduction" to a section of

179

articles by the author's students in an NEH summer seminar,[2] paradoxically calls attention to the authority of a critic who can, in effect, make
what is marginal the center of attention. The dialectic of marginality/
centrality—or the dialectical nature of the "middle" itself—implicates
both critic and text in the ironies of what we have come to call deconstructive criticism. "Narrative Middles" is at once a radical and
conservative document. On one hand, it is an attempt to restructure—or
de-center—critical discourse, less polemical than many of Miller's other
essays,[3] yet significant for what it suggests about his own criticism and
about the *style* of deconstruction in America. On the other, however, it
also demonstrates implicitly the difference between the "central" texts of
deconstruction—notably Derrida's—and the "marginal" strategies of
interpretation that inform those peculiarly American hybrids: deconstructive "readings" of individual texts. The dialectic of center and
margins, then, can be rewritten, at least in regard to Miller's article, as
the dialectic of conservative and radical energies that define—and often
divide—postmodern criticism.

Miller, like Hartman and de Man, has both benefitted and suffered
from having his works conflated with Derrida's under the rubric of
"deconstruction." This identification has been at least implicitly encour-
aged by the Yale critics and frequently taken for granted by both their
defenders and detractors. It is one measure of the significance of the Yale
School that its exegesis of Derrida's thought dominates popular con-
ceptions of what deconstruction is or might be; one finds even in the
work of Frank Lentricchia, Jonathan Culler, Atkins, and Leitch that the
English and Comparative Literature Departments in New Haven have to
a large extent set the ground rules for critical debate.[4] "Deconstruction"
as it is perceived, taught, and practiced in the United States is often
reified as a programmatic method of reading or a metaphysics of absence
set against the metaphysics of presence—of logocentrism—that Derrida
critiques.[5] Such misreading of Derrida is not a lesson that Miller,
Hartman, and de Man have consciously taught but a redaction, a
simplification, of the stylistic element of deconstruction that critics have
found in their works. By mistaking rhetorical strategies for metaphysical
absolutes, a number of second-generation commentators have contributed to the hazy assumption that Miller and de Man are merely disciples
or popularizers of Derrida. These critics have, in effect, suppressed the
differences between two kinds of reading, domesticating deconstruction
for their own purposes.

In an important sense, to read the works of the Yale critics is to become involved in the complex process of disentangling their assumptions and values from Derrida's. To restore some sense of perspective to our reading of "Narrative Middles," then, it seems worth the effort to emphasize briefly the differences between Derrida's analysis of the suppression of writing in major *philosophical* texts—in the works of Saussure, Rousseau, Husserl, Hegel, Plato, Heidegger, Foucault, and Freud—and what the Yale critics see as the reflexive deconstruction of writing in *literary* texts. The generic—and ultimately institutional or ideological—difference here is subtle but significant. Derrida's project is the careful demonstration of the contradictions inherent in western philosophical writing, of the complicity of "oppositions" such as presence/absence, speech/writing, inside/outside, origin/history. Hartman, Miller, and de Man, however, displace or "de-form" Derrida's demystification of philosophical "truth" to emphasize that all texts—in effect—deconstruct themselves. "Deconstruction," says Miller, "is not a dismantling of the structure of a text but a demonstration that it has already dismantled itself."[6] The rhetorical shift from Derrida's work characterizes the conservative tendency of the Yale School's version of deconstruction, its insistence, to borrow Hartman's title, on saving the text. Applying deconstruction to literature, Miller tells us, "clearly cannot occur as abstract theory but only by way of reflection about concrete acts of interpreting particular works."[7] As radical or unsettling as the criticism of the Yale School may sometimes seem, it is grounded in the traditional, "concrete" act of interpretation.

Miller's rhetoric of conservation, then, manages to be both a faithful continuation and a deliberate warping of Derrida's radically historical re-reading of western philosophy.[8] American deconstruction, as defined by Miller and Hartman, is frankly, even enthusiastically, dualistic: it presents itself as both a radical challenge to traditional ways of reading and as an attempt to preserve the text as an object of study, as part of an ongoing literary tradition. The conclusion of Miller's seminal article, "Stevens' Rock and Criticism as Cure" reveals this dialectic at work:

> Stevens' poem is an abyss and the filling of the abyss, a chasm and a chasmy production of icons of the chasm, inexhaustible to interpretation. Its textual richness opens abyss beneath abyss, beneath each deep a deeper deep, as the reader interrogates its elements and lets each question generate an answer which is another question in its turn. . . . Such a poem is incapable of being encompassed in a single logical formulation. It calls forth potentially endless commentaries, each one of which, like this essay, can only formulate and reformulate its *mise en abyme*.[9]

Miller's language in this passage verges on the deliberately hypnotic; it becomes both a challenge to the conventional critical style of "logical formulation" and a homage to the poem as an icon of the inexhaustibility of interpretation. "Criticism" is a deformation and a conservation of the text, not an attempt at explication. "The critic," Miller suggests, "is not able by any 'method' or strategy of analysis to 'reduce' the language of the work to clear and distinct ideas. He is forced at best to repeat the work's contradictions in a different form."[10] The critical act exists only as a marginal *repetition* of the text, an imperfect rendering of its *mise en abyme*, or one of the "potentially endless commentaries" that demonstrates its own inadequacy.

The authority of this passage, then, is stylistic rather than ideational. The assertion that no ultimate truth exists in the text cannot be logically demonstrated, or for that matter logically disproved or countered. Miller's authoritative rejection of a definitive interpretation of the poem simply states the obvious ideological point that the institution of literary criticism will, given enough time, produce a seemingly endless string of readings of Stevens' poem. But this passage cannot really be paraphrased. Its point, in an important sense, is its style. Deconstruction is manifest here not as a system of ideas, not as a method of reading, but as an incantatory rhetoric, a summoning of Derrida's specter to scatter and preserve the fictions of western metaphysics. As Leitch suggests, Miller may play "the role of the visionary magician," but he also acts as a kind of shaman, purging the text and the tradition of clotted meanings and mundane logic, of a language that reduces the mystery of literature to the barren rhetoric of explication.[11]

It is worth repeating that Derrida's "influence" in this passage and throughout Miller's work is stylistic as well as ideational or philosophical. Deconstruction offers the Yale critics an alternative to critical formulations about "truth" and "meaning," a convincing demonstration that the "central" rhetoric of logical analysis is less supple, less suggestive, and (let's face it) much less fun than a deliberately marginal, self-interrogating rhetoric of irony, paradox, and repetition. The style of deconstruction allows the critic to perceive himself/herself as writing a continuation of the text, not merely a parasitic commentary; it holds out the exhilirating opportunity of investigating not merely local meanings but the problematic of meaning, the silences, the abyss, of western metaphysics. The critic becomes an explorer venturing into the heart of darkest logomachy. In short, deconstruction offers itself (or offered itself in the mid and late seventies) as a means of reinvigorating literary studies by channelling critical energies away from what most perceptive critics (including traditionalists like Richard Levin[12]) have begun to recognize as an increasingly absurd and self-defeating hunt for definitive interpretations of individual texts. The project of the Yale critics, in this sense, might be defined as a strategic revolution within the languages, if not the institution, of criticism.

"Narrative Middles," like "Stevens' Rock and Criticism as Cure," foregrounds its stylistic authority rather than a "single logical formulation" of the text's complexities. Miller's article is, at once, a rewriting of both *Tristram Shandy* and the rules of critical discourse. It contains, for example, no citations to any other critics of Sterne or Schlegel (though Miller does acknowledge his debt to Ronald Paulson's reading of Hogarth). This lack of footnoting, of any reference to critical tradition, implies a hierarchical distinction between what we might call "originary" repetitions (those of a deconstructive criticism) that "continue" the text and parasitic repetitions (those of "monological" criticism) that, it seems, are not worth repeating. "Narrative Middles," in this respect, celebrates as a kind of positive knowledge the recognition that the critic "cannot by any means get outside the text, escape from the blind alleys of language he finds in the work. He can only rephrase them in other, allotropic terms."[13] The criticism of *Tristram Shandy*, or of Stevens' poems, or of any text, can end only in the repetition of the author's dilemma; critics fail "only by stopping short, by taking something for granted in the terminology one is using rather than interrogating it, or by not pushing the analysis of the text in question far enough so that the impossibility of a single definitive reading emerges."[14] Precisely because its ending is foretold, the critical act becomes ritualistic, a purging of the critic's hubris in his/her effort to repeat the dilemmas—the mysteries— of the text. And his/her success is determined largely by the *style* with which the text is repeated, continued, deformed.

In "Narrative Middles," this process becomes a retracing, a delineation of the narrative line—its inevitable doublings and disruptions—from Hogarth to Sterne to Schlegel. Miller does not try to interpret Sterne's novel but offers instead a "continuation" of *Tristram Shandy*'s "magnificent demonstration" of "the impossibility of distinguishing irrelevance from relevance, digression from the straight and narrow" (p. 381). If other of Miller's recent essays spend a good deal of time playing with etymologies, with the "traces" of words (like "cure") that resist attempts to pin down their meanings and remain "stubbornly heterogeneous,"[15] "Narrative Middles" extends and transforms this kind of wordplay to include playing with the image of the line and the multiple meanings that linearity at once engenders and resists. This article is structured less as an argument than as a labyrinthine tracing of various "lines" and their "filiations": the inevitably broken lines of narrative progression, of journeying, of logical argumentation, of history, of moral rectitude, "of a row of cabbages in a garden" (playing on Sterne's image), of geometry, of gravitation, of Sterne's "erotic pun" on the Hogarthian "line of beauty" (p. 381). As a repetition of the novel, Miller's text transforms criticism into child's play, a game of pick-up-sticks or disconnect the dots. [16] In this respect, as Miller calls attention to Sterne's subversion of linear rationality, his own text calls into question its own "line" of argument, its own "filiations," as it interrogates the values and assumptions of a traditional, logocentric criticism.

The playfulness that characterizes Miller's rhetoric, then, tests—and redefines—the limits of critical discourse. His strategies of isolating, expanding upon, and charting the metamorphoses of key words and images describe what I would call a rhetoric of *delay*—not the outright rejection of the interpretive act but its open-ended deferral. In this regard, *Tristram Shandy* becomes a particularly appropriate work for deconstructive criticism to "repeat": it celebrates the irrevocable delay and deferral of writing. Again and again, Sterne calls attention to his narrator's comic failure to translate experience into words, to Tristram's recognition that the longer he lives, the farther behind he falls in his account of his life:

> I am this month one whole year older than I was this time twelve-month, and having got, as you perceive, almost into the middle of my fourth volume— and no farther than to my first day's life—'tis demonstrative that I have three hundred and sixty-four days more life to write just now, than when I first set out; so that instead of advancing, as a common writer, in my work with what I have been doing at it—on the contrary, I am thrown so many volumes back—. . . at this rate I should just live 364 times faster than I should write—It must follow, an' please your worships, that the more I write, the more I shall have to write—and consequently, the more your worships read, the more your worships will have to read. [17]

The fiction of Sterne's novel—that it is a "realistic" narrative forever deferred to a future writing—might serve as a metaphor for the paradox of deconstructive criticism that Miller celebrates: by delaying interpretation indefinitely, repetition makes possible the critic's recognition that following the line of critical argument through to its "end" is impossible. Like Tristram, the critic paradoxically regresses along the line he/she wishes to follow; the more one writes, the more remains to be written. For Miller, deconstructive criticism delays both the entry into and the next step within the labyrinth, the *mise en abyme*, of interpretation. Paradoxically, the beginning and the continuation of the critical text become indistinguishable. *Tristram Shandy*, for example, may be all "middles," all digression, but it is also all beginnings, each new thrust or doubling of the narrative line offering the seductive freedom of a new start, a new direction, an ironic release from repetition. The "filiations" of deconstructive criticism, in this respect, represent neither a line nor a linear method; they are the images in Miller's texts of irrevocable delays—criticism as the infinitely receding moment of recognition, as a style poised on the brink of metaphoric revelation.

As it repeats and continues *Tristram Shandy*, as it interrogates its own claims to linear coherence, "Narrative Middles" necessarily parodies and challenges the traditional critical essay. It ironically appropriates and undermines the languages of authority and assertion that we expect to find in articles appearing in *Genre*, *Critical Inquiry*, or *PMLA*. In his concluding paragraph, Miller deals specifically with the ironies of his critical stance:

> I have followed here a brief historical line going from Hogarth through Sterne to Friedrich Schlegel. The sequence indicates various possible uses of the image of the line as a figure for narrative continuity or discontinuity, for all that part of the story in the middle, between start and finish. My line is itself a middle, since Hogarth is not by any means its beginning, nor Friedrich Schlegel its end, as I have indicated. The line stretches indefinitely before and after. Out of this truncated series I have made a little story of my own, a line not much undermined, except retrospectively at the end, by irony. The sequence I have followed would need to be tested against many actual narratives in order to be confirmed or rejected as an adequate interpretive model giving a comprehensive range of possible middles. That remains to be done. (p. 387)

This paragraph effectively demonstrates the productive tension within Miller's work between the radically destabilizing language of deconstruction and the imperatives of Anglo-American criticism as an institution: its seeming inability to do anything except interpret individual texts. What may be ironically undermined in this conclusion to "Narrative Middles" is the critic's shift to a language of rational experimentation and objectivity ("tested," "confirmed or rejected," "adequate interpretive model"), his turning away from the playfully assertive style of the article's first twelve pages. This change in voice, this falling back into the pseudo-scientific language of pre-1970 semiotics, however, is less a "retreat" than an inevitable articulation of the historical situation of criticism that Miller's essay both describes and questions. Its concluding paragraph, then, does not offer an interpretation of a text but a gloss, a marginal note, on the possibility of interpretation itself.

In this respect, Miller's brand of deconstruction raises a fundamental question about postmodern criticism and theory: if literature is not linear, not rationally determined, not morally impeccable, how can it be described by a logical, linearly progressive, and logocentric criticism? "Narrative Middles" does not answer this question so much as it poses (like "Ariadne's Thread" and "Stevens Rock and Criticism as Cure") a corollary: by interrogating its own premises, it forces us to question exactly what it is that deconstructive criticism does. Miller approaches this reflexive irony in two ways. In "Theory and Practice," he defines the critic's role as one of resisting "monological" readings "in order to name the special mode of uncanniness in the work in question,"[18] to describe the particular ways in which individual texts reveal their incoherence. To the sceptical, this may seem like rewriting criticism as an infinitely repeating *haiku*:

The words reform, draw back into themselves.
See! the labyrinthine shell.

But this resistance to authoritative reading, this emphasis on the "uncanniness" of the literary text, reflects Miller's—and the Yale critics'— basic desire to rewrite what is meant by "interpretation." The icon of the text, for Miller, Hartman, and particularly Bloom, can never truly be isolated as an object distinct from its "filiations," its complex geneaologies. To a great extent, their criticism insists on redefining not merely the problematic of the text but the "uncanniness," the mystery, of tradition itself.[19]

For deconstructive criticism, the text is less an artifact than an occasion for re-examining and rewriting the traditions of which it is part. In "Narrative Middles," *Tristram Shandy* offers itself as an opportunity for yet another filiation of the critical line precisely because its status as a literary work has already been assured; it is, to borrow Miller's phrasing, part of the "traditional canon" whose authors "both express that system and reveal what is problematic about it."[20] In an important sense, Miller's decision to "repeat" Sterne becomes an act that re-establishes

Tristram Shandy within the "system" and that defers to the priority of the novel *within* the tradition of literature. The fact that the text is worth "repeating" or "continuing" testifies to its value, to its "originary" significance as the *occasion* for the act of criticism. For Miller, the critical text becomes both an act of homage to a pre-existent tradition and a nearly heroic assertion of indeterminacy that reinvests the text with historical—that is, traditional—significance. The critic who demonstrates the "uncanniness" of the text, who resists the imposition of determinate meanings, ensures that the tradition of literature remains open to investigation, that the stylistic options of a deconstructive criticism remain accessible, a necessary part of the dialectic that attempts to reconcile the demands of innovation and tradition.

Miller's perception of literature and literary studies, then, is not, as some critics have charged, ahistorical. Like Derrida, Miller attempts to redefine "history" itself in relation to criticism. "The novelty of an innovative criticism," he argues, "is in large part its institutionalization, in the mode of its insertion into the teaching or reading of literature at a given historical moment, rather than any absolute originality of terminology or insight."[21] Deconstruction, in other words, defines its radical or destabilizing nature not in an abstract, metaphysical sense but in its challenges to Anglo-American traditions of teaching and reading literature. As an historical style, it distinguishes itself from both the "naive . . . millenial or revolutionary hopes . . . present even in sophisticated Marxism" and "the false specter of nihilism."[22] What "Narrative Middles" or *Fiction and Repetition* promises is not an agenda for social change but an initiation into a new "ethics of reading" that might make possible "more or less radical changes within the institution, changes in the style and content of teaching, changes in the organization of courses, curricula, and departments."[23] In statements like these, deconstruction emerges as a strategy for restructuring institutions as well as for changing our reading habits. The critical text, in this respect, is never an isolated or solipsistic act but a sign that indicates a new direction in the study of western metaphysics. The "marginal" strategies of deconstruction, for Miller, ultimately represent a *re*-centering of the institutional interests of literary study.[24]

Miller's perception of history and his attempts to conserve and radicalize tradition have provoked critics of both the right and left. The more substantive of these attacks, as Miller himself recognizes, now seem to be coming from Marxist critics. In a recent review of *The Yale Critics: Deconstruction in America*, Leitch suggests that the "historicizing" of deconstruction has already begun.[25] "History," as he and the editors of and contributors to *The Yale Critics* use it, is a Marxist concept that, in their minds, subsumes the strategies of deconstruction as part of its dialectical focus. But the relationship between Marxism and deconstruction remains unsteady; those Marxist critics who have made use of deconstructive strategies of reading—Jameson, Eagleton, Lentricchia, Michael Ryan, and Catherine Belsey, among others—disagree sharply about whether Derrida and his American counterparts are initiating or struggling against the kind of revolutionary change they envision.[26] This debate, though, seems to reflect the essential ironies of deconstruction as much as the divisions within contemporary Marxist criticism. The "filiations" of the critical lines sketched by Miller, Hartman, and de Man describe no single pattern or design, no one object of critical praise or attack. The refusal of Derrida and the Yale critics to politicize their rewriting of the textual tradition has provoked Eagleton and others to attack the "failure" of deconstruction to interrogate its material, social, and economic values as well as its ideational assumptions. For Pease in *Deconstruction in America*, Miller plays the role of Kerensky to the contributors' Bolsheviks; he becomes the classical (and largely ineffectual) liberal whose historical function is to get swept away by the rising tide of an inevitable revolutionary change.

But it would be a mistake to describe the debate between the Yale School and its Marxist critics solely as a conflict between the political agendas of liberal humanism and radical historicism. The confrontation that takes place in *The Yale Critics* is one of style as well as substance. The Marxist claim that deconstruction in America merely rewrites bourgeois criticism and Miller's contention that deconstruction subsumes the "naive," "millenial" hopes of Marxist criticism are rhetorical sallies as much as they are ideological statements. What is at stake in "Narrative Middles," *The Yale Critics*, or, for that matter, in Eagleton's *Literary Theory* is the metaphorics of criticism in the 1980s and beyond, the stories we will tell ourselves and our students about Shakespeare, Sterne, and Dickens. Miller, more than Pease or Cain, recognizes that the institutionalization of deconstruction—or of any new criticism—must take place on both symbolic and intellectual levels: it must manifest itself as a convincing rhetoric, a seductive style, and not simply as a political program. Miller's deconstructive criticism, then, is polemical precisely to the extent that it engages us imaginatively. The further it descends into the "deeper deeps" of indeterminacy, the more it encourages us to evaluate its success by the languages it creates rather than the readings it produces.

What we are witnessing now in the "postdeconstructive" criticism is, as Leitch suggests, an effort to recast the work of the Yale critics in the Marxist and historical languages of Jameson and Foucault. This rewriting of recent critical history, in one sense, reasserts the teleological values of literary or cultural studies; it tries to suppress "style," in order to define criticism metonymically rather than metaphorically. Although I am sympathetic to much of the work of Jameson, Eagleton, and such cultural historians as Foucault, Hayden White, and Christopher Hill, I think it would be a mistake to underestimate either the stylistic successes of Miller and his Yale colleagues or the imaginative hold that their work exercises on critics of all political persuasions. The "story" of the narrative line that Miller spins in "Narrative Middles" will, in subsequent filiations, be retold again and again by other critics "repeating" other texts; and the languages these critics employ will likely have their origins in his example. It is, after all, the style of deconstructive criticism that has given us the vocabulary to rewrite the history of contemporary theory.

NOTES

1. See J. Douglas Atkins, *Reading Deconstruction/Deconstructive Reading* (Lexington: University of Kentucky Press, 1983), pp. 64–88; Vincent Leitch, "The Lateral Dance: The Deconstructive Criticism of J. Hillis Miller," *Critical Inquiry*, 6 (1980), 593–607; William E. Cain, "Deconstruction in America: The Recent Literary Criticism of J. Hillis Miller," *College English*, 41 (1979), 367–82; and Donald Pease, "J. Hillis Miller: The Other Victorian at Yale," *The Yale Critics: Deconstruction in America*, ed. Jonathan Arac, Wlad Godzich, and Wallace Martin (Minneapolis: University of Minnesota Press, 1983). On Sterne see Melvyn New, "Surviving the Seventies: Sterne, Collins, and their Recent Critics," *The Eighteenth Century: Theory and Interpretation*, 25 (1984), 3–24.

2. See Miller's note (p. 375) in "Narrative Middles: A Preliminary Outline," *Genre*, 11 (1978), 375–87. Subsequent references to this article will be noted parenthetically in the text.

3. Most of Miller's defenses of deconstruction can be found in his major articles of the mid-seventies. The ones which I am particularly concerned with include "Ariadne's Thread: Repetition and the Narrative Line," *Critical Inquiry*, 3 (1976), 57–77; "Stevens' Rock and Criticism as Cure," *Georgia Review*, 30 (1976), 5–31; 330–48; "Ariachne's Broken Woof," *Georgia Review*, 31 (1977), 44–60; "The Critic as Host," *Critical Inquiry*, 3 (1977), 439–47; and "Theory and Practice: Response to Vincent Leitch," *Critical Inquiry*, 6 (1980), 609–14. Miller has, of course, produced many other valuable pieces of criticism. For a bibliography, see *The Yale Critics*, pp. 209–12.

4. See Frank Lentricchia, *After the New Criticism* (Chicago: University of Chicago Press, 1980); Jonathan Culler, *On Deconstruction: Theory and Criticism after Structuralism* (Ithaca: Cornell University Press, 1982); Atkins, *Reading Deconstruction/Deconstructive*

Reading; and Leitch, *Deconstructive Criticism: An Advanced Introduction and Survey* (New York: Columbia University Press, 1983).

5. For one critique of such "counterfeit Derrideanism," see Brian McCrea, "The Theoretician as Saran Wrap," *The Eighteenth Century: Theory and Interpretation*, 25 (1984).

6. "Stevens' Rock and Criticism as Cure, II," p. 341.

7. "Theory and Practice," p. 614.

8. My reading of Derrida is closer to Lentricchia's than to Terry Eagleton's in *Literary Theory: An Introduction* (Minneapolis: University of Minnesota Press, 1983). Eagleton finds Derrida's work "grossly unhistorical, politically evasive" (p. 148); Lentricchia in *After the New Criticism* (pp. 174–75) sees Derrida's deconstruction as an historically important critique of western metaphysics.

9. "Stevens' Rock," p. 31.

10. "Stevens' Rock, II," p. 333.

11. Leitch, "The Lateral Dance," p. 599.

12. See Richard Levin, *New Readings vs. Old Plays: Recent Trends in the Reinterpretation of English Renaissance Drama* (Chicago: University of Chicago Press, 1979).

13. "Stevens' Rock," p. 331.

14. "Ariadne's Thread," p. 74.

15. "Stevens' Rock," p. 10.

16. Pick-up-sticks begins by one's dumping short, straight sticks into a pile. One's opponent then attempts to pick up the sticks, one at a time, without disturbing the others. Eventually, he moves the wrong sticks and the original dumper gets a turn to try her luck. The winner, having removed the final stick, has reduced the pile to nothing.

17. *The Life and Opinions of Tristram Shandy, Gentleman*, ed. Ian Watt (Boston: Houghton Mifflin, 1965), p. 214.

18. "Theory and Practice," p. 610.

19. See especially Harold Bloom, *The Anxiety of Influence: A Theory of Poetry* (New York: Oxford University Press, 1973) and *Agon: Towards a Theory of Revisionism* (New York: Oxford University Press, 1982).

20. "Theory and Practice," p. 612.

21. "Stevens' Rock," p. 332.

22. "Theory and Practice," p. 612.

23. "Theory and Practice," p. 613.

24. On Miller's view of the role of deconstruction in the teaching of English, see "The Function of Rhetorical Study at the Present Time," *ADE Bulletin*, 62 (1979), 10–18; and "On Edge: The Crossways of Contemporary Criticism," *Bulletin of the American Academy of Arts and Sciences*, 32 (1979), 13–32.

25. In *MLN* 98 (1983), 1305–08.

26. For an interesting treatment of the relationship of Marxism and deconstruction, see Michael Ryan, *Marxism and Deconstruction: A Critical Articulation* (Baltimore: Johns Hopkins University Press, 1982).

Some Versions of Rhetoric:
Empson and de Man

Christopher Norris
University of Wales
Institute of Science and Technology

i

Deconstruction has been seen by some of its opponents as a mere continuation of the "old" New Criticism by more sophisticated technical means. Both movements, it is argued, took rise from a narrow preoccupation with "the text" which effectively cuts criticism off from a sense of its larger (intellectual and social) obligations. In each case the appeal is to a privileged *rhetoric*—or theory of linguistic figuration—which drives a wedge between textual meaning and the logic of "normal," communicative discourse. The New Critics made do with a homespun vocabulary of tropes like ambiguity, paradox and irony, figures that required no elaborate theory by which to back up their ontological claims about the nature of poetic language. Deconstruction developed out of the specialized idiom of post-Saussurian linguistics, coupled to a critique of philosophical concepts far more ambitious than anything dreamt of in New Critical theory. Nevertheless—so the argument runs—this added sophistication cannot disguise the basic continuity of method and aims. Deconstruction merely pushes to its furthest extreme that divorce between rhetoric and reason which the "old" New Criticism sought to impose. An ultra-refined model of linguistic structure is joined to a thoroughgoing Nietzschian scepticism as regards the possibility of achieving any knowledge outside the random play of textual meaning. Thus, for all its protestations to the contrary, deconstruction is put down as simply a more exotic, updated version of New Critical dogma.

This view has a certain limited plausibility, especially when applied to some proponents of so-called "American" deconstruction. The peculiar kinds of licence that were once extended to poetic language—the suspension of logic by a rhetoric of paradox, ambiguity, etc.—are now claimed by critics as rightfully theirs also to exploit. Where New Criticism drew

191

a firm disciplinary line between poem and commentary, deconstruction makes a virtue of crossing that line wherever possible, allowing the critic a speculative style in keeping with the text he or she interprets. Some, like Geoffrey Hartman, have pushed this new-found freedom to the point of dissolving all putative distinctions between "literature," "criticism" and "theory."[1] The erstwhile structuralist dream of a *science* of literature—an orderly taxonomy of forms and devices—gives way to the joyous post-structuralist assertion that theory is one variety of text among others, and hence no longer subject to the grim paternal law of scientistic method. Hartman's punning virtuosity of style goes along with his commitment to a range of hermeneutic models and theories more adventurous than anything allowed for in old New-Critical practice. To abandon the protocols of academic criticism—what Hartman calls "the Arnoldian concordat"—is to come out on the far side of any distinction between "primary" (creative) and "secondary" (critical) texts. Henceforth interpretation is to grasp its proper destiny as a free and equal partner in the intertextual dance of meaning. For Hartman, this is the promised land which Arnold glimpsed but failed to possess, interpreting his own as an age of criticism indeed, but one that could only serve as a prelude to some coming creative revival.[2] Such melancholy tonings will seem beside the point, Hartman suggests, if criticism casts off its old inferiority complex *vis-à-vis* the literary text.

Undoubtedly, this is the guise in which deconstruction has made its greatest impact on American literary studies. Its attractions are evident enough, and nowhere seen to more beguiling effect than in Hartman's style of speculative musing on and around the margins of the text. Yet the opponents of deconstruction have a point when they argue that this is, after all, just one more episode in the history of failed attempts to move beyond the confines of "old" New-Critical method. The liberty that Hartman so brilliantly exploits is still a licence to *interpret* texts, albeit in a manner scarcely thinkable to the high priests of orthodox formalism. W. K. Wimsatt was quick to see the threat in an essay, published in 1970, which reasserted the "ontological" argument—the poem as "verbal icon"—against any kind of newfangled critical theory which blurred the distinction between text and commentary.[3] A large weight of dogma, aesthetic and ethical, rested upon Wimsatt's rearguard response. Yet in retrospect it looks as if the threat came not so much from this textual-libertarian quarter as from another, more rigorous form of deconstruction which Wimsatt (one guesses) had yet to encounter.

Of course it is open to debate whether any such distinction can or should be drawn. If there are, as I am suggesting, "hard" and "soft" varieties of deconstructionist thought, then any such loaded comparison will quickly be dismantled (or rhetorically undone) by proponents of the hard-line persuasion. Besides, it is notoriously difficult to define what should count as argumentative "rigour" in the context of deconstruction. Certainly there exist no normative *logical* grounds for distinguishing rigorous from non-rigorous forms of deconstruction. If philosophy is blind to the rhetorical complications which threaten its sovereign logic—as Nietzsche argued, and as the deconstructors never cease to point out—then clearly no appeal to logical consistency will serve to make the needful distinction. Yet there is—in the texts of a critic like Paul de Man—a power of "rigorous" or consequential argument which sets them firmly apart from Hartman's exuberant, virtuoso style. The upshot of de Man's close-readings may be an affront to every standard notion of logical sense and consistency. But to follow them stage by stage through the process of his tortuous yet scrupulous argument is to experience something very different from the heady fascinations of Hartman's writing.

It might seem extravagantly wrong-headed to apply this same distinction in the case of Derrida's texts. Certainly a hard-line deconstructor would have ample Derridean warrant for rejecting any putative difference between "serious" and "non-serious," "rigorous" and "playful" forms of deconstructionist discourse. That philosophy has always clung to such distinctions as a self-promoting strategy of true (i.e. "rigorous") knowledge is a lesson that Derrida constantly drives home. From Plato on the sophists to Searle on Derrida, it has always been a contest between "serious" philosophy, aimed at the one, authoritative truth, and on the other hand a rhetoric which knows and exploits its own irreducibly figural status.[4] All the more reason to reject any straightforward distinction, on philosophic grounds, between rigorous and non-rigorous forms of deconstruction. To fall back into that prejudiced habit of thought is to ignore what Derrida's texts most forcefully proclaim: the liberation of rhetoric (or writing) from its age-old subjugation at the hands of philosophic reason.

Clearly there are pressing institutional motives for this readiness among literary critics to accept the broader drift of Derrida's arguments. It is agreeable to be told, after all—and on good "philosophical" authority—that criticism is not just a poor relation of philosophy but possesses the rhetorical means to dismantle philosophy's claims-to-truth. But there remains a great different between Derrida's scrupulous thinking-through of these issues and the way that his *conclusions* are taken as read by many of his American admirers. Again, deconstruction would reject in principle any attempt to discriminate "original" or first-order deconstructive thinking from its "derivative," secondary or non-original forms. Such distinctions would merely betoken the lingering hold of an outworn metaphysical prejudice, a harking-back to notions of authority, presence and origins. The slightest acquaintance with deconstructive theory is sufficient to reduce these notions to the status of ungrounded myths or metaphors. So one might gather from reading, for instance, J. Hillis Miller's ingenious meditations on the mazy etymology of "host" and "parasite," figuring between them the strange ("undecidable") relation of dependence between "primary" and "secondary" texts.[5] Such manoeuvres certainly inhibit any talk of first-order deconstructive thinkers on the one hand and mere camp-followers on the other. But it still makes sense—albeit problematically—to single out certain deconstructionist texts for the unsettling power and acuity of their arguments. These texts provoke a sharp and continuing discomfort, a generalized "resistance to theory" which de Man was quick to diagnose.[6] Unlike the products of mainstream "American" deconstruction, they hold out against the domesticating pressures which work to assimilate all new ideas to the basically conformist practice of interpretation. In short, these texts stand decidedly apart from the kind of deconstructive activity which—for all its new-found sophistication—still looks increasingly like "old" New Criticism under a different rhetorical guise.

What creates such acute discomfort in the reading of Derrida and de Man is the disciplined rigour of their arguments, coupled with the seemingly irrational conclusions to which those arguments lead. The New Critics were content to suppose that "literary" language had its own peculiar logic of paradox, irony and other such safely accommodating tropes. Rational explication was the interpreter's business, but only in so far as he or she respected the saving difference—the radical autonomy—of poetic language. Wimsatt takes his stand on precisely this ground when he argues (against Miller) that criticism needs to maintain a firm sense of the ontological difference between poem and commentary. And it is *this* distinction that de Man most flagrantly transgresses by refusing to separate the logic of commentary from that other, less answerable "logic" of poetic figuration. For de Man, the mutual questioning of text and critique is pressed to a point where reason itself becomes enmeshed in "undecidable" contexts of argument beyond its power to comprehend or control. What de Man won't accept is the convenient escape-route which holds that poems just *are* paradoxical and ambiguous, since that is the way that literary language works, as distinct from the language of rational prose discourse. This was the assumption of New Critics like Wimsatt and Cleanth Brooks. It undergoes a radical extension of kinds in Hartman's or Miller's argument that *all* texts are figural through and through, whatever their self-professed "logical" status. At times this is certainly de Man's position. But along with it—and so closely intertwined as to make this a clumsy way of formulating the difference—there emerges a refusal simply to take refuge in the all-embracing realm of poetic figuration. It is this "perverse" tenacity of argument which sets de Man apart from critics like Hartman, and which probably accounts for the extreme hostility that his writings often provoke.

A programmatic statement from *Allegories of Reading* may help to make this point more clearly. The context is de Man's opening discussion of rhetorical questions, as in Yeats's line from "Among School Children": "How can we know the dancer from the dance?" In such cases, de Man writes, "the same grammatical pattern engenders two meanings that are mutually exclusive."[7] The question simultaneously asks to know the difference and denies (rhetorically) that such knowledge is possible. Yeats's line presents a simple enough case, but it serves to introduce a series of antinomies which de Man exploits to extraordinary effect in subsequent chapters. In particular, it signals his unwillingness to opt—like the "old" New Critics—for some inclusive rhetoric of poetic figuration which would simply suspend all questions of logical accountability. It is not just the case, de Man writes,

> that the poem simply has two meanings that exist side by side. The two readings have to engage each other in direct confrontation, since the one reading is precisely the error denounced by the other and has to be undone by it. Nor can we in any way make a valid decision as to which of the readings can be given priority over the other; none can exist in the other's absence. (*AR*, p. 12)

This passage demonstrates the unsettling coexistence, in de Man's critical language, of a rhetoric of textual *undecidability* and a constant demand for *logical* precision. That there is no valid procedure for deciding between readings is a message that Brooks and Wimsatt would happily endorse. A deconstructor like Hartman would be just as much at home with the notion of an open-ended textual "freeplay" beyond all governance of critical method. What complicates matters in de Man's case is the insistence that each reading must "undo" the other, and that meanings cannot simply be conceived to coexist in a peaceful state of aesthetic suspension. There remains an irreducibly *logical* tension between the "literal" and the "figurative" senses of language, such that criticism is brought up sharply against the limits of its own linguistic competence.

This is how de Man deconstructs the opposition between "literary" and "critical" discourse. It is no longer a question of laying down firm categorical limits within which poetry can safely exercise its penchant for ambiguity and paradox. Text and critique are henceforth involved in a shuttling exchange of priorities which allows of no protective buffer-zone between the two. But neither is it a case—as with Hartman—of simply submerging all limits and distinctions in the undifferentiated play of textuality. De Man may indeed double back and forth across the notional line between "literature" and "commentary." At one moment he will valorize criticism for its power to demystify the "normative pathos" vested in literary language. At the next, he will elevate the literary text as implicitly *acknowledging* its own rhetorical character, and thus making a dupe of the literal-minded critic who seeks to articulate its truth. But this strategy works to complicate—rather than collapse—the system of tentative checks and resistances set up between text and commentary. It requires, that is to say, a kind of shifting, provisional boundary-line, even if the line is constantly blurred by the two-way traffic of interpretative sense that flows across it.

This is why de Man's allegories of reading are enacted in a space which is undecidably both "in" the texts he interprets and "in" the deconstructive reading that brings them to light. Simply to collapse that distinction—to merge text and commentary in Hartman's manner—would amount to a denial that criticism could achieve any kind of articulate knowledge beyond that provided by literature itself. Such would indeed appear to be de Man's position at a certain late stage of the deconstructive process. But in order to *reach* that stage his argument must undergo the passage through a constant reciprocating dialogue of text and critique which requires at least some residual sense of the difference between them. In the end it may appear, as Barbara Johnson says, that criticism is often "the straight man whose precarious rectitude and hidden risibility, passion and pathos are precisely what literature has somehow already foreseen."[8] But on the way to this *dénouement*—and in order to achieve it—theory has to pass through successive encounters with its own "undecidable" status *vis-à-vis* the literary text. And this entails a certain operative distinction between "text" and "theory," no matter how often that distinction is overthrown by the devious logic of intertextuality. On the one hand de Man can argue that "poetic writing is the most advanced and refined mode of deconstruction" (*AR*, p 17). On the other, he is constantly obliged to set a distance between them, at least as a kind of heuristic device whereby to plot their convergence. Thus:

> It seems that as soon as a text knows what it states, it can only act deceptively . . . and if a text does not act, it cannot state what it knows. The distinction between a text as narrative and a text as theory also belongs to this field of tension. (*AR*, p. 270)

This passage certainly works to deconstruct any firm categorical distinction between literature and theory. It implicates both within the "allegory of reading" that constitutes the only possible form of demystified textual knowledge. Yet even here de Man is constrained to make the point by provisionally separating "narrative" from "theory" in terms of his own dialectic.

This sets de Man apart from that strain of deconstructionist thinking which breaks with New Criticism only by dissolving all limits to the play of figurative language. He remains, one might say, a *philosopher* of language—a conceptual rhetorician—precisely in so far as his texts resist the drift toward pure, undifferentiated freeplay. Philosophy may turn out, in de Man's words, as "an endless reflection on its own destruction at the hands of literature" (*AR*, p. 115). But the means of that reflection derive unmistakably from philosophic discourse, that "labour of the negative" installed within philosophy from Hegel to Adorno. De Man's overriding drive to demystify language goes along with his adherence to the protocols of logical argument, no matter how strange or paradoxical their upshot.

ii

It is to William Empson, and not the New Critics, that attention might be turned in seeking a precursor for de Man's kind of strongly interrogative reading. Empson's techniques of verbal analysis were of course taken up by critics like Cleanth Brooks, but not without certain doctrinal reservations. The problem was that Empson insisted on *rationalizing* poetry, not merely seeking out multiple meanings but attempting to fit them into some kind of logical structure. This led the New Critics to view with suspicion Empson's habits of homely prose paraphrase and his constant drawing-out of underlying philosophical arguments. Philip Wheelwright suggested that the term "ambiguity" was partly to blame, since it allowed for a logical "either/or" response as well as the inclusive "both/and" of genuine poetic language.[9] "Plurisignification" was Wheelwright's preferred candidate; "irony" and "paradox" likewise served to raise a protective fence around the privileged domain of the poem as "verbal icon."

I have argued elsewhere that Empson's kind of sturdy rationalism was especially offensive to the New Critics when he brought it to bear on religious poets like George Herbert and Milton.[10] Poetry and theology both demand respect for their peculiar, uniquely sanctioned varieties of figural language. To read them in Empson's manner—drawing out their logical contradictions—is to open up their mysteries to a secular critique which would threaten that saving autonomy. John Crowe Ransom registered this sense of unease with Empson's method when he spoke of "the reading of the poet's muddled mind by some later, freer and more self-conscious mind.[11] To inquire too closely into the logical workings of poetic language is to forget that poetry occupies a separate realm of complex but non-discursive meaning. Thus Ransom remarks, in another context, that any putative "logic of poetic figure" would always be self-contradictory, suggesting in effect "a logic of logical aberrations, applicable to the conventions of poetic language."[12] New Criticism sought to avoid such confusions of realm by drawing a firm categorical line between critical theory and the inwrought structures of poetic irony and paradox. Theory has to do with the broadest questions of interpretative method, and had better not become too closely involved with the actual *reading* of poetry. Thus Brooks legislates flatly that "the principles of criticism define the area relevant to criticism; they do not constitute a method for carrying it out."[13]

Empson and de Man have this much in common: they refuse to make any such clear-cut distinction between the structure of poetic meaning and the logic of critical argument. They both insist on pressing their analysis of figural language to the point where it offers a maximal resistance to the habits of straightforward rational thought. But where New Criticism simply suspends those habits—accepting that poetry just *is* paradoxical, and quite beyond reach of logic—Empson and de Man make a point of keeping the logical problems in view. In de Man, this leads to a species of negative hermeneutic which deconstructs the very grounds and assumptions of normative reading. In Empson, it takes a more overtly "commonsense" form, but runs none the less into regions of textual doubt and self-questioning which often approach the stage of deconstructive aporia. And this comes about precisely through Empson's refusal to let go of logic in pursuit of some other, paradoxical quality invested in poetic language.

The effect is most marked in what Empson classifies as "ambiguities of the seventh type." These occur when "the two meanings of the word, the two values of the ambiguity, are the two opposite meanings defined by the context, so that the total effect is to show a fundamental division in the writer's mind."[14] *Seven Types* is a loosely-organized book, and Empson makes no claims for any clear-cut, orderly progression of "types." There is, however, a marked development of interest which leads from vaguely *inclusive* ambiguities—cases where the mind doesn't need to choose one way or the other—to instances of full-blown logical *conflict*, such as make up the seventh type. Thus Empson can be seen to turn on its head the New Critical idea that poetic ambiguity is properly a matter of "both/and," rather than "either/or" tension. For Empson, the most powerful and productive ambiguities are those which maintain the *logical* tension between two or more "incompatible" meanings. Like de Man, he resists any premature retreat to a ground of aesthetic reconciliation where opposites can peacefully coexist within a structure of irony, paradox, etc. "The conditions for this verbal effect," Empson writes, "are not those of a breakdown of rationality" (*Seven Types*, p. 198).

The most sustained and striking instance of Empson's seventh "type" comes with his reading of George Herbert's poem "The Sacrifice." Here, if anywhere, the method gives reason for those orthodox New Critical fears about the effects of a "logical" approach to the mysteries of poetry and religion. Empson reads "The Sacrifice" as riven by internal contradictions, its surface mood of placid acceptance everywhere subject to harsh self-inflicted ironies. Christ is depicted, in Empson's words, as

> scapegoat and tragic hero; loved because hated; hated because godlike; freeing from torture because tortured; torturing his torturers because all-merciful; source of all strength to men because by accepting he exaggerates their weakness; and, because outcast, creating the possibility of society. (*Seven Types*, pp. 232–3)

These paradoxes are *not* entertained in the spirit of a formalist criticism which would take them (so to speak) on faith, as evidence of poetry's power to reconcile conflicting states of mind. Rather, they are presented as an outright affront to the logic of rational thought, effective as poetry only in so far as reason measures their irrational appeal.

In de Man, likewise, there is an ethical compulsion behind the will to demystify certain predominant poetic tropes and devices. This compulsion is most evident where de Man deconstructs that species of rhetorical bad faith which he associates with Romanticism and its attempts to transcend the antinomies of rational (post-Kantian) thought. These are the stakes in de Man's classic essay "The Rhetoric of Temporality," first published in 1969. The essay turns on the cardinal distinction between "symbol" and "allegory," conceived not so much as two distinct orders of language—since symbol, for de Man, always resolves back into allegory—but as two strategies for *making sense* of linguistic figuration. The rhetoric of Symbolism is that which seeks a transcendent unifying vision atop all the hateful antinomies of subject and object, time and eternity, word and idea. It deludedly hopes that such distinctions may simply fall away in the moment of unmediated, purified perception towards which poetry strives. De Man quotes Coleridge, among others: the Symbol is characterized by "the translucence of the special in the individual, or of the general in the special, or of the universal in the general; above all, by the translucence of the eternal through and in the temporal."[15]

It is this last claim especially that vexes de Man, and which opens up the gap between logic and rhetoric that his essay proceeds to exploit. Romanticism achieves its moments of delusory transcendence only by ignoring or suppressing the *textual* operations that underwrite its will-to-truth. Refusing to distinguish between experience and the representation of experience, Romanticism seeks to collapse all those awkward distinctions that force an awareness of the secondary, mediating character of language. The ethos of the Symbol is precisely this belief that language can attain to a pure ideality where subject and object, mind and nature would at last coincide without the interposition of mere arbitrary signs. And this would also mean—as suggested in the passage from Coleridge—that thought might be momentarily redeemed from its enslavement to the *temporal* condition of language. The "translucence of the eternal through and in the temporal" is the aim of every discourse founded on the Symbol as a means of reconciling logical antinomies. It is the arbitrary nature of the sign—the perpetual slippage between signifier and signified—which enforces the ineluctably time-bound condition of all discursive thought. The language of Symbolism seeks to overcome this predicament by abolishing the distance between sign and meaning, language and the orders of inward and outward experience. With "the assumed superiority of the Symbol in terms or organic substantiality"

(*Blindness*, pp. 192–3), language takes on a new-found conviction of its power to transcend all merely intellectual antinomies.

It is precisely this assumed superiority that de Man sets out to deconstruct by juxtaposing symbol and allegory as rival modes of understanding. He notes how "the valorization of symbol at the expense of allegory" goes along with the rise of a cult of aesthetic transcendence aimed at securing the radical autonomy of poetic imagination. This process is reversed point for point by substituting "allegory" for "symbol" as the ground of all linguistic understanding. Allegory becomes the demystifying trope *par excellence*, the determinate negation of everything claimed on behalf of symbolic transcendence. To interpret allegorically is to read in the knowledge that there always exists, in the nature of language, a constitutive gap between words and experience, signs and the reality they seek to evoke. Allegory perpetually redirects attention to its own *arbitrary* character, the fact that any meaning there to be read is the product of interpretative codes and conventions with no claim to ultimate, authentic priority. It is, thus, in terms of allegory—as de Man interprets it—that thought comes to recognize the temporal predicament of all understanding. There is no present moment of self-possessed meaning where signs would so perfectly match up with experience as to obviate the need for further interpretation. Allegory in de Man exerts something like the power of deconstructive leverage that Derrida brings to bear through his key-term *différance*.[16] That is to say, it introduces the idea of a differential play within language that everywhere prevents (or constantly *defers*) the imaginary coincidence of meaning and intent. For de Man, this recognition can only be suspended by the workings of a covert ideology—that of transcendental aesthetics—which wills its own blindness to the rhetoric of temporality.

The following passage brings out the underlying ethical dimension of de Man's argument:

Whereas the symbol postulates the possibility of an identity or identification, allegory designates primarily a distance in relation to its own origin, and, renouncing the nostalgia and the desire to coincide, it establishes its language in the void of this temporal difference. In so doing, it prevents the self from an illusory identification with the non-self, which is now fully, though painfully, recognised as a non-self. It is this painful knowledge that we perceive at the moments when early romantic literature finds its true voice. (*Blindness*, p. 207)

The choice thus posed—"painful" recognition or mystified, evasive strategy—is cast in terms of an almost existentialist drive toward authentic self-knowledge. For de Man the only truth to be grasped through language is that "truth" is always non-self-identical, a fugitive knowledge that nowhere coincides with the moment of its own, self-sufficent revelation. Allegorical reading drives this lesson home by constantly revealing the interpretative slide from moment to moment in the chain of signification. Thus "the prevalence of allegory always corresponds to the unveiling of an authentically temporal destiny" while this unveiling takes place "in a subject that has sought refuge against the impact of time in a natural world to which, in truth, it bears no resemblance" (*Blindness*, p. 206).

Hence de Man's relentless critique of organicist metaphors in the discourse of post-romantic thought. Such figures seek to impose an equivalence between processes of natural growth on the one hand and products of spontaneous creativity on the other. Both are conceived as totalizing movements which contain within themselves the shaping principle that assures their intelligible form. For de Man, such metaphors are merely another species of the will to mystify critical discourse, to lift interpretation outside the temporal existence which endlessly defers its own closure. Literary "form," de Man writes, is "the result of the dialectic interplay between the prefigurative structure of foreknowledge and the intent at totality of the interpretative process" (*Blindness*, p. 31). Criticism builds its mistaken ontological assumptions on the failure to recognize that metaphors like "organic form" can never be more than stopgap expedients in the face of an authentically temporal self-understanding. "Form is never anything but a process on the way to its completion," a sentence which typically self-deconstructs around its own incompatible terms.

Empson comes closest to full-dress deconstructive reading in his pages on Wordsworth's "Tintern Abbey" as the crowning example of fourth-type ambiguity.

> And I have felt
> A presence that disturbs me with the joy
> Of elevated thoughts; a sense sublime
> Of something far more deeply interfused
> Whose dwelling is the light of setting suns,
> And the round ocean and the living air,
> And the blue sky, and in the mind of man:

A motion and a spirit, that impels
All thinking things, all objects of all thought,
And rolls through all things.

To a formalist like Brooks, any logical problems about Wordsworth's poetry can always be turned aside by declaring them strictly irrelevant. "What Wordsworth wanted to say demanded his use of paradox, . . . could only be said powerfully through paradox."[17] Empson, on the other hand, holds out against any such willing suspension of logical disbelief. Wordsworth, he argues, "seems to have believed in his own doctrines," and this makes it only reasonable to interrogate the poetry for "definite opinions on the relations of God, man and nature, and on the means by which such relations can be known" (*Seven Types*, p 152).

I wouldn't want to suggest that Empson's kind of sturdy scepticism is just another version of de Man's rigorously negative hermeneutics. Nevertheless, it produces a reading of Wordsworth which leads to some strikingly similar conclusions. Empson shares with de Man a principled mistrust of any totalizing rhetoric which would simply gloss over the elements of strain and contradiction in Wordsworth's inspirational language. He positively wrestles with the poem's syntax and logical connections, only to conclude that they cannot be sorted into any kind of rational-discursive order. In particular, Empson sees fit to resist the heady rhetorical drift which assimilates man and nature to a realm of undifferentiated spirit, with the vague implication that both are subsumed within the mind of God. For Empson, as for de Man, such elisions of the subject/object dichotomy are products of a synthesizing rhetoric which needs to be questioned, not taken on faith.

I must now quote Empson at sufficient length to bring out the deconstructive bearings of his argument. In the passage from "Tintern Abbey," he suggests,

> the *something* may possibly dwell only in the natural objects mentioned, ending at *sky*; the *motion* and the *spirit* are then not thought of at all as *interfused* into nature, like the *something*; they are things active *in the mind of man*. At the same time they are similar to the *something*; thus Wordsworth either *feels* them or *feels a sense* of them . . . (so that) man has a spirit immanent in nature in the same way as the spirit of God, and is decently independent from him. Or the *something* may also *dwell in the mind of man*, and have the *motion* and the *spirit* in opposition to it; under this less fortunate arrangement a God who is himself nature subjects us at once to determinism and predestination. (*Seven Types*, p. 153)

In a footnote to the second edition of *Seven Types*, Empson records the objection of M. C. Bradbrook that Wordsworth's logical imprecisions are nothing to the point, since "his theme is the transcendence of the subject-object relationship." But Empson rejects this accommodating line, insisting still that "the more seriously one takes the doctrine . . . the more this expression of it seems loose rhetoric" (p. 153).

What Empson is trying to pinpoint here is the tension (or divergence) between logic and rhetoric which de Man will later formulate in deconstructionist terms. In both cases there is a flat refusal to simply go along with the suasive rhetoric and leave the logical antinomies to sort themselves out into some kind of order. Empson protests that he enjoys this poetry, though he clearly feels a nagging mistrust as to the sources and nature of that enjoyment. His case, like de Man's, has ethical implications: poetry may use its rhetorical power to insinuate varieties of plainly irrational belief. In de Man, this suspicion takes the form of an unrelenting will to recall language to its "authentic" (temporal) condition, rather than permit the tropes to get away with their mystifying work. In Empson, the tone is more frankly puzzled than charged—like de Man's—with a kind of displaced existential pathos. But the object is likewise to resist what Empson sees as the irrational synthesizing claims of Wordsworth's rhetoric. Thus he writes:

> The reason why one grudges Wordsworth this source of strength is that he talks as if he owned a creed by which his half-statements might be reconciled, whereas, in so far as his creed was definite, he found these half-statements necessary to keep it at bay. (*Seven Types*, p. 154)

At one level this reflects Empson's rooted dislike of Christianity and the kinds of instituted paradox to which such beliefs give rise. But his critique of Wordsworth's "shuffling" argumentation—"this attempt to be uplifting yet non-denominational"—also leads into regions of specifically textual contradiction and aporia.

iii

De Man wrote admiringly about Empson in an essay called "The Dead-End of Formalist Criticism" (1956), first published in *Critique* by way of introducing French readers to recent Anglo-American developments. The "dead-end" in question was that represented by I. A. Richards's early attempts to put criticism on a "scientific" basis by reducing it to a matter of applied psychology. De Man finds problems—

as might be expected—with Richards's confident assumption that poetry serves to *communicate experience* from one mind to another. On this
highly simplified model, the author's task (as de Man describes it)
consists in "constructing a linguistic structure that will correspond as
closely as possible to the initial experience."[18] This "structure" will exist
for the reader as well, so that "what is called communication can then
occur." Criticism thus has its work cut out describing these kinds of
complex experience, determining their modes of verbal organization and
removing any obstacles to a full and free response on the reader's part.
There may be "numerous possibilities of error" in the carrying-out of
these pedagogic aims, but Richards is never in any doubt that "in every
case a correct procedure can be arrived at" (*Blindness*, p. 232).

De Man characteristically denies that interpretative "errors" can be
simply removed by the adopting of any such straight forward propedeu-
tic model. Richards's criticism, he writes, can be seen to rest on some
"highly questionable ontological presuppositions," foremost among
them the assured idea "that language, poetic or otherwise, can *say* any
experience, of whatever kind, even a simple perception" (*Blindness*, p.
232). Where Richards goes wrong is in failing to recognize the complex
mediations and the structures of perhaps *unmasterable* difference that
open up within the always error-prone activity of reading. Thus his
method assimilates *meaning* to *perception*, and both in turn to a theory of
poetic form which likewise ignores its own problematic status. While
admitting the attractions of this simplified creed—not least its pedagi-
gical usefulness—de Man is constrained to point out the difficulties in its
way. Richards makes do with a commonsense–empiricist theory of
language that effectively collapses all distinctions between perceptual,
aesthetic and critical-reflective orders of cognition. His method runs
together the two distinct elements of "a theory of constituting form" and
"a theory of signifying form" (p. 232). And this prevents Richards from
seeing that errors of interpretative insight may not be simply a matter of
corrigible reading-habits. As de Man writes:

> It can be said that there is a perceptual consciousness of the object and an
> experience of this consciousness, but a working out of a *logos* of this experience
> or, in the case of art, of a *form* of this experience, encounters considerable
> difficulties. (p. 23)

These problems, he argues, are constitutive of textual understanding, at
least where pursued with sufficient dialectical rigor and hermeneutic
tact. Richards can avoid facing up to them because he founds his poetics

on a purely *affective* psychology of imputed reader-response. Poetry, according to Richards, deals in varieties of "emotive" pseudo-statement which give no hold for any logical or cognitive account. Again, de Man sees the usefulness of this as a means of "saving" poetry for the purposes of humanist edification. But he also insists that Richards's position allows him to sidestep some crucial questions of interpretative theory and practice.

What de Man finds in Empson is a salutary knowledge that criticism cannot sink ontological differences in this brusque and question-begging manner. Empson's "ambiguity," unlike Richards's "emotive" language, preserves a keen sense of the problems involved with negotiating the passage from poetry to criticism. To anticipate the language of de Man's later texts, Ambiguity finds room for those "allegories of reading"—or self-reflexive moments of interpretative error—which result from the perpetual non-coincidence of poetic *meaning* and critical *method*. It resists, that is to say, the prematurely totalizing rhetoric of closure that Richards (like his followers, the American New Critics) raised to a high point of principle. The New Critics rejected what they saw as Richards's subjectivist bias, his appeal to psychological states of mind in the reader rather than "objective" structures of meaning in the poem.[19] But they managed to bypass epistemological problems by simply translating Richards's criteria (of "complexity," "equillibrium," etc.) to a notional image of the poem itself as objective verbal construct. Richards thus provided a working model for the basic New Critical strategy of *containing* awkward antinomies by always appealing to a higher, synthetic ground of unified perception. "Richards," says de Man, "did recognize the existence of conflicts, but he invoked Coleridge, not without some simplification, to appeal to the reassuring notion of art as the reconciliation of opposites" (*Blindness*, p. 237). This simplification led on directly to the formalist avoidance of those problems about mind and nature, subject and object which idealist aesthetics failed to resolve but refused to simply set aside.

It is at this point that Empson's "ambiguity" figures as a counter-trope in de Man's dialectical structure of argument. Ambiguity holds out against the synthesizing drive of Ricardian poetics and its various formalist offshoots. The source of that resistance, according to de Man, is the sheer impossibility of tracking language back to a moment of self-possessed original *experience* that would serve to ground the communicative process. Richards thinks of poetry as preserving such moments from "the lives of exceptional people," capturing a state where "their control and command of experience is at its highest degree."[20] Empson, on the contrary, shows poetry pressing the signifying potential of language to a point where Ambiguity outruns any possible grounding in experience. This lesson is most aptly figured for de Man in Empson's ambiguities of the seventh type, cases where the question of "conscious" or "unconscious" meaning becomes lost in a labyrinth of textual undecidability. At this stage criticism has to acknowledge its powerlessness to halt the figural drift of language in the name of some recuperative humanist ideal. "All of its basic assumptions have been put into question: the notions of communication, form, signifying experience, and objective precision" (*Blindness*, p. 241). As thought measures up to the problems engendered by linguistic figuration, so it comes to recognize the instability of its own ontological presuppositions. Even within the stronghold of American New Criticism, rhetoric proves more powerful and subversive than anything envisaged by the formalist program. "Terms such as paradox, tension and ambiguity abound . . . to the point of nearly losing all meaning" (*Blindness*, p. 241).

Up to now it might seem that de Man's own reading of Empson tends to confirm what I have been arguing here. Certainly it draws some similar conclusions about the inability of formalist criticism to think beyond the terms of its own self-supporting dialectic of method and meaning. It likewise agrees in setting up Empsonian "ambiguity" as a kind of conceptual stalking-horse whereby to reveal the inbuilt errors and delusions of a prematurely totalizing rhetoric. Ambiguity forces interpretation to the point of an unsettling self-knowledge where in "experience sheds its uniqueness and leads instead to a dizziness of the mind" (*Blindness*, p. 235). It is in this role that Empson serves de Man's argument as a kind of proto-deconstructionist thinker, a conceptual rhetorician willing to forego the easy satisfactions of normative criticism. But this undoing of naive ontological assumptions is only one side of de Man's argumentative strategy. Along with it there goes a rather different set of emphases, a rhetoric which treats Ambiguity as the product of some deep, aboriginal swerve within the being of language itself. This Heideggerian strain is very marked in de Man's early essays. It is mostly set off against a countervailing drive to demystify the kind of metaphysical pathos which would posit an *authentic* origin or ground, now lost beyond recall through the multiplied errors of linguistic figuration. Where de Man encounters such themes—as in Heidegger's reading of Hölderlin[21]—he interprets them as symptoms of a recurrent delusion, a nostalgic mystique of origins deeply complicit with the history of Western metaphysics. Yet the essay on Empson seems oddly disinclined to deconstruct this Heideggerian thematic. It enlists Ambiguity as bearing witness to the fundamental split between experience and language that language itself must constantly disguise *and* expose. Clearly de Man is not arguing that there once existed a state of linguistic innocence and grace when no such fallen condition prevailed. But the rhetoric of his essay often carries such suggestions, if only by way of contesting the reductive positivist assumptions of a critic like Richards.

Thus de Man writes of Empson that "he develops a thought Richards never wanted to consider: true poetic ambiguity proceeds from the deep division of Being itself, and poetry does no more than state and repeat this division" (*Blindness*, p. 237). Such formulations are a great deal less circumspect and rigorous than de Man's later idiom in *Allegories Of Reading*. They evoke a Heideggerian ethos of primal authenticity even in the process of denying that condition as a species of impossible and self-deluded dream. This ambivalance is yet more pronounced in other passages. Thus:

> The ambiguity poetry speaks of is the fundamental one that prevails between the world of spirit and the world of sentient substance: to ground itself, the spirit must turn itself into sentient substance, but the latter is knowable only in its dissolution into non-being. The spirit cannot coincide with its object and this separation is infinitely sorrowful. (*Blindness*, p. 237)

This Hegelian dialectic of the "unhappy consciousness" descends more by way of Kierkegaard than Nietzsche. It carries a charge of existential pathos that is still present—though nothing like as overt—in de Man's later writing. Certainly it seems very remote from the style of "enlightened" rationalist critique that Empson adopts towards most of his examples in *Seven Types of Ambiguity*. Empson says flatly that his kind of verbal analysis is meant to provide a "machinery of reassurance" for the reader uncertain as to how far his or her responses might bear such close inspection. If the results may sometimes seem "lacking in soul," then that is still preferable—Empson argues—to the attitude that puts up barriers of principled incomprehension between poem and reader. This assurance is important, moreover, since Empson admits that he is "treating the act of communication as something very extraordinary, so that the next step would be to lose faith in it altogether" (*Seven Types*, p. 243). De Man, of course, takes this decisive "next step" when he cites Empson's readings as witness to the ways in which "true poetic ambiguity" subverts the very logic of communicative language. But in mounting this argument de Man is constrained to read Empson according to a certain predisposed rhetoric of crisis by no means self-evident in Empson's text.

The same disposition is at work in de Man's reading of Empson's later book *Some Versions Of Pastoral* (1935). Empson defines pastoral in the broadest possible terms as a matter of "putting the complex into the simple." Under this rubric he treats a wide variety of texts—Shakespeare, Marvell, Gray's "Elegy," *The Beggars' Opera, Alice In Wonderland*—as instances of literature's striving to reconcile the claims of a "complex" imaginative life with the "simple" requirements of social equality and justice. His opening chapter ("Proletarian Literature") itself gives expression to this "pastoral" complex of motives by attempting to square the book's line of interest with the current pronouncements of Soviet Socialist Realism. Now de Man sees clearly that Empson's theme is nothing like as "simple" as might be thought, either by a Marxist or a literary scholar of more orthodox persuasion. Empson may choose to conduct his argument "under the deceitful title of a genre study." What he has actually written, de Man suggests, is a full-scale "ontology of the poetic," strategically disguised by "some extraneous matter that may well conceal the essential" (*Blindness*, p. 239).

Here again, de Man's language makes room for metaphysical presuppositions which his later writing would more rigorously call into question. It winnows the "essential" from the merely "extraneous" in the name of an authentically "ontological" concern which supposedly constitutes the truth of Empson's text. And this truth can only consist, for de Man, in that state of divided or "unhappy" consciousness theorized by Hegel and endlessly rehearsed in the self-reflexive tropes of poetic language. There is no denying that de Man's preoccupations answer to one—elusive but persistent—line of development in Empson's book. This aspect is most evident in the chapter on Marvell's "The Garden," which de Man understandably singles out for close attention. Empson reads the poem as a sustained meditation on the antinomies of conscious and unconscious thought, a compressed phenomenology of mind worked out through successive metaphorical exchanges between "outward" nature and "inward" thought.[22] He is plainly more at ease with Marvell's style of wittily discursive "metaphysics" than with Wordsworth's more earnest and high-toned reflections on a similar theme. And this is what de Man's reading must needs pass over in its desire to harness Empson's versions of pastoral to its own interpretative purpose. De Man seeks out ontological perplexities which will—he assumes—work everywhere to baffle and complicate the aims of normative interpretation. Empson is aware of these deep-seated problems, but treats them as a topic of speculative fancy, finally amenable to some kind of reasoned and more-or-less persuasive statement.

De Man's account of Empson on "The Garden" has the effect of reversing this clearly-marked preference and reading Empson (as well as Marvell) on distinctly Wordsworthian terms. Empson is quite explicit in drawing the relevant contrast here. Marvell's poem has the pastoral lightness of touch that allows it to suggest all manner of "transcendent" antinomies and mystical truth-claims without undermining its own witty logic. According to Empson, this also applies to "Romantic nature poetry" like Wordsworth's, though sometimes the wit is less in evidence and the truth-claims pitched too high.

> A hint of the supreme condition is thus found in the actual one (this makes the actual one include everything in itself), but this apparently exalted claim is essentially joined to humility; it is effective only through the admission that it is only a hint. Something of the tone of pastoral is therefore inherent in the claim; the fault of the Wordsworthian method seems to be that it does not show this. (*Some Versions*, p. 112)

This is the aspect of Empson's criticism that de Man fails to notice through his own preoccupation with the "deep" ontological problems of poetic language. To borrow de Man's terminology, the "insights" of his reading are tightly bound up with the "blindness" it exhibits toward other, less congenial elements of Empson's thought.

The path of this divergence can be tracked with some precision through the course of de Man's argument. His account of Empson on "The Garden" starts out from a point where he can almost paraphrase *Some Versions* yet manage to imply, in the same form of words, the "ontological" bearing of Empson's remarks. Thus de Man: "a reflection is not an identification, and the simple correspondence of the mind with the natural, far from being appeasing, turns troublesome" (*Blindness*, p. 239). By the next paragraph the argument has moved to a somewhat higher level of generalization. "What is the pastoral convention," de Man asks, "if not the eternal separation between the mind that distinguishes, negates, legislates, and the originary simplicity of the natural?" (p. 239). Such language evokes ontological depths and perplexities which belong more properly to what Empson calls "the Wordsworthian method," rather than Marvell's witty play of self-possessed pastoral conceits.

And then, within a page or so, de Man reaches the point of effectively declaring his revisionary bias. Pastoral figures as the counter-trope to *history*, in particular the Marxist understanding of history as the ground-principle of all interpretation. Empson has a good deal to say about the tensions between Marxist aesthetics (conceived, rather narrowly, as the call for "proletarian literature") and the different, more complicated workings of pastoral convention. Yet, so far from rejecting the Marxist set of claims, he examines their implications in a closely-argued chapter, and then goes on to interpret his various texts in terms which always relate—however obliquely—to changing conditions of history and class-consciousness. No doubt *Some Versions* contains many statements which would seem politically suspect or evasive from a Marxist viewpoint. The pastoral strategy of "putting the complex into the simple" produces a degree of ambivalence which affects both the genre and Empson's sympathetic treatment of it. But there is too much history and class-based analysis in Empson's pages for the book to be read as some kind of cryptic anti-Marxist tract.

Empson comes nearest to explaining his position in some comments on the topic of dialectical materialism. "I do not mean to say that the philosophy is wrong," he writes; "for that matter pastoral is worked from the same philosophical ideas . . .—the difference is that it brings in the absolute less prematurely" (*Some Versions*, p. 25). The "absolute" in question is the grand Hegelian idea of a totalizing movement in thought and history whereby mind would eventually transcend the crass contingencies of time and place. Empson has his doubts about the effect of such idealist residues in Marxist thinking. As with Wordsworth, he resists the synthesizing claims of a rhetoric all too willing to collapse such merely logical obstacles to thought as stand in its way. The virtue of pastoral, Empson suggests, is to handle these claims with a certain ironic "humility" and tact which saves them from turning into premature absolutes.

De Man is right enough to perceive the tensions that exist between pastoral and the claims of any hard-line materialist dialectic. But the upshot of his reading is to force Empson's text toward another kind of "absolute," one that negates historical understanding in the name of a more authentic, "ontological" concern. It is the great strength of Empson's criticism, de Man writes, that it "stands as a warning against certain Marxist illusions." And again, more specifically: "the problem of separation inheres in Being, which means that social forms of separation derive from ontological and meta-social attitudes" (*Blindness*, p. 240). De Man is able to quote convincingly from Empson to support this

ontological reading. But he also has to ignore many passages that allow
for no such smooth transition to the realm of metaphysical absolutes.
What his reading most actively works to achieve is the subjugation of
historical thought to a rhetoric of crisis and division descended from
Hegel's "unhappy consciousness." As de Man interprets it,

> the pastoral problematic, which turns out to be the problematic of Being
> itself, is lived in our day by Marxist thought, as by any genuine thought.
> Marxism is, ultimately, a poetic thought that lacks the patience to think its
> own conclusions to their end. (p. 240)

De Man finds this all the more striking for the fact that Empson sets out
from a broadly political or sociological set of concerns. *Some Versions*
should therefore be read, he argues, as an allegory of modern critical
consciousness forced to acknowledge the inherent limitations of its own
grounding concepts. Pastoral begins "under the aegis of Marxism" the
better to demonstrate the gulf which opens up between those twin
fascinations of present-day theory, poetry on the one hand and politics on
the other. Where Marxism holds out positive "solutions," poetry remains resistant to the point of disrupting all attempts to contain its
problematic nature. Empson thus serves de Man's argument in two
exemplary roles. Ambiguity unfolds into a powerful critique of the
assumptions underlying any formalist aesthetic of premature reconciliation between language and experience. Pastoral then completes this
process by implicitly contesting the truth-claims vested in the Marxist
dialectic of history and consciousness.

iv

I have argued that de Man's is a strong misreading of Empson, an
appropriative reading deeply committed to its own preoccupations of
method and intent. But I also hope to have shown that Empson's
criticism presses the analysis of poetic language to a stage where com-
parisons with de Man are still very much to the point. Empson's attitude
of sturdy rationalism makes him far more resistant to the kinds of
deep-rooted ontological perplexity which deconstruction discovers
everywhere at work. His reading of Wordsworth shows Empson refusing
to go along with the poetry and raise metaphysical paradoxes to the level
of transcendent (if problematic) truths. The example of Wordsworth, he
writes, "may show how these methods (i.e. those of verbal analysis) can
be used to convict a poet of holding muddled opinions rather than to

praise the complexity of the order of his mind" (*Seven Types*, p. 154). De Man's is essentially the opposite persuasion: that poetry is "authentic" only in so far as it reveals the inability of language to disguise its own self-divided and problematic nature.

Hegel, Kierkegaard and Heidegger stand as exemplars for de Man's conviction that knowledge can only be achieved through a chastening of its own positive truth-claims, a *via negativa* of ontological doubt. Empson, on the contrary, assumes that language should always be accountable to some kind of rational argument, even where the process leads—as with Wordsworth—into regions of obscurely paradoxical sense. Rather than equate such obscurity with philosophic "depth," Empson treats it as a habit of thought which may, on occasion, produce good poetry, but still needs explaining in logical terms. Thus, Wordsworth "sometimes uses what may be called philosophical ambiguities when he is not sure how far this process can tolerably be pushed" (*Seven Types*, p. 151). Such breakdowns in the logic of communicative sense are a symptom of *confusion* on Wordsworth's part, and not—as always for de Man—a symptom of language pushed up against the limits of figural undecidability.

Yet Empson and de Man have a good deal in common beyond the obvious fact that both represent a form of textual close-reading that often works to problematize poetic language. They each hold out against the formalist desire to sacralize the poem as a "verbal icon," a self-enclosed structure of rhetorical devices exempt from the sense-making context and conditions of language at large. In both, there is a will to demystify aesthetics and to press far beyond the kinds of compromise solution which New Criticism sought to impose. In the end, as I have argued, de Man must be seen as espousing a form of negative hermeneutics profoundly at odds with Empson's outlook of enlightened rationalist critique. But in the detailed working-out of these divergent positions they offer some exceptionally interesting grounds for comparison.

NOTES

1. See especially Geoffrey Hartman, *Saving the Text: literature/Derrida/philosophy* (Baltimore: Johns Hopkins University Press, 1981).
2. See Hartman, *Criticism In The Wilderness: the study of literature today* (New Haven: Yale University Press, 1980).
3. W. K. Wimsatt, "Battering The Object: the ontological approach," in Bradbury and Palmer eds, *Contemporary Criticism* (London: Edward Arnold, 1970).
4. See Derrida, "Signature Event Context," in *Margins Of Philosophy* trans. Alan Bass (Chicago: Chicago University Press, 1982), pp. 307–30.

5. J. Hillis Miller, "The Critic As Host," in *Deconstruction And Criticism* (New York: Seabury Press, 1979).

6. Paul de Man, "The Resistance To Literary Theory," *Yale French Studies*, 63 (1982), 3–20.

7. Paul de Man, *Allegories Of Reading: figural language in Rousseau, Nietzsche, Rilke, and Proust* (New Haven: Yale University Press, 1979), p. 9. Further page references to this book will be noted in the text along with *AR*.

8. Barbara Johnson, *The Critical Difference: essays in the contemporary rhetoric of reading* (Baltimore: Johns Hopkins University Press, 1980), p. xii.

9. Philip Wheelwright, "On The Semantics Of Poetry," *Kenyon Review*, 2 (1940), 264–83.

10. See, for instance, Cleanth Brooks, "Empson's Criticism," *Accent* (Summer, 1944), 208–16.

11. John Crowe Ransom, "Mr. Empson's Muddles," *The Southern Review*, 4 (1938), 334.

12. Ransom, quoted in William Rueckert, *Critical Responses to Kenneth Burke* (Minnesota: Minnesota University Press, 1969), p. 156.

13. Cleanth Brooks, "My Credo" (contribution to "The Formalist critics: a Symposium"), *Kenyon Review*, 18 (1951), 72–81.

14. William Empson, *Seven Types Of Ambiguity* (Harmondsworth: Penguin, 1961), p. 192. All further references to *Seven Types* are given by page-number in the text.

15. Paul de Man, *Blindness And Insight: essays in the rhetoric of contemporary criticism*, Second Ed., Revised and Enlarged, ed. Wlad Godzich (London: Methuen, 1983). "The Rhetoric of Temporality" appears among the supplementary essays, pp. 187–228. Quotation from Coleridge, p. 192. All further references given by page number in the text.

16. See Jacques Derrida, "Differance," in *Margins Of Philosophy* trans. Alan Bass (Chicago: Chicago University Press, 1982), pp. 3–27.

17. Cleanth Brooks, *The Well Wrought Urn* (New York: Dobson, 1949), p. 138.

18. Paul de Man, "The Dead-End Of Formalist Criticism," in *Blindness And Insight*, pp. 229–45. All further references given in the text.

19. Brooks, *The Well Wrought Urn*, p. 237.

20. I. A. Richards, *Principles Of Literary Criticism* (London: Kegan Paul, Trench, Trubner, 1926), p. 32.

21. Paul de Man, "Heidegger's Exegeses Of Hölderlin," in *Blindness And Insight*, pp. 246–66.

22. William Empson, "Marvell's Garden," in *Some Versions Of Pastoral* (Harmondsworth: Penguin, 1966), pp. 97–119. All subsequent references given by page-number in the text.

The Anxiety of Allegory:
De Man, Greimas, and the
Problem of Referentiality

Ronald Schleifer
University of Oklahoma

> It would be quite foolish to assume that one can lightheartedly move away
> from the constraint of referential meaning.
>
> —Paul de Man

i

Consistently central to scientific semantics, to speech-act philosophy,
and to literary criticism is the question of reference. In fact, "to understand," Paul de Man has written,

> primarily means to determine the referential mode of a text and we tend to
> take for granted that this can be done. We assume that a referential discourse
> can be understood by whoever is competent to handle the lexicological and
> grammatical code of a language. Neither are we helpless when confronted
> with figures of speech: as long as we can distinguish between literal and
> figural meaning, we can translate the figure back to its proper referent. (*AR*,
> p. 201)[1]

Linguistics, above all, seems to take for granted that this can be done in
its very use of what A. J. Greimas calls a "metalanguage" for describing
linguistic facts; yet to do so, it seems to suspend—or, more radically,
"behead"—the referential function of language.

De Man himself refers to such suspension of reference as the "arbitrary
power play of the signifier" which "from the point of view of the subject
. . . can only be experienced as a dismemberment, a beheading or a
castration" (*AR*, p. 296). The arbitrary play of the signifier is language
without reference—"the entirely gratuitous and irresponsible text" (*AR*,
p. 296)—that "contemporary semiotics" seeks to analyze (*AR*, p. 207).
Thus in Chapter Four of *Structural Semantics*, Greimas attempts to
describe the manifestation of signification in discourse by analyzing the
organization of the elementary units of signification (which he calls

215

"semes") within a particular word ("lexeme"). The word he chooses by way of example is "head," and taking his examples from the dictionary, he notes at the beginning of his analysis that while the "fundamental definition from which all the others derive . . . is its representation as part (of the body),' " "none of the examples cited by Littré illustrates the word *tête* as part of the body" (*SS*, p. 47).[2] That is, the most extended example that *Structural Semantics* offers is one that explores signification in terms of what Greimas calls "a radiating source of 'meanings' more or less 'figurative' " (*SS*, p. 47): headsplitting noise, head of cattle, to be over one's head in debt, head of a line, head of a pin, etc. Greimas's is a significant example, however, because it demonstrates the constant gesture of linguistics to suspend the opposition between the figurative and the literal by postulating minimal semic oppositions that inform signification.

This opposition can be suspended because in significant ways reference is suspended. Summing up the philosophical debate about the nature of reference, John Searle describes it as "reference to" a *unique pre-existing object*: "a fully consummated reference is one in which an object is identified unambiguously for the hearer."[3] That is, the referent is, as de Man says, "extralinguistic" and has "prior existence" to its reference (*AR*, pp. 106, 121). The elements of linguistics, however, exist in diacritical rather than referential relationships. The *"seme,"* Greimas writes, "has no existence on its own and can be imagined and described only in relation to something that it is not, inasmuch as it is only part of a structure of signification" (*SS*, p. 118). What Greimas is doing—what structural linguistics does—is to attempt the grammatization of language. Thus, Greimas can write an essay entitled "Narrative Grammar," and he structures his semantic description of language in *Structural Semantics* in close relationship to syntactic and combinatory models.

That is, both Greimas and structural linguistics in general attempt, as de Man says, to create a grammar:

> The system of relationships that generates the text and that functions independently of its referential meaning is its grammar. To the extent that a text is grammatical, it is a logical code or a machine. And there can be no agrammatical texts. . . . Any nongrammatical text will always be read as a deviation from an assumed grammatical norm. But just as no text is conceivable without grammar, no grammar is conceivable without the suspension of referential meaning. Just as no law can ever be written unless one suspends any consideration of applicability to a particular entity including, of course,

oneself, grammatical logic can function only if its referential consequences are disregarded. (*AR*, pp. 268–69)

Grammar, like the law, has to be blind; it has to suspend what Emile Benveniste calls "the instances of discourse,"[4] and with that the possibility of reference. For this reason de Man argues that an enabling postulate of "contemporary semiology" is the reduction of the referential function of language "to being just one contingent linguistic property among others" (*AR*, p. 207), and Greimas substantiates this in calling for "the rejection of the supplementary dimension of the *referent*" (*SS*, p. 12). "Any discourse, we know," he writes, "presupposes a nonlinguistic situation of communication. This situation is covered by a certain number of morphological categories, which make it explicit linguistically but introduce at the same time in the manifestation a *parameter of subjectivity* which is not pertinent to the description . . ." (*SS*, p. 175). Linguistics, Greimas continues, must eliminate categories of person, time, deixis, and the phatic element in general.

Grammar, in short, must function without regard to person or position, like a machine rather than a monarch—who has in his person, as de Man says, the power to execute, and is defined *against* the law: "the divergence . . . in the relationship between the citizen and the executive is in fact an unavoidable estrangement between political rights and laws on the one hand, and political action and history on the other" (*AR*, p. 266). "Machine," as de Man goes on to show, is a good metaphor for grammatization because it is defined against the body: "The text as body, with all its implications of substitutive tropes ultimately always retraceable to metaphor, is displaced by the text as machine and, in the process, it suffers the loss of the illusion of meaning" (*AR*, p. 298). Thus, it is precisely *against* the symbolism of Gilbert Durand, based upon "an apparent systematization of bodily gestures" (*SS*, p. 62), that Greimas defines the semiological level of language.

"Beheading," then, is what linguistics attempts: to suspend the silly "(silliness being deeply associated with reference)" (*AR*, p. 209), the accidents of emotion (fear, self-love, doubt, even anxiety), and what Shoshana Felman calls the "trivial" in *The Literary Speech Act* (p. 116),[5] in favor of describing language in a way that excludes psychic energies. "As soon as the text is said not to be a figural body but a machine," de Man writes, ". . . far from seeing language as an instrument in the service of a psychic energy, the possibility now arises that the entire construction of drives, substitutions, repressions, and representations is the aberrant, metaphorical correlative of the absolute randomness of language, prior to any figuration of meaning. It is no longer certain that language, as excuse, exists because of a prior guilt but just as possible that since language, as a machine, performs anyway, we have to produce guilt (and all its train of psychic consequences) in order to make the excuse meaningful" (*AR*, p. 299). The confusion concerning the priority or antecedence of guilt is the confusion of referentiality: it is not the confusion of possible referents but the confusion—the "un-decidability"—of whether or not referentiality is possible.

ii

De Man's reading of *Julie*, for instance, is an allegory of the (illusory) relationship between meaning and referent narrated in the transformation of the pathos of "referential indeterminacy" (*AR*, p. 197) into religious belief, "the articulation of the figural mode with an ethical tonality" (*AR*, p. 188). De Man articulates this more concretely later in this essay in terms of the body when he notes "the lines of a face produce a semiological as well as a physical connotation, and appear as the inscription, on the surface of the face, of the soul's meaning" (*AR*, p. 211). In fact, it is in his discussion of *Julie* that he attempts to define *pathos*:

> The more the text denies the actual existence of a referent, real or ideal, and the more fantastically fictional it becomes, the more it becomes the representation of its own pathos. Pathos is hypostatized as a blind power or mere 'puissance de vouloir,' but it stabilizes the semantics of the figure by making it 'mean' the pathos of its undoing. (*AR*, pp. 198–99)

"Pathos" is a recurring word in de Man—along with "seduction" it is the term he uses to describe the affects of language—and, as we shall see, it marks the problem of the body in discourse, the question of "beheading," which is closely tied, as a defining case, to referentiality. For just as the law must intend yet suspend referentiality and linguistics must assert yet suspend the meaning-effects of language,[6] so the opposition between discourse and the body—what Felman calls "the dichotomy between self-referentiality and linguistic referentiality" (Felman, p. 81) and de Man describes as the dichotomy between cognition and act—is both enabling and distortive. For a central concern of language—whether it be literary criticism or speech-act theory or even structural linguistics—is the question of how it is that language can *provoke* (to use a term of Greimas's) physical responses, what psychology calls conversion reactions. How is *pathos*—the quality or power, the dictionary says, in literature, music, speech, or other expressive forms, of evoking a feeling—possible? To "behead" language is to make its pathos "mean"; it is to erase the materiality of language. This is the structuralist enterprise—not only Greimas in his elimination of the phatic elements of language, but also Lévi-Strauss in his attempt, as he says in *The Raw and the Cooked*, to inscribe the materiality of body functions such as the heartbeat and the pulse within the signifying structures of music.[7]

Here is the center of de Man, his allegories of reading. Allegory for de Man is the reading of statement against enunciation, the spirit against the letter, the ethics of (impossible) grammatical meaning against the pathos of (illusory) material reference. In the first half of *Julie*, he argues, "the value system and the narrative promote each other's elaboration; hence the relative ease of the narrative pattern in . . . the story of passion in the first part of *Julie* which is said to be 'like a live source that flows forever and that never runs dry' " (*AR*, p. 206). In the second part, however, when Julie turns from the love of Saint-Preuve to the love of God,

> The concatenation of the categories of truth and falsehood with the values of right and wrong is disrupted, affecting the economy of the narration in decisive ways. We can call this shift in economy *ethical*, since it indeed involves a displacement from *pathos* to *ethos*. Allegories are always ethical, the term ethical designating the structural interference of two distinct value systems. In this sense, ethics has nothing to do with the will (thwarted or free) of a subject, nor *a fortiori*, with a relationship between subjects. . . . Morality is a version of the same language aporia that gave rise to such concepts as "man" or "love" or "self," and not the cause or the consequence of such concepts. (*AR*, p. 206)

The structural interference of two value systems that de Man describes are the systems of grammar and rhetoric: the nonreferentiality of grammar interfering with the referentiality of rhetoric. In "Pascal's Allegory of Persuasion" de Man approvingly cites Hegel's distinction between allegory and enigma "in terms of allegory's 'aim for the most complete clarity. . . .' The difficulty of allegory," de Man continues, "is rather that this emphatic clarity of representation does not stand in the service of something that can be represented."[8] The nature of allegory, then, is its structurality; it "initiates and continually revivifies its own desire," as Joel Fineman has described it, "a desire born of its structurality. . . . This is the formal destiny of every allegory insofar as allegory is definable as continued metaphor. Distanced at the beginning from its source, allegory will set out on an increasingly futile search for a signifier with which to recuperate the fracture of and at its source."[9] As a "continued metaphor," allegory is referential language without a referent. The structure of allegory is the incongruity at its source, the discrepancy between the spirit and the word, the material word and that to which it refers.

The ease with which de Man moves from pathos to ethics, from a tropological to a cognitive sense of language, is remarkable: it is, I believe, parallel to the ease with which Lévi-Strauss moves from bodily functions to semiotic systems and the ease with which Greimas can dismiss what he might call the "affectivity" of language. For Greimas, the "reception" of language is purely cognitive: the problem in language, he argues, is that of "grasping" signification (SS, p. 114). Yet the pathos of language is not cognitive but tropological: "seductive," "forceful," a kind of "power." It is what de Man calls "referential error" and designates in the discussion of *Julie* as "desire":

> Like "man," "love" is a figure that disfigures, a metaphor that confers the illusion of proper meaning to a suspended open semantic structure. In the naively referential language of the affections, this makes love into the forever-repeated chimera, the monster of its own aberration, always oriented toward the future of its repetition, since the undoing of the illusion only sharpens the uncertainty that created the illusion in the first place. In this same affective language, the referental error is called desire, and the voice of this desire can be heard throughout Rousseau's writings. . . . (*AR*, p. 198)

Such troping is the will to power de Man describes in Nietzsche's conception of "positing" rather than "knowing" (*AR*, p. 121). Knowing, in this sense, is *referential*: "to know," de Man writes, "is a transitive function that assumes the prior existence of an entity to be known and that predicates the ability of knowing by ways of properties" (*AR*, p. 121). What knowledge does most of all is erase "the pathos of a temporal predicament in which man's self-definition is forever deferred" (*AR*, p. 199). It does so not simply for those who naively imagine an unproblematic referent for discourse, but (more pathetically) for de Man himself. Knowledge is "a dismemberment, a beheading or a castration"—"the symbol manifests itself first of all," as Lacan has said, "as the murder of the thing"[10]—yet such violence, for de Man, responds to the greater violence of what is "random," and it results simply in anxiety— the anxiety of allegory.

This anxiety is a result of the fact that, despite what de Man says earlier in the essay, pathos itself—the pathos of affect—cannot "mean":

> The heterogeneous texture of Rousseau's allegorical narratives is less surprising if one keeps in mind that his radical critique of referential meaning never implied that the referential function of language could in any way be avoided, bracketed, or reduced to being just one contingent linguistic property among others, as is postulated, for example, in contemporary semiology which . . . could not exist without this postulate. Rousseau never allows for a "purely" aesthetic reading in which the referential determination would remain suspended or be nonexistent. Such a reading is inconceivable on the epistemological, premoral level, where it would be the mere play of a free signifier, nor does it exist in allegory, when the undoing of signification has taken on ethical dimension. . . . Suspended meaning is not, for him, disinterested play, but always a threat or a challenge. . . . But since the convergence of the referential and the figural signification can never be established, the reference can never be a meaning. In Rousseau's linguistics there is room only for "wild" connotation; the loss of denominational control means that every connotation has claim to referential authority but no statute in which to ground this claim. . . .
>
> The persistence of the referential moment (which is to be distinguished from the noncognitive, performative function of language) prevents the confinement of allegory to an epistemological and ethical system of valorization. Since the epistemological mediation is known to be unreliable, and since the narrative of its discovery *cannot be left suspended* in the contemplation of its own aesthetic gratification, the allegory speaks out with the referential efficacy of a *praxis*. The ethical language of persuasion has to act upon a world that it no longer considers structured like a linguistic system but that consists of a system of *needs*. (AR, pp. 207–09; first italicization added)

Reference can never be meaning because the world (unlike Lacan's unconscious) is *not* structured like a language. Pathos, here, is precisely the pathos of needs, of necessity beyond language, the necessities of contingent bodily existence: the fact that "nonverbal entities" are "random" rather than meaningful, in an unsponsored world where sense and reference cannot coincide and the pleasures of aesthetics do not allow us to forget the "threat" and "challenge" of suspended meaning. Not only does de Man suggest that psychic energies are possibly "the aberrant, metaphorical correlative to the absolute randomness of language" (AR, p. 299), but more darkly he asserts that bodily death is inscribed in language. *The Triumph of Life*, he writes in "Shelley Disfigured," is inscribed with—indeed, "mutilated" by (p. 67)—its "decisive textual articulation: its reduction to the status of a fragment brought about by the actual death and subsequent disfigurement of Shelley's body" (p. 66). *"The Triumph of Life,"* he concludes,

> warns us that nothing, whether deed, word, thought or text, ever happens in relation, positive or negative, to anything that precedes, follows or exists elsewhere, but only as a random event whose power, like the power of death, is due to the randomness of its occurrence. (p. 69)[11]

The pathos of suspended meaning, then, is "worse than madness: the mere confusion of fiction with reality, as in the case of Don Quijote, is mild and curable compared to this radical dyslexia" (*AR*, p. 202).

In what is perhaps the most chilling assertion of *Allegories of Reading*—one that is the opposite to the "lightheartedness" of my epigraph (and of Nietzsche, Felman, and Derrida)[12]—de Man cites Nietzsche: " 'Only as an *aesthetic phenomenon* is existence and the world forever *justified*': the famous quotation, twice repeated in *The Birth of Tragedy*, should not be taken too serenely, for it is an indictment of existence rather than a panegyric of art" (*AR*, p. 93). Harold Bloom has offered the image of Oedipus as a metaphor for this reading—"the blind Oedipus is the human, the total coherence that knows life cannot be justified as an aesthetic phenomenon, even when that life is wholly sacrificed to the aesthetic realm"[13]—and de Man later allegorizes this "sense" of existence (located in the nonconvergence of the random possibilities of reference and the certainty of meaning) in the allegory of reading with which he concludes his study of *Julie*: "The readability of the first part is obscured by a more radical indeterminacy that projects its shadow backwards and forwards over the entire text. Deconstructions of figural texts engender lucid narratives which produce, in their turn and as it were within their own texture, a darkness more redoubtable than the error they dispel" (*AR*, p. 217). This "darkness" is the origin and opposite of discourse, both its referent (in the rhetorical sense of antecedent) and its meaning (in the grammatical sense of "the possibility of unproblematic dyadic meaning"—*AR*, p. 19). It is this random absence of relations which gives rise to the linguistic assertion of relations: the darkness of death. "Discourse," Derrida has written,

> if it is originally violent, ... as the avowal of violence, is the least possible violence, the only way to repress the worst violence, the violence of primitive and prelogical silence, of a unimaginable night which would not even be the opposite of nonviolence: nothingness and pure nonsense.[14]

For de Man "needs"—necessity beyond language—offer a referent, like "darkness," "threat," and the unserenity of "pathos," which lies in the lesser (discursive) violence of the uncertainty between reference and meaning: "the entire assumption of a nonverbal realm governed by needs may well be a speculative hypothesis that exists only . . . *for the sake of language*" (*AR*, p. 210). Such an understanding of needs creates the possibility of meaning against darkness and unimaginable night: "needs," de Man concludes, "reenters the literary discourse as the aberrant proper meaning of metaphors *against* which the allegory constitutes itself" (*AR*, p. 210).

iii

In this conception of metaphor (and passion and nonverbal entities) the referential aspects of language are more complex than de Man's earlier statements about grammatical machines suggest. Metaphor is a complication of reference, seemingly situated both within and outside the grammatization of discourse. In his discussion of the metaphors of "cold" and "hot" in Rousseau's *Pygmalion* de Man notes that

> this coldness has nothing in common with the coldness of the original stone; Bachelard's thermodynamics of the material imagination would find nothing to feed on in *Pygmalion*. "Hot" and "cold" are not, in this text, derived from material properties but from a transference from the figural to the literal that stems from the ambivalent relationship between the work as an extension of the self and as a quasi-divine otherness. (*AR*, p. 178)

The transference de Man describes is the complication of reference, not its suspension. The metaphors "hot" and "cold" refer, at least in part, to those psychic energies that he claims elsewhere the "machine" of grammar excludes. More generally, de Man defines "*text*" as "any entity that can be considered from such a double perspective: as a generative, open-ended, non-referential grammatical system and as a figural system closed off by a transcendental signification that subverts the grammatical code to which the text owes its existence"; "a text is defined by the necessity of considering a statement, at the same time, as performative and constative, and the logical tension between figure and grammar is repeated in the impossibility of distinguishing between two linguistic functions which are not necessarily compatible" (*AR*, p. 270). It is this "impossibility" that Derrida calls the "violence" inscribed in language. In de Man's example the "transference from the figural to the literal" is the translation of "cold" as a metaphor for a feeling to what Greimas calls

the "substantifying" (SS, pp. xli, 138) of that feeling as such, a quasi-
divine manifestation of the feeling's energy, as if from somewhere else.
This is the "literalization" of metaphor, the fact that "metaphor literal-
izes its referential indetermination into a specific unit of meaning" (AR,
p. 153): it "transfers" the metonymic "cold" of the stone into something
to which the substitutive metaphoric "cold" refers.

In large part the whole thrust of Allegories of Reading is predicated on
the metaphorical articulation of passion as de Man describes it in the
discussion of Rousseau's Second Discourse.

> The fact that Rousseau chose fear as an example to demonstrate the priority of
> metaphor over denomination complicates and enriches the pattern to a
> considerable degree, for metaphor is precisely the figure that depends on a
> certain degree of correspondence between "inside" and "outside" proper-
> ties. . . . The metaphor is blind, not because it distorts objective data, but
> because it presents as certain what is, in fact, a mere possibility. The fear of
> falling is "true," for the potentially destructive power of gravity is a verifiable
> fact, but the fear of another man is hypothetical. . . . By calling him a
> "giant," one freezes hypothesis, or fiction, into fact and makes fear, itself a
> figural state of suspended meaning, into a definite, proper meaning devoid of
> alternatives. The metaphor "giant," used to connote man, has indeed a
> proper meaning (fear), but this meaning is not really proper: it refers to a
> condition of permanent suspense between a literal world in which appearance
> and nature coincide and a figural world in which the correspondence is no
> longer a priori posited. Metaphor is error because it believes or feigns to
> believe in its own referential meaning. (AR, p. 151)

This definition of metaphor as presenting "mere possibility" as certain is
central to the distinction that is posited and deconstructed throughout
Allegories of Reading between the literal and the figurative. "Mere
possibility" is what Greimas refers to as "a Saussurean 'great cloudiness' " (SS, p. 67), that is, as Louis Hjelmslev's conception of the
undifferentiated "substance of the content," "an unanalyzed, amorphous
continuum, on which boundaries are laid by the formative action of the
languages."[15] Greimas bases his definition of the elementary structure of
signification on this Hjelmslevian model, and he locates both the "form
of the content" and the "substance of the content" within the linguistic
universe (arguing that the semantic axes of language constitute the
"substance"—see SS, pp. 26–28). But most importantly, he asserts that
"Hjelmslev's concept of the form of the content . . . signified the death
of formalism" (SS, p. 68). In this, he is following Lévi-Strauss who has
argued that "Form is defined by opposition to material other than itself.

But *structure* has no distinct content; it is content itself, apprehended in a logical organization conceived as a property of the real."[16]

In this conception, the problem of referentiality is not "suspended" as simply one contingent linguistic property among others, but made in significant ways a *function* of language (in both the ordinary and mathematical senses of the word: what languages *does* and what is dependent upon language). "Without language," Saussure notes, "thought is a vague, uncharted nebula [a "great cloudiness"]. There are no preexisting ideas, and nothing is distinct before the appearance of language."[17] "Language," he continues, "might be called the domain of articulations" (pp. 112–13), and by "articulation" he means "the subdivision of the chain of meanings into significant units": "what is natural to mankind is not oral speech but the faculty of constructing a language, i.e. a system of distinct signs corresponding to distinct ideas" (p. 10).

It is on the basis of this argument that Hjelmslev distinguishes between the "form of the content" and the "substance of the content": "If we maintain Saussure's terminology," he writes, "it becomes clear that the substance depends on the form to such a degree that it lives exclusively by its favor and can in no sense be said to have independent existence" (*Prolegomena*, p. 50). In *Structural Semantics* Greimas borrows Hjelmslev's "now famous example of the color specturm (*Prolegomena*, p. 53)" to demonstrate this *structural* distinction:

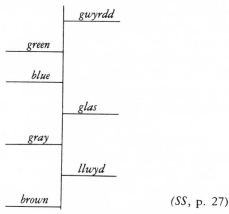

(*SS*, p. 27)

As this chart shows, colors articulated in English and Welsh do not coincide. Rather, as Hjelmslev notes, "behind the paradigms that are furnished in the various languages by the designations of color, we can . . . disclose such an amorphous continuum, the color spectrum, on which each language arbitrarily sets its boundaries" (*Prolegomena*, p. 52).

Such a conception of language makes the "objects" of reference problematic. It accomplishes, as Felman argues in *The Literary Speech Act* (not in terms of Hjelmslevian linguistics, but in terms of speech-act theory), a "*change in status* of the referent as such" (Felman, p. 75). "Contrary to the traditional conception of the referent, however," she continues,

> referential knowledge of language is not envisaged here as constative, cognitive knowledge: neither for psychoanalysis nor performative analysis is language a *statement* of the real, a simple reflection of the referent or its mimetic representation. Quite to the contrary, the referent is itself produced by language as its own *effect*. . . . This means that between language and referent there is no longer simple opposition (nor is there identity, on the other hand): language makes itself part of what it refers to (without, however, being all that it refers to). Referential knowledge of language is not knowledge *about* reality (about a separate and distinct entity), but knowledge that *has to do with reality*, that acts within reality, since it is itself—at least in part—what this reality is made of. The referent is no longer simply a preexisting *substance*, but an *act*, that is, a dynamic movement of modification of reality. (pp. 76–77)

Despite the gesture in Greimas (and in Hjelmslev as well) to seemingly "bracket" the referent, this "structural" conception of reference, in fact, reinscribes referentiality in relation to the "grammatical" relationships that define language. This change in status escapes the oppositional alternatives of language and referent, certainty and possibility. Even Searle agrees that color is an object in the world that preexists its linguistic "description" (not "articulation"): speaking of the "preexistence" of fictional "entities" as susceptible to reference—"one can refer to them *as fictional characters* precisely because they do *exist in fiction*" (Searle, p. 78) he writes—Searle asserts that "it is essential to realize that even in 'Little Red Riding Hood,' 'red' means red" (p. 79).[18]

Moreover, besides the color spectrum (which, it could be argued, functions like Locke's "secondary characteristics"), Hjelmslev also offers five sentences in different languages (the English version of which is "I do not know") to show that this purport could be "analyzed from many points of view, to be subjected to many different analyses, under which it would appear as so many different objects" (*Prolegomena*, p. 51). Greimas, too, adds that the articulations of the form and content of the substance "characterize, of course, not only the color spectrum but a great number of semantic axes" (*SS*, p. 27). What structural semantics does, then, is not to abandon the referent, but to reconceive it. "It seems to be true," Hjelmslev notes,

> that a sign is a sign for something, and that this something in a certain sense lies outside the sign itself. Thus the word *ring* is a sign for that definite thing on my finger, and that thing does not, in a certain (traditional) sense, enter into the sign itself. But that thing on my finger is an entity of content-substance, which, through the sign, is ordered to a content-form and is arranged under it together with various other entities of content-substance (*e.g.*, the sound that comes from my telephone). That a sign is a sign for something means that the content-form of a sign can subsume that something as content-substance. . . .
>
> . . . [Thus] it appears more appropriate to use the word *sign* as the name for the unit consisting of content-form and expression-form. . . . If *sign* is used as the name for the expression alone or for a part of it, the terminology, even if protected by formal definitions, will run the risk of consciously or unconsciously giving rise to or favoring the widespread misconception according to which a language is simply a nomenclature or a stock of labels intended to be fastened on pre-existent things. (*Prolegomena*, pp. 57–58)

Like the linguistic performance of marriage Austin describes or its breach in seduction Felman describes, reference here is "a sign *for* something" which is neither simply a signified nor simply some *thing*. Rather, the activity of reference is always inscribed within another context in which reference "has to do with reality." Reference, in this conception, can be compared to a child's discourse imitating that of his parents: his word refers to the object his parents hold and name—a wedding ring, for instance—but such "reference," like the ring itself, is inscribed within another network of relations (of love or fear or simply the desire for community) which *do occur* as powerfully as death precisely because they are as "random" as death. [19]

This conception of reference, then, forces us to reconceive what de Man says about the avoidance, bracketing, and reduction of the referential function in contemporary semiotics (*AR*, p. 207). If, in fact, structure articulates "the real," then the question of reference is more complicated than de Man seems to indicate in his distinction between certainty and possibility. That is, the only "certainty" (which de Man seems so anxious to achieve) is the ambiguous culturally determined "certainty" of linguistic articulation. The articulations of the form of the content, Greimas argues, "are only different categorizations of the world, which define, in their specificity, cultures and civilizations" (*SS*,

p. 27). Given this method of understanding the function of reference in language—and Hjelmslev has shown it is a central consequence of Saussurean linguistics—de Man's distinction between the possibility and certainty of reference seems somewhat naive.

iv

Elsewhere, in his distinction between metaphor and metonymy, de Man seems to offer a more complicated sense of this distinction:

> The distinction between metonymic aggregates and metaphorical totalities, based on the presence, within the latter of a "necessary link" that is lacking in the former, is characteristic of all metaphorical systems, as is the equation of the principle of totalization with *natural* process. After the deconstruction of the metaphorical model has taken place, the attribute of naturalness shifts from the metaphorical totality to the metonymic aggregate, as was the case for the "state of nature" in the *Second Discourse* or for "sensation" in the *Profession de foi*. (AR, p. 259)

The distinction between metonymic aggregates and metaphorical totalities, like that between blue and gray in the English articulation of the color spectrum, is purely an arbitrary and performative one.[20] Metaphor creates certainty by substantifying experience through the principle of totalization, yet that substantification can *always* be deconstructed since, given the relational nature of language, the "certainty" and unity of substance can always be "exploded" into the aggregation of relationships: "Whenever one opens one's mouth to speak of relationships," writes Greimas in *Du Sens*, "they transform themselves, as if by magic, into substantives, that is into terms whose meaning we must negate by postulating new relationships, and so on and on."[21]

A central feature of structural analysis—one to which Derrida repeatedly calls attention[22]—is its tendency to undermine its own enabling oppositions. It is as if the radically relational nature of what Greimas calls "the elementary structure of signification" necessarily erases as it posits its structures. Thus Fineman says that

> allegory initiates and continually revivifies its own desire, a desire born of its own structurality. Every metaphor is always a little metonymic because in order to have a metaphor there must be a structure, and where there is a structure there is already piety and nostalgia for the lost origin through which the structure is thought. Every metaphor is a metonymy of its own origin, its structure thrust into time by its very structurality.[23]

For Greimas this is inscribed in the global double analysis of *Structural Semantics* which understands its "objects" of analysis sometimes as "discrete units . . . presented as unitary objects" producing the meaning-effect of "The idea of 'substance,' " and sometimes as "integrated units" presented as in integrated collection of determinations (*SS*, p 138).

This process of "undermining" is a version of deconstruction, and Greimas's "semiotic square"—which Fredric Jameson describes as the mapping of "the logical structure of reality itself"[24]—inscribes within itself what Greimas calls the "explosion" of a unity into an aggregate, the elementary into complexity (see *SS*, pp. xxxii–xxxv). Elsewhere Jameson describes this "explosion" as "a decisive leap, . . . a production or generation of new meaning"[25], and throughout *Allegories of Reading* de Man charts the explosive confusion of metaphor and metonymy, of continuous texts and discontinuous formulations (*AR*, p. 101), the "disruptive intertwining of trope and persuasion or—which is not the same thing—of cognitive and performative language" (*AR*, p. ix). This "confusion" is not simply muddled, but rather, in Greimas's square, stands outside the oppositional terms: "non *a*" becomes "neither *a* nor non *a*"; as de Man says, "a statement of distrust is neither true nor false" (*AR*, p. 150). Thus, rather than simple negation in binary opposition to the positive, "the reversal from denial to assertion implicit in deconstructive discourse never reaches the symmetrical counterpart of what it denies" (*AR*, p. 125).

This is the "radical negativity" Felman explores in *The Literary Speech Act*:

> This radical negativity is not simply "negative"; it is—in a very complex way—positive, it is fecund, it is affirmative. . . .
>
> Thus negativity, fundamentally fecund and affirmative, and yet without positive reference, is above all *that which escapes the negative/positive alternative*. . . .
>
> Radical negativity (or "saying no") belongs neither to *negation*, nor to *opposition*, nor to *correction* ("normalization"), nor to *contradiction* (of the positive and the negative, the normal and the abnormal, the "serious" and the "unserious," "clarity" and "obscurity")—it belongs precisely to *scandal*: to the scandal of their nonopposition. This scandal of the *outside of the alternative*, of a negativity that is neither negative nor positive. . . . (pp. 141–42)

The "scandal" Felman is speaking of is, as the French title of her book says, *Le Scandale du corps parlant*, "the scandal of the *seduction* of the human body insofar as it speaks" (p. 12). It is, as she suggests, the scandal, not of referentiality, but of the affectivity of language, its possibility of creating bodily responses (such as fear, or passion, or distrust, or even anxiety). As de Man says, this is the "impossible" situation where "the ethical language has to act upon a world that it no longer considers structured like a linguistic system" (*AR*, p. 209) yet which, impossibly, it still affects. The scandal of the speaking body is precisely the nonopposition of the difference between body and word, what both Felman and de Man describe as the "seductive" power of language (the former in terms of pleasure, the latter in terms of pathos).

In *Allegories of Reading* de Man narrates the scandalous negativity of deconstruction:

> Deconstruction does not occur between statements, as in a logical refutation or in a dialectic, but happens instead between, on the one hand, metalinguistic statements about the rhetorical nature of language and, on the other hand, a rhetorical praxis that puts these statements into a question. The outcome of this interplay is not mere negation. *The Birth of Tragedy* does more than just retract its own assertions about the genetic structure of literary history. It leaves a residue of meaning that can, in its turn, be translated into statement, although the authority of this second statement can no longer be like that of the voice in the text when it is read naively. The nonauthoritative secondary statement that results from the reading will have to be a statement about the limitations of textual authority. (*AR*, pp. 98–99)

This "residue of meaning" is "ignorance," always in de Man—under the denotations of "impossibility," "undecidability," "undeterminable," "an intolerable semantic irresolution . . . worse than madness: the mere confusion of fiction with reality . . . is mild and curable compared to this radical dyslexia" (p. 202)—the scandal of reference.

That is, the central will to truth in de Man—his sense, as he argues throughout *Allegories of Reading* that the opposition truth vs. falsehood (based upon the traditional sense of referentiality) cannot be suspended, that its "confusion" is a threat, a challenge, a pathos, an occasion for anxiety that cannot lightheartedly or easily be dismissed—underlines the difference between the reference and grammar of language which Felman erases. De Man needs this opposition to maintain the distinction between the literal and the figurative—he needs it, as we can see in his definition of "understanding," to make knowledge itself possible—yet he continually sees it deconstructed in Rousseau and the other texts he examines: "all language," he asserts, "*has to be* referential but can never signify its actual referent" (*AR*, p. 160).

For him, unlike Felman, this uncertainty is simply anxious—an anxiety about the possibility of knowledge that is itself remarkable. In a revealing passage towards the end of "Semiology and Rhetoric," he says

> We end up therefore, in the case of the rhetorical grammatization of semiology, just as in the grammatical rhetorization of illocutionary phrases, in the same state of suspended ignorance. Any question about the rhetorical mode of a literary text is always a rhetorical question which does not even know whether it is really questioning. The resulting pathos is an anxiety (or bliss, depending on one's momentary mood or individual temperament) of ignorance, not an anxiety of reference. . . . (AR, p. 19)

It is ignorance, the impossibility of truly understanding what one is doing with language, what language itself could possibly do in reference to the world, rather than any possible contingent mistake, that most troubles de Man: "the problem" he writes, "is not that Julie remains mystified, but that a totally enlightened language . . . is unable to control the recurrence . . . of the errors it exposes" (AR, p. 219n). Yet he does not make the pathos of this "problem"—a subjective feeling, "bliss," "fear," "anxiety" itself—a criterion for deciding (or even deciding "undecidability" best "understands" the situation). The opposite of "knowledge" for de Man is not an "error" in reference—error is a complicated and fecund category in de Man, related to Felman's discussion of the possibility of infelicity in speech-act theory[26]—but it is *ignorance*. In Felman its opposite is *pleasure* (i.e. "bliss"), which is simply the negative to de Man's ignorance; while in Greimas it is *power*.

v

Power, for Greimas, is a complex category that, as in J. L. Austin's speech-act theory, modifies the syntax of knowledge with the modalities of adverbs. Greimas describes power as the power to do, as know-how ("savoir faire"), or, more generally, as a function of the modal category of "will"—"we would be somewhat tempted to consider it as a modulation of *will*" (SS, p. 152)—or "will to act" (SS, p. 206). That is, while he describes *knowledge* in terms of a syntactic model (what de Man describes as the self-consistent, nonreferential logic of "grammar"), he situates *power* in relation to modal "aspects" of discourse, embodied, for instance, in the adverbial modifiers "*willingly* vs. *unwillingly*" (SS, p. 206) (what de Man describes in the hypostazation of pathos as "puissance de vouloir"). Austin also calls attention to adverbs, and Felman cites this passage in Austin as an example of the radical negativity of Austinian speech-act theory: "A belief in opposites and dichotomies encourages, among other things, a blindness to the combinations and dissociations of adverbs that are possible, even to such obvious facts that we can act at once on impulse and intentionally" (Felman, p. 141). As I have argued elsewhere, the introduction of modalities which "lack a syntactic model" (*SS*, p. 205) to describe actants puts into question the *nonfigurative* aim of Greimas's structural semantics and thus is a breach in the "grammatization" of his semantics (see *SS*, pp. xlix–liv). Since, as de Man argues, "figural discourse is always understood in contradistinction to a form of discourse that would not be figural" (*AR*, p. 201) and thus figures *always* imply a referent (see p. 90), the category *power* reinscribes the referent in Greimas's semantics. That is, adverbs—which, modifying sentences as a whole, seem to presuppose a nonlinguistic situation yet are metalinguistic and, as Felman says, "without positive reference" (Felman, p. 141)— breach de Man's opposition of pure rhetoric vs. pure grammar (*AR*, p. 9). With this breach, adverbs introduce the "radically negative" Hjelmslevian sense of the referent into Greimasian semiology.

The inscription of the referent in Greimas can be described in an actantial as well as a grammatical (structural) way. In his actantial schema, *power* manifests a teleological relationship between the subject and its object (the "object of desire") as opposed to *knowledge* which inscribes an etiological understanding of the object (the "object of communication") (*SS*, Chap. 10). In *Structural Semantics* Greimas inscribes the six *actants* of narrative in the following chart (*SS*, p. 207; see also p. xliii).

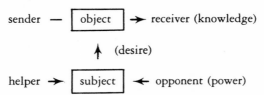

This chart describes the fact, as Greimas understands it, that any message both presents the "syntax" of knowledge and represents the positioning or "drama" of power (see *SS*, p. xliii). Syntax, to use de Man's description of Nietzsche, is "a speech *fact*," which is "nonpositional with regard to the properties" of an object and does not "*have to be* spoken since the order of things does not depend on its predicative power for its existence" (*AR*, p. 122); while the drama of power, what de Man calls "the positional power of language in general" (*AR*, p. 123), *posits* an object. In Greimas's actantial schema, the "object" remains the same (even though it "alternates" through the "nonopposition" of syntax and drama), and despite his "rejection of the supplementary dimension of the *referent*" (*SS*, p. 12), the *object* of both power and knowledge is the world: the opposition knowledge vs. power is inscribed on the semantic axis— the "substance of the content"—of "object" (referent).

For de Man this is different: the opposite of knowledge is *ignorance*, and this opposition is inscribed on the axis of "communication" (meaning). De Man's "anxiety of ignorance"—explicitly opposed, in his discourse, to the "anxiety of reference"—brackets the referent by reducing it to an element of aporia: the self-contradictory nature of language which must, yet cannot, be referential. Both can be inscribed in a semiotic square:

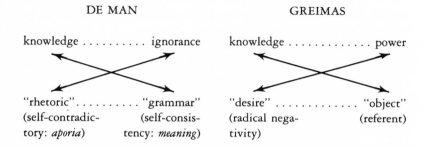

DE MAN   GREIMAS

knowledge . . . . ignorance   knowledge . . . . power

"rhetoric" . . . . "grammar"   "desire" . . . . "object"
(self-contradic-   (self-consis-   (radical nega-   (referent)
tory: *aporia*)   tency: *meaning*)   tivity)

If "rhetoric" in de Man (which, like "desire," occupies Greimas's "explosive" position: neither knowledge nor ignorance) is understood as "affectivity," then a kind—a Hjelmslevian kind—of "referent" is reinscribed in his model. It becomes a form of desire, "neither knowledge nor power," the *needs* de Man describes outside "the language-structured discourse of passion" (*AR*, p. 209). (It is just this possibility, I suspect, that governs Felman's playful valorization of seduction, her reading of de Man carried out throughout *The Literary Speech Act* even though she rarely cites him.) Yet de Man does not—it seems he cannot—"understand" the persuasive power of rhetoric beyond the "intricate set of feints and ruses" of "seduction" (*AR*, p. 159). Like the hypostazation of pathos, for de Man "seduction" is more "formal" than "material," a function of the grammatical aporetic "illusion" of referential meaning rather than an activity of language in the world. Thus he writes that in reading *Julie*, "from the first, one has to expect a mental attitude that is highly self-reflective, persistently aware of the discrepancies between the formal and the semantic properties of language, fully responsive to the seductive plays of the signifier yet wary of their powers of semantic aberration"

(*AR*, p. 207). What is "seductive" are "semiological fantasies about the adequation of sign to meaning" (*AR*, p. 262), and for de Man "responsiveness" has to be tempered by cognition. Seduction for him, then, is not the scandal of the speaking body—the scandal to thought of "nonopposition"—but the scandal of language, which is defined (according to de Man by Rousseau) as "the possibility of contingent error" (*AR*, p. 156). That is, language is scandalously defined in opposition to a nonlinguistic world and thus institutes the impossible oppositions of meaning and reference, knowledge and ignorance. With a twist of the wrist, language, as Felman argues, can become positive, fecund, affirmative, yet de Man, with his aporetic imagination in *Allegories of Reading*, never quite escapes "the negative/positive alternative."

Ignorance, as de Man asserts, can be either anxious or blissful "depending on one's momentary mood or individual temperament" (p. 19), but for him anxiety seems the over-riding response. Such anxiety is a kind of pathos of distrust: de Man reinscribes "the entire assumption of a nonverbal realm governed by needs" into the "speculative hypothesis" of language (*AR*, p. 210), but doing so, in his discourse, he also inscribes his own need for certainty rather than what Keats describes as the capability "of being in uncertainties, Mysteries, doubts, without any irritable reaching after fact & reason." "Coleridge, for instance," Keats goes on, "would let go by a fine isolated verisimilitude caught from the Penetralium of mystery, from being incapable of remaining content with half knowledge."[27] De Man is severely capable of doubt, yet he is irritable as well, and *Allegories of Reading* continually demonstrates a kind of courage of accepting, anxiously rather than contentedly, the irritation of the half-knowledge of ignorance.

Yet like Coleridge, he also misses, I believe, isolated *verisimilitudes* of reference—of lightheartedness, of trusting beyond distrust, of childishness, of bliss as well as anxiety—in an imagination which is, at once, skeptical and totalizing. De Man does not lightheartedly move away from the constraints of referential meaning, yet he anxiously deconstructs them and allegorizes his anxiety in work whose strength and weight come from a rigorous commitment to truth. "No man," writes Yeats,

> believes willingly in evil or in suffering. How much of the strength and weight of Dante and of Balzac comes from unwilling belief, from the lack of it how much of the rhetoric and vagueness of all Shelley that does not arise from personal feeling?[28]

His unwilling belief comes from a will to truth—another "nonlinguistic situation." For all the redoubtable darkness of his unwilling belief, there is no rhetoric or vagueness in de Man—his difficulties are the human difficulties of the relationships between knowledge and ignorance, language and needs—yet his discourse is neither serene nor does it possesss the "authority" of the constative. At its best it articulates rigorously— *willfully*—the necessity of not being complacent in our pleasures and commitments. His commitment to truth—to reference—is a difficult one fraught with doubt, uncertainty, anxiety; it is, as Wlad Godzich says, an "almost obsessive preoccupation."[29] Yet such a preoccupation, even if it is configured in error, is not confused or life-denying or simply a mistake. Rather, it is what Hillis Miller calls a species of de Manian "error," delimiting the ground of commitment altogether and understanding literature as an articulation and response to our impossible situation within language and in the world.

NOTES

1. Paul de Man, *Allegories of Reading: Figural Language in Rousseau, Nietzsche, Rilke, and Proust* (New Haven: Yale University Press, 1979); abbreviated *AR* throughout the text.

2. A. J. Greimas, *Structural Semantics: An Attempt at a Method*, trans. Daniele McDowell, Ronald Schleifer, Alan Velie, with an Introduction by Ronald Schleifer (Lincoln: University of Nebraska Press, 1983); abbreviated *SS* throughout the text. (Roman numerals refer to the Introduction.)

3. John Searle, *Speech Acts: An Essay in the Philosophy of Language* (New York: Cambridge University Press, 1969), p. 82; see pp. 72–97. For a concise and thoughtful account of the philosophical debate about referentiality, see Robert Con Davis, "The Case for a Post-Structuralist Mimesis: John Barth and Imitation," *American Journal of Semiotics*, forthcoming. My work on this paper has benefited from Davis's careful readings and advise.

4. Emile Benveniste, *Problems in General Linguistics*, trans. Mary Elizabeth Meek (Coral Gables: University of Miami Press, 1971), pp. 217–22.

5. Shoshana Felman, *The Literary Speech Act: Don Juan with J. L . Austin, or Seduction in Two Languages*, trans. Catherine Porter (Ithaca: Cornell University Press, 1983).

6. Fredric Jameson, in *The Prison-House of Language* (Princeton: Princeton University Press, 1972), describes "meaning-effect" in terms of the essentially abstract nature of structural linguistics: it is "as though, having taken all meaning for our object, we can no longer speak about it in terms of signification as such, and find ourselves obliged somehow to take a position outside the realm of meanings in order to judge what they all, irrespective of the content, have formally in common with each other" (p. viii). By "content" Jameson means, at least in part, "reference."

7. For a discussion of the relationship between biological and semiological aspects of music, see *The Raw and the Cooked*, trans. John and Doreen Weightman (New York: Harper Books, 1975), "Overture," esp. p. 14. I discuss this matter in a review essay examining Greimas's and J. Courtés', *Semiotics and Language: An Analytic Dictionary* in "Language, Semiotics, and Criticism," *Criticism*, 25 (1983), 267–76.

8. "Pascal's Allegory of Persuasion," in *Allegory and Representation*, ed. Stephen Greenblatt (Baltimore: Johns Hopkins University Press, 1981), p. 1.

9. "The Structure of Allegorical Desire," in *Allegory and Representation*, pp. 44–45.

10. *Écrits: A Selection*, trans. Alan Sheridan (New York: Norton, 1977), p. 104. For a discussion of Lacan and Greimas, see my "The Space and Dialogue of Desire: Lacan, Greimas, and Narrative Temporality," *MLN*, 98 (1983), 871–89.

11. "Shelley Disfigured," in *Deconstruction and Criticism*, ed. Harold Bloom et. al. (New York: Continuum Books, 1979). For an interesting suggestion of de Man's existential—and especially Sartrean—sympathies, see Frank Lentricchia's chapter in *After the New Criticism* (Chicago: University of Chicago Press, 1980), "Paul de Man: The Rhetoric of Authority." Lentricchia's essay is marred in part, I think, by misreading de Man's rigorous commitment to truth and the tone of his work occasioned by his genuine doubts and anxiety about its possibility—what Lentricchia calls its "atmospherics" (p. 299).

12. Throughout Derrida there is a sense of what Felman, speaking of Austin, calls "the *fun* or enjoyment" of philosophy, a "joyous," "pleasing," "gratifying" "*festival* of knowledge" (Felman, p. 102)—that (at least "theoretically"—that is to say, "constatively") informs Nietzsche as well. For a statement of this attitude, see, for instance, the peroration of "Differance," in Derrida's *Speech and Phenomena*, trans. David Allison (Evanston: Northwestern University Press, 1973). For an exception to the "fun" in Felman, see Jonathan Culler, *On Deconstruction* (Ithaca: Cornell University Press, 1982), p. 118.

13. *The Anxiety of Influence: A Theory of Poetry* (New York: Oxford University Press, 1973), p. 106.

14. "Violence and Metaphysics: An Essay on the Thought of Emmanuel Levinas," in *Writing and Difference*, trans. Alan Bass (Chicago: University of Chicago Press, 1978), p. 130. For a reading of violence in Derrida and Greimas, see Nancy Mergler and Ronald Schleifer, "The Plain Sense of Things: Violence and the Discourse of the Aged," forthcoming in a special issue of *Semiotica* on "Violence" edited by Nancy Armstrong.

15. Louis Hjelmslev, *Prolegomena to a Theory of Language*, trans. Francis J. Whitfield (Madison: University of Wisconsin Press, 1961), p. 52.

16. "Structure and Form: Reflections on the Work of Vladimir Propp," in *Structural Anthropology*, vol. II, trans. Monique Layton (New York: Basic Books, 1976), p. 155.

17. Ferdinand de Saussure, *Course in General Linguistics*, trans. Wade Baskin (New York: McGraw-Hill, 1959), p. 112.

18. Colors are used throughout *Speech Acts* as recurring examples of objects of reference: "for Frege," Searle writes, "an object is anything that can be referred to by a sigular noun phrase, whether it is a property [such as color—see p. 86], a particular, a number or whatnot" (p. 100). In an example he educes to explain the relationship between Nominalism and Realism, he writes:

> if two philosophers agree on the truth of a tautology, such as e.g. "everything coloured is either red or not red", and from this one concludes that the property of being red exists, and the other refuses to draw this conclusion; there is and can be no dispute, only a failure to understand. Either they mean something different by the derived proposition or, counter to hypothesis, they do not understand the original proposition in the same way. (pp. 105–06)

The "understanding" that Searle does not take into account is to see the naive sense of referentiality in the hypothesis: "either red or not red," as Hjelmslev shows in the comparison of English and Welsh color articulations, is not exhaustive. There is also "neither red nor not red."

19. The relationship of context to reference is a problematic one. In both speech-act theory and its various deconstructions—by Derrida, de Man, and Felman—it has been the object of vigorous debate. See the exchange between Derrida and Searle in *Glyph* 1 and 2 (1977); Culler's discussion in *On Deconstruction*, "Meaning and Iterability"; Davis's discussion in "Post-Structuralist Mimesis." De Man, as we have seen, distinguishes "the referential moment" from the "performative function of language" (*AR*, p. 208), yet is is a distinction—along with the possibility of a "referential moment"—that he continually calls into question.

20. It is for this reason, I believe, that "metaphor" itself can denote both the global sense of all figurative language (including "metonymy") and also the figure of substitution (as opposed to the contiguity of metonymy). In its totalizing and global sense it substitutes the most abstract sense of "substitution" for the aggregate of particular kinds of figuration—including the figure of metaphor narrowly conceived as simple substitution based on resemblance (see *AR*, p. 146).

21. *Du Sens* (Paris: Seuil, 1970), p. 8.

22. See, for instance, "Force and Signification" and "Structure, Sign, and Play in the Discourse of the Human Sciences," in *Writing and Difference*.

23. Fineman, p. 44.

24. *The Political Unconscious* (Ithaca: Cornell University Press, 1981), p. 46.

25. *The Prison-House of Language*, p. 166.

26. A large part of Felman's discussion of Austin hinges on the "misfirings" of language. See also, Stanley Corngold, "Error in Paul de Man," in *The Yale Critics: Deconstruction in America*, ed. Jonathan Arac, Wlad Godzich, Wallace Martin (Minneapolis: University of Minnesota Press, 1983).

27. John Keats, *Selected Poems and Letters*, ed. Douglas Bush (Boston: Houghton Mifflin, 1959), p. 261.

28. W. B. Yeats, *Explorations* (New York: Macmillan, 1962), p. 277.

29. "The Domestication of Derrida," in *The Yale Critics*, p. 25.

Bibliography

Hartman, de Man, Miller

Note by compiler: This is a comprehensive bibliography of the works of Geoffrey Hartman, Paul de Man, and J. Hillis Miller. Publications by them are listed alphabetically by title to facilitate locating particular works. I have also included a selective list of essays dealing with their work and notable reviews of their work, in both cases listed under the writer's or reviewer's name. I am indebted to Professors Hartman and Miller for their cheerful cooperation. Indispensable to this bibliography were the bibliographies compiled by Wallace Martin in *The Yale Critics: Deconstruction in America* (Minneapolis, Minn.: Univ. of Minnesota Press, 1983) and by Richard Barney in "Deconstructive Criticism: A Selected Bibliography" (*SCE Reports*, No. 8 [1980]). —Gita Rajan

The Works of Geoffrey H. Hartman

"The Aesthetics of Complicity." *Georgia Review*, 28 (1974), 384–88.

Akiba's Children. Emory, Va.: Iron Mountain Press, 1978.

André Malraux. London: Bowes and Bowes, 1960.

"Between the Acts: Jeanne Moreau's Lumière." *Georgia Review*. 31 (1977), 237–42.

Beyond Formalism: Literary Essays 1958–1970. New Haven, Conn.: Yale Univ. Press, 1970.

"Blessing the Torrent: On Wordsworth's Later Style." *PMLA*, 93 (1978), 196–204.

"Centaur—Remarks on the Psychology of the Critic." *Salmagundi*, 43 (1979), 130–39.

"Communication, Language, and the Humanities." *ADE Bulletin*, No. 70 (1981), n. pag.

"The Concept of Character in Lawrence's First Play." *Bulletin of the Midwest Modern Language Association*, 10, No. 1 (1977), 38–43.

Criticism in the Wilderness: The Study of Literature Today. New Haven, Conn.: Yale Univ. Press, 1980.

"Diction and Defense in Wordsworth." In *The Literary Freud: Mechanisms of Defense and the Poetic Will*. Ed. Joseph H. Smith. New Haven, Conn.: Yale Univ. Press, 1980, pp. 205–15.

239

Easy Pieces: Literary Essays and Reviews. New York: Columbia Univ. Press, forthcoming (1985).

The Fate of Reading and Other Essays. Chicago: Univ. of Chicago Press, 1975.

"The Fullness and Nothingness of Literature." *Yale French Studies*, No. 16 (1955–56), pp. 63–78.

"Hermeneutic Hesitation: A Dialogue between Geoffrey Hartman and Julian Moynahan." *Novel*, 12 (1979), 101–12.

Hopkins: A Selection of Critical Essays. Editor. Englewood Cliffs, N.J.: Prentice-Hall, 1966.

"How Creative Should Literary Criticism Be?" *New York Times Book Review*, April 5, 1981, pp. 11, 24–25.

"Humanistic Study and the Social Sciences." *College English*, 38 (1976), 219–23.

"The Interpreter's Freud." *Raritan Review*, Fall 1984, pp. 143–47.

"Literature as a Profession II: The Creative Function of Criticism." *Humanities*, 2 (Dec. 1981), 8–9.

"The Malraux Mystery." *New Republic*, Jan. 29, 1977, pp. 27–30.

"Nerval's Peristyle." *Nineteenth-Century French Studies*, 5 (1976–77), 71–78.

New Perspectives on Coleridge and Wordsworth. English Institute Essays. Editor. New York: Columbia Univ. Press, 1972.

"Plenty of Nothing: Alfred Hitchcock's *North by Northwest.*" *Yale Review*, 71 (1981), 13–27.

"The Poetics of Prophecy." *High Romantic Argument: Essays for M. H. Abrams.* Ed. Lawrence Lipking. Ithaca, N.Y.: Cornell Univ. Press, 1981, pp. 15–40.

"Preface." *Deconstruction and Criticism.* Ed. Harold Bloom et al. New York: Seabury, 1979, pp. vii–ix.

"Preface." *The Gaze of Orpheus and Other Literary Essays.* By Maurice Blanchot. Barrytown, N.Y.: Station Hill, 1981, pp. ix–xi.

"Preface." *Papers in Comparative Studies*, 1 (1981), 5–8.

"Preface." *Psychoanalysis and The Question of the Text.* Editor. Baltimore, Md.: Johns Hopkins Univ. Press, 1978.

"Preface." *Romanticism: Vistas, Instances, Continuities.* Coeditor, with David Thornburn. Ithaca, N.Y.: Cornell Univ. Press, 1973.

"Reading Insight—Keat's 'Ode to Psyche'." In *Centre and Labyrinth.* Eds. E. Cook et al. Toronto, Ontario: Univ. of Toronto Press, 1983, pp. 21–26.

"Recent Studies in the Nineteenth Century." *Studies in English Literature*, 6 (1966), 753–82.

"Reflections on Romanticism in France." *Studies in Romanticism*, 9 (1970), 233–48.

Saving the Text: Literature / Derrida / Philosophy. Baltimore, Md.: Johns Hopkins Univ. Press, 1981.

"Shakespeare—Division of Experience." Review of work by Marilyn French. *New York Times Book Review*, Dec. 13, 1981, pp. 11–12.

"Signs and Symbols." Review of *Image—Music—Text* and *A Lover's Discourse*, by Roland Barthes. *New York Times Book Review*, Feb. 4, 1979, pp. 12–13, 34–35.

"The Taming of History." *Yale French Studies*, 18 (1957), 114–28.

"To Bedlam and Part Way Back." In *Anne Sexton: The Artist and Her Critics*. Ed. J. D. McClatchy. Bloomington, Ind.: Indiana Univ. Press, 1978, pp. 118–21 (first published in *Kenyon Review*, 22 [1960], 691–700).

"A Touching Compulsion: Wordsworth and the Problem of Literary Representation." *Georgia Review*, 31 (1977), 345–61.

The Unmediated Vision: An Interpretation of Wordsworth, Hopkins, Rilke, and Valéry. 2d ed. New York: Harcourt, 1966.

"The Use and Abuse of Structural Analysis: Riffaterre's Interpretation of Wordsworth's 'Yew-Trees'." *New Literary History*, 7 (1975), 165–80.

"Words, Wish, Worth: Wordsworth." In *Deconstruction and Criticism*, ed. Harold Bloom et al., New York: Seabury, 1979, pp. 177–216.

"Wordsworth." *Yale Review*, 58 (1969), 507–25.

Wordsworth: Selected Poetry and Prose. Editor & Intro. New York: New American Library, 1970.

Wordsworth's Poetry, 1748–1814. 3d ed. New Haven, Conn.: Yale Univ. Press, 1971.

Works About Hartman

Culler, Jonathan. "Reading and Misreading." Review of *The Fate of Reading*, by Hartman. *Yale Review*, 65 (1975), 88–95.

Donoghue, Denis. "Reading about Writing." Review of *Criticism in the Wilderness*, by Hartman. *New York Times Book Review*, Nov. 9, 1980, pp. 11, 32–33.

Fletcher, Angus. Review of *Beyond Formalism*, by Hartman. *College English*, 34 (1972), 414–25.

Garber, Frederick. Review of *The Fate of Reading*, by Hartman. *Comparative Literature*, 30 (1978), 172–78.

Johnson, Barbara. "Nothing Fails Like Success." *SCE Reports*, No. 8 (1980), pp. 7–16.

Langbaum, Robert. "Magnifying Wordsworth." Review of *Wordsworth's Poetry*, by Hartman. *ELH*, 33 (1966), 271–78.

Lawall, Sarah. Review of *Criticism in the Wilderness*, by Hartman. *Comparative Literature*, 34 (1982), 177–81.

Leitch, Vincent B. "The Book of Deconstructive Criticism." *Studies in the Literary Imagination*, 12 (1979), 19–39.

————. *Deconstructive Criticism: An Advanced Introduction and Survey*. New York: Columbia Univ. Press, 1982.

Marshall, Donald. "Criticism and Creativity." Review of *Criticism in the Wilderness* and *Saving the Text*, both by Hartman. *Yale Review*, 71 (1981), 129–138.

Martin, Wallace. "Hermeneutic Hesitation: The Stuttering Text." Review of *Criticism in the Wilderness*, by Hartman. *Boundary 2*, 9, No. 1 (1980), 211–32.

————. "Literary Critics and Their Discontents: Response to Geoffrey Hartman." *Critical Inquiry*, 4 (1977), 397–406.

Moynihan, Robert. "Interview with Geoffrey Hartman, Yale University, March 19, 1979." *Boundary 2*, 9 (1980), 191–215.

Poirier, Richard. Review of *The Fate of Reading*, by Hartman. *New York Times Book Review* Apr. 20, 1975, pp. 21–26.

Riddel, Joseph N. Review of *Beyond Formalism*, by Hartman. *Comparative Literature*, 25 (1973), 178–80.

Sprinker, Michael. "Aesthetic Criticism: Geoffrey Hartman." In *The Yale Critics: Deconstruction in America*. Eds. Jonathan Arac et al. Minneapolis, Minn: Univ. of Minnesota Press, 1983. pp. 43–65.

The Works of Paul de Man

Allegories of Reading: Figural Language in Rousseau, Nietzsche, Rilke, and Proust. New Haven, Conn.: Yale Univ. Press, 1979.

"Allegorie und Symbol in der europäischen Frühromantik." In *Typologia Litterarum*. Eds. Stefan Sondereger et al. Zurich: Atlantis, 1969, pp. 403–35. Trans. as "The Rhetoric of Temporality" (q.v.).

"Autobiography as De-Facement." *MLN*, 94 (1979), 919–30.

"Blanchot." In *Modern French Criticism: From Proust and Valéry to Structuralism*. Ed. John K. Simon. Chicago: Univ. of Chicago Press, 1971, pp. 255–76.

Blindness and Insight: Essays in the Rhetoric of Contemporary Criticism. 2d ed. Minneapolis, Minn.: Univ. of Minnesota Press, 1983.

"The Crisis of Contemporary Criticism" *Arion*, 6 (1967), 38–57. Revised in *Blindness and Insight* (q.v.), pp. 3–19.

"La Critique thématique devant le thème de Faust." *Critique*, 13 (1957), 387–404.

"Dialog and Dialogism (The Relationship Between Fact and Fiction in the Novel)." *Poetics Today*, 4 (1983), 99–107.

"The Epistemology of Metaphor." *Critical Inquiry*, 5 (1978), 13–30.

"Les Exégèses de Hölderlin par Martin Heidegger." *Critique*, 11 (1955), 800–19.

Foreword. *The Dissimulating Harmony*, by Carol Jacobs. Baltimore, Md.: Johns Hopkins Univ. Press, 1978, pp. vii–xiii.

"Giraudoux." Review of *Plays*, by Jean Girandoux, trans. Christopher Fry. *New York Review of Books*, Nov. 28, 1963, pp. 20–21.

"Hegel on the Sublime." In *Displacement: Derrida and After*. Ed. Mark Krupnick. Bloomington, Ind.: Indiana Univ. Press, 1983, pp. 139–53.

"Heidegger Reconsidered." Review of *What is Existentialism?* by William Barrett, *New York Review of Books*, April. 2, 1964, pp. 14–16.

"Hölderlins Rousseaubild." *Hölderlin-Jahrbuch*, 1967–68. (Tubingen: Mohr, 1969), pp. 180–208. Originally published as "L'Image de Rousseau dans la poésie de Hölderlin" (q.v.).

"Hypogram and Inscription: Michael Riffaterre's Poetics of Reading." *Diacritics*, 11, No. 4 (1981), 17–35.

"L'Image de Rousseau dans la poésie de Hölderlin." *Deutsche Beiträge für geistigen Überlieferung*, 5 (1965), 157–83.

"Intentional Structure of the Romantic Image." In *Romanticism and Consciousness*. Ed. Harold Bloom. New York: Norton, 1970, pp. 65–77.

Introduction. *Toward an Aesthetics of Reception*, by Hans Robert Jauss. Minneapolis, Minn.: Univ. of Minnesota Press, 1982, pp. vii–xxv.

"Keats and Hölderlin." *Comparative Literature*, 8 (1956), 28–45.

"A Letter from Paul de Man." *Critical Inquiry*, 8 (1982), 509–13.

"Literature and Language: A Commentary." *New Literary History*, 4 (1972), 181–92.

"The Literature of Nihilism." Review of *The Artist's Journey into the Interior*, by Erich Heller, and *The German Tradition in Literature, 1871–1945*, by Ronald Gray. *New York Review of Books*, June 23, 1966, pp. 16–20.

"Lyric and Modernity." *Forms of Lyric: Selected Papers from the English Institute*. Ed. Reuben A. Brower. New York: Columbia Univ. Press, 1970, pp. 151–76.

Madame Bovary, by Gustave Flaubert. Trans. and Editor. New York: Norton, 1965.

"Madame de Staël et Rousseau." *Preuves*, no. 190 (Dec. 1966), pp. 35–40.

"The Mask of Albert Camus." Review of *Notebooks 1942–1951*, by Albert Camus. *New York Review of Books*, Dec. 23, 1965, pp. 10–13.

"A Modern Master." Review of *Dreamtigers and Labyrinths*, by Jorge Luis Borges. *New York Review of Books*, Nov. 19, 1964, pp. 8–10.

"Modern Poetics: French and German." In *Princeton Encyclopedia of Poetry and Poetics*. Eds. Alex Preminger et al. Princeton, N.J.: Princeton Univ. Press, 1965, pp. 518–23.

"Montaigne et la transcendance." *Critique*, 9 (1953), 1011–22.

"Le Néant poétique: Commentaire d'un sonnet hermétique de Mallarmé." *Monde nouveau*, No. 88 (1955), pp. 63–75.

"New criticism et nouvelle critique." *Preuves*, No. 188 (Oct. 1966), pp. 29–37. Revised in *Blindness and Insight* (q.v.) pp. 20–35.

"A New Vitalism." Review of *The Visionary Company*, by Harold Bloom. *Massachusetts Review*, 3 (1962), 618–23.

"Pascal's Allegory of Persuasion." In *Allegory and Representation*. Ed. Stephen J. Greenblatt. Baltimore, Md.: Johns Hopkins Univ. Press, 1981, pp. 1–25.

The Portable Rousseau. Editor. New York: Viking, forthcoming.

"Professing Literature—The Return to Philology," *Times Literary Supplement*, 1982: 1355–56.

"The Resistance to Literary Theory." *Yale French Studies*, No. 63 (1982), pp. 3–20.

Review of *The Anxiety of Influence*, by Harold Bloom. In *Comparative Literature*, 26 (1974), 269–75.

Review of *De la grammatologie*, by Jacques Derrida. *Rousseau*, 37 (1966–68), 284–88.

"The Rhetoric of Romanticism." In *Studies in Romanticism*, 18 (1979), 495–99.

The Rhetoric of Romanticism. New York: Columbia Univ. Press. 1984.

"The Rhetoric of Temporality." In *Interpretation: Theory and Practice*. Ed. Charles S. Singleton. Baltimore, Md.: Johns Hopkins Univ. Press, 1969, pp. 173–209.

"The Riddle of Hölderlin." Review of *Poems and Fragments*, by Friedrich Hölderlin, trans. Michael Hamburger. *New York Review of Books*, Nov. 19, 1970, pp. 47–52.

"Sartre's Confessions." Review of *The Words*, by Jean-Paul Sartre, *New York Review of Books*, Nov. 5, 1964, pp. 10–13.

Selected Poetry of Keats. Editor. New York: New American Library, 1966.

"Shelley Disfigured." In *Deconstruction and Criticism*. Eds. Harold Bloom et al. New York: Seabury, 1979, pp. 39–74.

"Sign and Symbol in Hegel's Aesthetics." *Critical Inquiry*, 8 (1982), 761–75.

"Sign and Symbol in Hegel's Aesthetics." Response to Guss and Raymond, *Critical Inquiry*, 10 (1983), 383–90.

"Situation du Roman." *Monde nouveau*, No. 11 (June, 1956), pp. 57–60.

"Spacecritics." Review of *The Disappearance of God*, by Hillis Miller, and *The Widening Gyre*, by Joseph Frank. *Partisan Review*, 31 (1964), 640–50.

"Structure intentionelle de l'image romantique." *Revue International de Philosophie*, 14 (1960), 68–84. Trans. as "Intentional Structure of the Romantic Image" (q.v.).

"Symbolic Landscape in Wordsworth and Yeats." In *In Defense of Reading*. Eds.

Reuben A. Brower and Richard Poirier. New York: Dutton, 1962, pp. 22–37.

"Tentation de la permanence." *Monde nouveau*, No. 93 (1955), pp. 49–61.

"What is Modern?" Review of *The Modern Tradition*, by Richard Ellman and C. Feidelson, Jr., *New York Review of Books*, Aug. 26, 1965, pp. 10–13.

"Whatever Happened to André Gide?" Review of *André Gide*, by Wallace Fowlie, and *Marshlands and Prometheus Misbound*, by André Gide. *New York Review of Books*. May 6, 1965, pp. 15–17.

"Wordsworth und Hölderlin." *Schweizer Monatshefte*, 45 (1966), 1141–55.

Works About de Man

Adams, Robert Martin. "Extension and Intension." Review of *Blindness and Insight*, by de Man. *Hudson Review*, 24 (1971–72), 687–96.

Arac, Jonathan. "Aesthetics, Rhetoric, History: Reading Nietzsche with Henry James." Review of *Allegories of Reading*, by de Man. *Boundary 2*, 9 (1981), 437–54.

Bové, Paul. *Destructive Poetics: Heidegger and Modern American Poetry*. New York: Columbia Univ. Press, 1980.

Christensen, Jerome C. "The Symbol's Errant Allegory: Coleridge and His Critics." *ELH*, 45 (1978), 640–59.

Culler, Jonathan. "Frontiers of Criticism." Review of *Blindness and Insight*, by de Man. *Yale Review*, 61 (1971–72), 259–71.

Donoghue, Denis. "Deconstructing Deconstruction." Review of *Deconstruction and Criticism*, eds. Harold Bloom et. al. and *Allegories of Reading*, by de Man. *New York Review of Books*, June 12, 1980, pp. 37–41.

———. *Ferocious Alphabets*. Boston: Little, Brown, 1981.

Ferguson, Frances. "Reading Heidegger." In *Martin Heidegger and the Question of Literature*, ed. William V. Spanos. Bloomington: Indiana Univ. Press, 1979, pp. 253–70.

Fletcher, Angus. " The Perpetual Error." Review of *Blindness and Insight*, by de Man, *Diacritics*, 2, No. 4 (1972), pp. 14–20.

Gans, Eric. "Anamorphose du cercle." *Critique*, 30 (1974), 927–40.

Garber, Frederick. Review of *Blindness and Insight*, by de Man. *Comparative Literature*, 26 (1974), 276–81.

Gasché, Rodolphe. "Deconstruction as Criticism." *Glyph*, 6 (1979), pp. 177–215.

———. " 'Setzung' and 'Übersetzung': Notes on Paul de Man." *Diacritics*, 11, No. 4 (1981), 56–59.

Godzich, Wlad. "Introduction: Caution! Reader at Work!" In *Blindness and Insight and Other Essays*, by de Man. 2d edition. Minneapolis, Minn.: Univ. of Minnesota Press, 1983.

Klein, Richard. "The Blindness of Hyperboles: The Ellipses of Insight." *Diacritics*, 3, No. 2 (1973), 33–44.

Lentricchia, Frank. *After the New Criticism.* Chicago: Univ. of Chicago Press, 1980.

MacCannell, Juliet Flower. "Memorial Essay: Paul de Man." *Semiotica*, forthcoming.

McLelland, Jane. Review of *Allegories of Reading*, by de Man. *MLN*, 96 (1981), 888–97.

Mellor, Anne K. "On Romantic Irony." *Criticism*, 21 (1979), 217–29.

Norris, Christopher. "Between Marx and Nietzsche: The Prospect for Critical Theory." *Journal of Literary Semiotics*, 32, No. 4, 104–15.

Riddel, Joseph. "Neo-Nietzschean Clatter—Speculation and the Modernist Poetic Image." *Boundary 2*, 9 (1981), 209–39.

Sabin, Margery. Review of de Man, *Allegories of Reading. Comparative Literature*, 33 (1981), 69–73.

Ulmer, Gregory L. "Jacques Derrida and Paul de Man on Rousseau's Faults." *Eighteenth Century: Theory and Interpretation*, 20 (1979), 164–81.

Wade, G. G. "Lacanian Study: de Man and Rousseau." *Eighteenth-Century Studies*, 12 (1979), 504–13.

The Works of J. Hillis Miller

Afterword. *Our Mutual Friend*, by Charles Dickens. New York: New American Library, 1964, pp. 901–11.

"The Anonymous Walkers." *Nation*, 190 (1960), 351–54.

"Antitheses of Criticism: Reflections on the Yale Colloquium." *MLN*, 81 (1966), 557–71.

"Ariachne's Broken Woof." *Georgia Review*, 31 (1977), 44–60.

"Ariadne's Thread: Repetition and the Narrative Line." *Critical Inquiry*, 3 (1976), 2–7.

"Beginning with a Text." *Diacritics*, 6 (1976), 2–7. Review of *Beginnings*, by Edward W. Said.

"Beguin, Balzac, Trollope et la Double Analogie redoublée." In *Albert Beguin et Marcel Raymond.* Paris: Corti, 1979, pp. 135–54.

"A 'Buchstabliches' Reading of the Elective Affinities." *Glyph*, 6 (1979), 1–23.

"Character in the Novel: A Real Illusion." In *From Smollet to James: Studies in the Novel and Other Essays Presented to Edgar Johnson.* Eds. Samuel J. Mintz et al. Charlottesville, Va.: Univ. Press of Virginia, 1981, pp. 277–85.

"Charles Dickens." In *The New Catholic Enclyclopedia*. New York: McGraw-Hill, 1967. Vol. IV.

Charles Dickens: The World of His Novels. Cambridge, Mass.: Harvard Univ. Press, 1958.

"The Creation of the Self in Gerard Manley Hopkins." *ELH*, 22 (1955), 293–319.

"The Critic as Host." *Critical Inquiry*, 3 (1977), 439–47.

"The Critic as Host." In *Deconstruction and Criticism*. Eds. Harold Bloom et al. New York: Seabury, 1979, pp. 217–53.

"Deconstructing the Deconstructers," Review of *The Inverted Bell*, by Joseph N. Riddel. *Diacritics*, 5, No. 2 (1975), 24–31.

The Disappearance of God. 2d ed. Cambridge, Mass: Harvard Univ. Press, 1976.

"The Disarticulation of the Self in Nietzsche." *Monist*, 64 (1981), 247–61.

"Dismembering and Disremembering in Nietzsche's 'Truth and Lies in a Non-Moral Sense.' " *Boundary 2*, 9 (1981), 41–54.

Fiction and Repetition: Seven English Novels. Cambridge, Mass.: Harvard Univ. Press, 1982.

"Fiction and Repetition: *Tess of the d'Urbervilles*." In *Forms of Modern British Fiction*. Ed. Alan Warren Freidman. Austin, Tex.: Univ. of Texas Press, 1975, pp. 43–71.

"The Fiction of Realism: Sketches by Boz, Oliver Twist, and Cruikshank's Illustrations." In *Charles Dickens and George Cruikshank*, by Miller and David Borowitz. Los Angeles: W. A. Clark Memorial Library, 1971, pp. 1–69. Rpt. in *Dickens Centennial Essays*. Eds. Ada Nisbet and Blake Nevius. Berkeley, Ca.: Univ. of California Press, 1971, pp. 85–153.

"The Figure in the Carpet." *Poetics Today*, 1, No. 3 (1980), 107–18.

Foreword. *Aspects of Narrative*, English Institutes Essays. Editor. New York: Columbia Univ. Press, 1971, pp. v–vii.

The Form of Victorian Fiction. Notre Dame, Ind.: Notre Dame Univ. Press, 1968; 2d ed., with a new preface, Arete Press, 1980.

"Franz Kafka and the Metaphysics of Alienation." In *The Tragic Vision and the Christian Faith*. Ed. N. A. Scott, Jr. New York: Association Press, 1957, pp. 281–305.

"The Function of Rhetorical Study at the Present Time." *ADE Bulletin*, No. 62 (Sept./Nov. 1979), pp. 10–18.

"Geneva or Paris: The Recent Work of Georges Poulet." *University of Toronto Quarterly*, 39 (1969–70), 212–28.

"The Geneva School: The Criticism of Marcel Raymond, Albert Beguin, Georges Poulet, Jean Rousset, Jean-Pierre Richard, and Jean Starobinski." *Critical Quarterly*, 8 (1966), 305–21. Rpt. with annotated bibliography in *Modern French Criticism*. Ed. John K. Simon. Chicago: Univ. of Chicago Press, 1972, pp. 277–310.

"Georges Poulet's 'Criticism of Identification.' " In *The Quest for Imagination*. Ed. O. B. Hardison, Jr. Cleveland, Ohio: Case-Western Reserve Univ. Press, 1971, pp. 191–224. Pp. 191–205 are revised from "The Literary Criticism of Georges Poulet" (q.v.); pp. 205–20 are from "Geneva or Paris" (q.v.).

"A Guest in the House." *Poetics Today*, 2, No. 10 (1980–81), 189–91.

"History as Repetition in Thomas Hardy's Poetry: The Example of 'Wessex Heights' " In *Victorian Poetry*. Eds. M. Bradbury and D. Palmer. London: Edward Arnold, 1972, pp. 222–53.

" 'I'd have my Life unbe': La Ricerca dell'obblio nell'opera di Thomas Hardy." *Strumenti Critici*, 3 (1969), 263–85.

"The Interpretation of *Lord Jim*." In *The Interpretation of Narrative*. Ed. Morton W. Bloomfield. Cambridge, Mass.: Harvard Univ. Press, 1970, pp. 211–28.

"The Interpretation of Otherness—Literature, Religion, and the American Imagination," *Journal of Religion*, 62 (1982): 290–304.

Introduction. *Bleak House*. Ed. Norman Page. Harmondsworth, England: Penguin, 1971, pp. 11–34.

Introduction. *Oliver Twist*, by Charles Dickens. New York: Holt, 1962, pp. v–xxiii.

Introduction. *The Well Beloved*. London: Macmillan, 1975, pp. 11–21.

"Kenneth Burke." In *International Encyclopedia of the Social Sciences*. New York: Free Press, 1979, Vol. 18, pp. 78–81.

"The Linguistic Moment in 'The Wreck of the Deutschland'." In *The New Criticism and After*. Ed. Thomas D. Young. Charlottesville, Va.: Univ. Press of Virginia, 1976, pp. 47–60.

"The Literary Criticism of Georges Poulet." *MLN*, 78 (1963), 471–88.

"Literature and Religion." In *Relations of Literary Study*. Ed. James Thorpe. New York: Modern Language Association, 1967, pp. 111–26.

"*Middlemarch*, Chapter 85: Three Commentaries." *Nineteenth-Century Fiction*, 35 (1980), 441–48.

"Myth as 'Hieroglyph' in Ruskin." *Studies in the Literary Imagination*, 8, No. 2 (1975), 15–18.

"Narrative and History." *ELH*, 41 (1974), 455–73.

"Narrative Middles: A Preliminary Outline." *Genre*, 11 (1978), 375–87.

"Nature and the Linguistic Moment." In *Nature and the Victorian Imagination*. Eds. U. C. Knoepflmacher and G. B. Tennyson. Berkeley, Calif.: Univ. of California Press, 1977, pp. 440–51.

"On Edge: The Crossways of Contemporary Criticism." *Bulletin of the American Academy of Arts and Sciences*, 32, No. 4 (1979), 13–32.

"Optic and Semiotic in *Middlemarch*." In *The Worlds of Victorian Fiction*. Ed.

Jerome H. Buckley. Cambridge, Mass.: Harvard Univ. Press, 1975, pp. 125–45.

" 'Orion' in 'The Wreck of the Deutschland'." *MLN* 76 (1961), 409–14.

Poets of Reality: Six Twentieth-Century Writers. Cambridge, Mass.: Harvard Univ. Press, 1965.

"The Problematic Ending in Narrative." *Nineteenth-Century Fiction*, 33 (1978), 3–7.

"Recent Studies in the Nineteenth Century." *Studies in English Literature*, 9 (1969), 737–53; 10 (1970), 183–214.

"The Rewording Shell: Natural Image and Symbolic Emblem in Yeats's Early Poetry." In *Poetic Knowledge: Circumference and Center.* Eds. Roland Hagenbuchle and Jospeh T. Swann. Bonn, West Germany: Bouvier, 1980, pp. 75–85.

"Some Implications of Form in Victorian Fiction." *Comparative Literature Studies*, 3 (1966), 108–18.

"The Sources of Dickens's Comic Art: From *American Notes* to *Martin Chuzzlewit*." *Nineteenth-Century Fiction*, 24 (1970), 467–76.

"Stevens' Rock and Criticism as Cure." *Georgia Review*, 30 (1976), 5–31, 330–48.

"The Still Heart: Poetic Form in Wordsworth." *New Literary History*, 2 (1971), 297–310.

"The Stone and the Shell: The Problem of Poetic Form in Wordsworth's 'Dream of the Arab'." In *Mouvements premiers: Études critiques offertes à Georges Poulet.* Paris: Corti, 1972, pp. 125–47.

"The Theme of the Disappearance of God in Victorian Poetry." *Victorian Studies*, 6 (1963), pp. 207–27.

"Theology and Logology in Victorian Literature." *Journal of the American Academy of Religion*, 47, No. 2, Supplement (1979), 345–61.

"Theoretical and Atheoretical in Stevens." In *Wallace Stevens: A Celebration.* Eds. Frank Doggett and Robert Buttel. Princeton, N.J.: Princeton Univ. Press, 1980, pp. 274–85.

"Theory and Practice: Response to Vincent Leitch." *Critical Inquiry*, 6 (1980), 609–14.

"Thomas Hardy: A Sketch for a Portrait." In *De Ronsard à Breton: Hommages à Marcel Raymond.* Paris: Corti, 1967, pp. 195–206.

Thomas Hardy: Distance and Desire. Cambridge, Mass: Harvard Univ. Press, 1970.

"Three Problems of Fictional Form: First-Person Narration in *David Copperfield* and *Huckleberry Finn*." In *Experience in the Novel.* Ed. Roy Harvey Pearce. New York: Columbia Univ. Press, 1968, pp. 21–48.

"Topography in *The Return of the Native* (Thomas Hardy)," *Essays in Literature*, 3, 1981, 119–34.

"Tradition and Difference." *Diacritics*, 2, No. 4 (1972), 6–13. Review of *Natural Supernaturalism*, by M. H. Abrams.

"Triptych and the Cross—Central Myths of George Eliot's Poetic Imagination." Review in *Notre Dame English Journal*, 12 (1979), 78–80.

"Trollope Thackeray." *Nineteenth Century Fiction*, 37 (1982), 350–57.

"The 2 Allegories." in *Allegory, Myth and Symbol*. Ed. M. W. Bloomfield. Cambridge, Mass.: Harvard Univ. Press, 1981, pp. 355–70.

"The 2 Relativisms: Point of View and Indeterminacy in the Novel *Absalom, Absalom!*." in *Relativism in the Arts*. Ed. B. J. Craige. Athens, Ga.: Univ. of Georgia Press, 1983, pp. 148–70.

"Virginia Woolf's All Soul's Day: The Omniscient Narrator in *Mrs. Dalloway*." In *The Shaken Realist*. Eds. Melvin J. Friedman and John B. Vickery. Baton Rouge, La.: Louisiana State Univ. Press, 1970, pp. 100–27.

"Wallace Stevens's Poetry of Being" *ELH*, 31 (1964), 86–105.

"Walter Pater: A Partial Portrait." *Daedalus*, 105, No. 1 (1976), 97–113.

" 'Wessex Heights': The Persistence of the Past in Hardy's Poetry." *Critical Quarterly*, 10 (1968), 339–59.

William Carlos Williams: A Collection of Critical Essays. Editor. Englewood Cliffs, N.J.: Prentice-Hall, 1966.

"William Carlos Williams: The Doctor as Poet." *Plexus*, 3, No. 4 (1968), 19–20.

"Williams's 'Spring and All' and the Progress of Poetry." *Daedalus*, 99 (1970), 405–34.

"*Wuthering Heights* and the Ellipses of Interpretation," *Notre Dame English Journal*, 12 (1980), 85–100.

"The Year's Books: J. Hillis Miller on Literary Criticism." *New Republic*, Nov. 1975, 29, pp. 30–33.

Works About Miller

Atkins, G. Douglas. "J. Hillis Miller: Deconstruction and the Recovery of Transcendence." *Notre Dame English Journal*, 13 (1980), 51–63.

Cain, William E. "Deconstruction in America: The Recent Literary Criticism of J. Hillis Miller." *College English*, 41 (1979), 367–82.

Leitch, Vincent, "The Lateral Dance: The Deconstructive Criticism of J. Hillis Miller." *Critical Inquiry*, 6 (1980), 593–607.

Norris, Christopher. "Deconstruction and the Limits of Sense." *Essays in Criticism*, 30 (1980), 281–92.

———. *Deconstruction, Theory and Practice*. London: Methuen, 1982.

———. "Derrida at Yale: The 'Deconstructive Moment' in Modernist Poetics." *Philosophy and Literature*, 4 (1980), 242–56.

Pease, Donald. "J. Hillis Miller: The Other Victorian at Yale." In *The Yale Critics: Deconstruction in America*. Eds. Jonathan Arac et al. Minneapolis, Minn.: Univ. of Minnesota Press, 1983, pp. 66–89.

Riddel, Joseph N. "A Miller's Tale." *Diacritics*, 5, No. 3 (1975), 56–65.

Rimmon-Kenan, Shlomith. "Deconstructive Reflection on Deconstruction: In Reply to Hillis Miller." *Poetics Today*, 2, No. 10 (1980–81), 185–88.

Said, Edward W. "A Configuration of Themes." *Nation*, 202 (1966), 659–61. Review of *Poets of Reality*, by Miller.

————. "Reflections on Recent American 'Left' Literary Criticism." *Boundary 2*, 8, No. 1 (1979), 11–30.

INDEX

253